Do-it-yourself Yearbook

Popular Science

Do-it-yourself Yearbook

1989

Published by
Popular Science Books, Danbury, CT

lovely logs

This sprawling ranch-style log home, with an attached three-car garage, was built from factory-made components.

Sleek vertical siding gives this log home a contemporary look.

Decorative windows and a five-sided sunroom reflect design changes.

Log homes have a place in the hearts of many Americans, perhaps because they symbolize pioneering efforts to carve out a place of one's own. By tradition, log homes are informal and individualistic, and while these design values still appeal to American taste, most people don't believe that a log home would really work for everyday living in an everyday neighborhood. That's a misconception, because log homes today aren't what they once were. Many of the new designs have squared-off corners, and exterior walls that look more like clapboards than logs. You'll see styles ranging from ranches to sleek contemporaries.

Reprinted by permission of Home-owner magazine.

foam-block house

On September 19, 1986, Nancy and Myron Kalinovich of Surrey, B.C., Canada, a Vancouver suburb, moved into a new house whose walls were built from the contents of six 45-gallon drums. What size house could be built with less than two cubic yards of materials? In this case it's a sprawling 2,300-square-footer—plus garage.

There were no tricks involved, just chemistry. Three of the drums held isocyanate resin; the other three held an organic compound called polyol. Mixed together and spewed into special molds, the liquids expanded to 30 times their original volume. The result: polyurethane; specifically, 3,300 polyurethane blocks—enough to build walls 240 feet long, 12 feet high, and 8 inches thick.

Superkids? Not these two; the foam-block wall section these two boys are holding weighs less than 16 pounds. Building an Insulock wall is fast and easy (opposite); no mortar is used. Walls naturally go up straight and plumb, forming walls that are airtight; thus there is no need to wrap the house in an infiltration barrier. Window and door openings can be cut with a hand saw. Finished foam-block house is indistinguishable from its neighbors. But owners Myron and Nancy Kalinovich of Vancouver, B.C., report exceptional quiet and comfort in their foam home.

The polyurethane blocks, made by Canadian Insulock Corporation of Vancouver, actually perform three functions in the house. First, they interlock side to side and top to bottom to form mortarless walls. Second, the hollow cores of the blocks act as formwork for reinforced concrete, which forms the post-and-beam structure of the house. And third, since polyurethane is a fine insulator, the blocks are the insulation. Foam-block houses are quick to build, require fewer skilled tradesmen, and need little maintenance. They are energy efficient and cost competitive—and the Kalinovichs report theirs is amazingly clean and quiet.

Canadian Insulock was founded by two brothers, Amin and Nazim Shivji, but the polyurethane blocks were invented by Keith Inness of Seattle, Washington. How the Shivjis and Inness got together is a surprising story.

The Shivji brothers, of Indian ancestry, were born and raised in Uganda, part of a family that had lived there for three generations. Nevertheless, Ugandan president Idi Amin deported them, along with all other "Asians," in 1972. "Each person could take only 55 pounds sterling in currency, a watch, a wedding band, and the shirt on his back," Nazim, then a high-school student, recalled. The Shivji family eventually landed in Vancouver, where Amin became a banker and Nazim a lawyer. The brothers were primarily interested in entrepreneurial enterprises, however, and decided that a tongue-and-groove concrete block would be a promising product.

"After months of trying we finally created a design that worked," Nazim told me. But in a patent search they discovered that a Canadian patent had already been issued for their design. They traced the patent to a Seattle firm called Insulock.

The brothers crossed the border for a visit and were amazed to find that the Seattle company (by then dormant) had made the interlocking blocks of polyurethane instead of concrete. "We liked the product so much we bought the company," Nazim said with glee. The deal included the technical expertise of Keith Inness.

That was in 1984. Two years and $2.5 million later, Canadian Insulock had developed a machine and a resin formula that would produce polyurethane blocks of consistent quality.

Insulock blocks are 8 by 8 by 16 inches, the same as a standard concrete block. The polyurethane blocks, however, weigh only 12 ounces each; concrete blocks weigh about 40 pounds.

Because they require no mortar and they interlock like Lego toy blocks, the Insulock blocks are quick and easy to lay, and walls pretty much go up straight and plumb. "If a wall does bow a bit, you just brace it till the concrete sets; that snugs it all up tight," said Nazim. Thus the blocks are ideal for do-it-yourselfers, and reduce the need for skilled labor on a construction site.

The blocks are surprisingly strong. Nazim, a stocky man, demonstrated this by taking one from a pile, putting it on the ground, then calmly stepping up on it. The block didn't even dent. And polyurethane is an excellent insulator. An Insulock block has an insulating value of R-22.

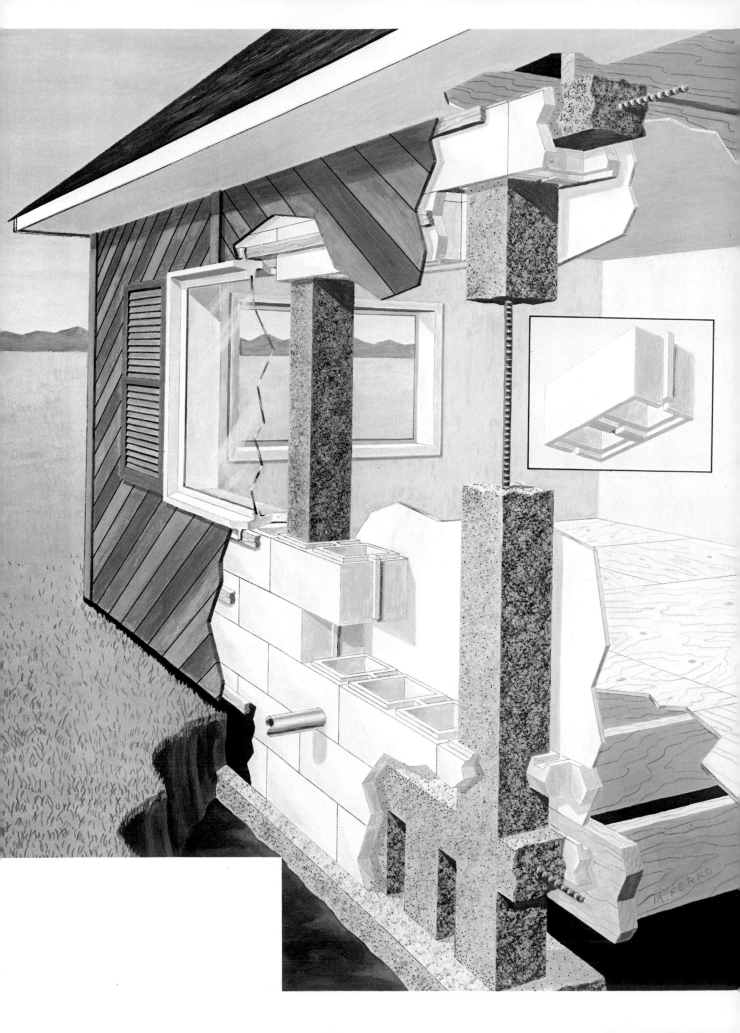

Insulock polyurethane blocks interlock side to side and top to bottom. Here's how a house is built:

Blocks for the foundation or basement rest on standard footings, and a steel reinforcing bar is placed in the hollow core of a block every 2 feet; concrete is poured in all cores. At the top of the foundation is a bond beam. To make this, workers use a special tool to cut a continuous channel in the blocks; then they place rebar and fill the channel with concrete. Waterproofing is applied to the exterior of the foam foundation.

Next the walls go up: Blocks are stacked, and every 2 to 4 feet (depending on the structural needs of the house) a rebar is placed in the block cores and a concrete post is poured. At the top, a reinforced-concrete lintel is formed (as with the foundation beam below). Plumbing and wiring can run in the hollow block cores. Roof construction is conventional. Inside, plasterboard is glued on with contact cement. Outside, furring strips are glued to the foam with construction adhesive, and siding is nailed to them; or stucco can be troweled on.

How does polyurethane behave in a fire? That was one of Myron Kalinovich's concerns, so he took scraps of the stuff and tried to burn them. "As long as you hold the heat source to the foam, it will continue to burn," he reported. "It turns black and charcoally. But as soon as you take the fire away, it stops burning." Tests have confirmed that its flame-spread rating is lower than that of red oak, the standard, and that the smoke produced is no more toxic than wood smoke.

Still, I wondered why this company used polyurethane, when most foam houses I've reported on are made of expanded polystyrene foam, which generally offers the greatest insulation for the dollar.

"We wanted to be able to make the blocks on site," Nazim explained. "You could do that with styrene, but it would take huge quantities of materials. With polyurethane, four 45-gallon drums hold enough chemicals to make the blocks for a small house." Polyurethane also offers the greatest insulation per *inch*, Nazim pointed out.

Canadian Insulock makes mobile block factories—small trailers full of molds, air compressors, and the other equipment required to make the blocks. They sell these and the requisite supplies to licensees.

Their first sale was to Gary and Irene Morgan, who live just across the border from Vancouver in Everson, Wash. The Morgans, stockholders in the original Insulock company, traced down the new company when they decided to enclose their swimming pool and wanted to avoid building with wood.

Itinerant butchers by trade, the Morgans live in a big white farmhouse with a classic red barn behind. The Insulock trailer sits in front of the barn, and son Mark was learning to make polyurethane blocks the day I was there. It was his third day on the job, and he was turning out three blocks every five minutes.

Inside the little white trailer a hose ran from each of two steel drums. The components for the polyurethane are metered out automatically in the proper ratio, Mark Morgan explained, and mixed before they emerge from the hose's nozzle. Compressed air forces the liquid out. Mark deftly directed the whitish stream in a figure-eight pattern, filling each of three molds and closing the lid on each as he worked. Five minutes later he unlatched the lids, and with a piercing hiss, the blocks popped up, pushed by jets of compressed air from below. Three more white, shiny Insulock blocks were ready to use. (The blocks come out white but ultraviolet radiation quickly yellows them to the color you see in the photos.)

The Morgans bought the little three-mold trailer for practice but intend to scale up their operation. A six-mold factory could produce 100,000 blocks a year with one shift—enough to build 30 good-size houses. They plan to go to a nine- or 12-mold operation.

The illustration and caption explain how an Insulock house is constructed. A few homes were built in the Seattle area seven years ago using the original Insulock blocks. The Kalinovich house is the first one built with Canadian Insulock's products.

Myron Kalinovich, formerly a building-materials salesman, liked the Insulock concept as soon as he learned of it. "But somebody had to convince me that it would work," he added. That job fell to Warren Jones, a custom builder who specializes in energy-efficient housing—the Kalinovichs' prime concern. Jones, a tall redhead who worked five years as a Canadian mounted policeman, speaks in the flat tones of his native Manitoba, which contrast sharply with the near-Scottish lilt of the Vancouver populace. *A Popular Science* subscriber for 14 years, Jones credits the magazine with stimulating his interest in energy-efficient housing.

Jones now works for Insulock as well as running his own contracting firm, Cortez Energy Efficient Homes, Ltd. When the Kalinovichs asked him to build their new house he convinced them to use Insulock blocks.

Finished, the Kalinovich house looks conventional, but the couple and their two sons enjoy some unconventional benefits because of the way the house is built. The first thing you notice is how quiet it is inside. "In our former house [right next door] there was always the din of traffic noise," said Nancy Kalinovich. "In this one we don't hear the traffic at all." About the only background sound comes from the fans and air movement created by the air-to-air heat exchanger. The house has a low natural infiltration rate without using a vapor or infiltration barrier, thanks to the interlocking foam blocks. So in order to keep the air fresh and healthy, forced ventilation is required. Filters on the heat exchanger ensure that the incoming air is clean.

Radiant electric ceiling panels heat the house. The Kalinovichs don't know how much energy they used last winter, but report satisfyingly low bills. This year they plan to monitor the energy consumption.

The house promises a long and low-maintenance lifetime. Rodents and termites don't dine on concrete and polyurethane. Dampness, mildew, and rot have no effect.

Bottom line

The Kalinovich house cost about $52 per square foot, turnkey. "That's about average for a well-appointed custom house in this area," Jones reported. Generally, an Insulock house will be cost-competitive with a frame house of similar insulation, meaning 2 × 6 stud walls plus an insulating sheathing on the outside, Jones noted.

An Insulock house also compares favorably in cost with concrete-block construction, the company claims. "In Ontario, block foundations cost three to six dollars a block, laid in place," Jones said. "Ours cost three dollars to three-and-a-quarter each, and you end up with a basement insulated to R-25, so why not use Insulock?" The company sells the blocks for $2 (U.S.) each and expects that price to decline as they buy resin in larger quantities.

Currently, one Insulock house is being built in Mount Vernon, WA; another is going up in Cleveland, OH; and one is just started in Toronto, Ont., Canada—*by V. Elaine Gilmore. Illustration by Mario Ferro.*

7 magnificent house designs

Popular Science's new home collection offers a wide range of truly original house plans from designers noted for devotion to single-family housing. These architectural designers, scattered along America's northeast and northwest coasts, were chosen on the basis of the popularity of their previous work in the magazine. *Popular Science* challenged them to produce innovative houses without sacrificing amenities or energy efficiency. We asked for designs that would be at home on a variety of sites, from suburban lots to country property. All seven houses avail themselves of passive solar energy by siting glass walls to the south. All feature skylights, and all are well insulated. The fourth house, indeed, was analyzed by Portland (OR) General Electric Company's Good Cents Qualifier calculations: Built locally, with a two-ton heat pump, it can be heated annually for $180.

Wherever you hope to build, and whether you plan to do most of the work yourself or hire a contractor, one of these houses should be right for you. Detailed construction drawings are available for each (see ordering data)—*by Al Lees.*

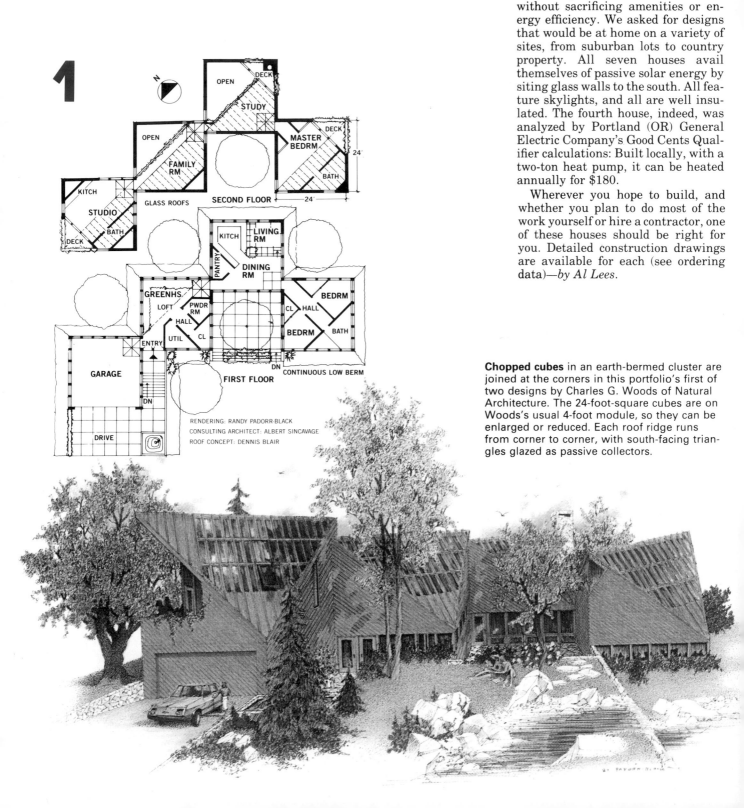

RENDERING: RANDY PADORR-BLACK
CONSULTING ARCHITECT: ALBERT SINCAVAGE
ROOF CONCEPT: DENNIS BLAIR

Chopped cubes in an earth-bermed cluster are joined at the corners in this portfolio's first of two designs by Charles G. Woods of Natural Architecture. The 24-foot-square cubes are on Woods's usual 4-foot module, so they can be enlarged or reduced. Each roof ridge runs from corner to corner, with south-facing triangles glazed as passive collectors.

2

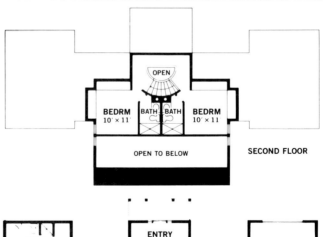

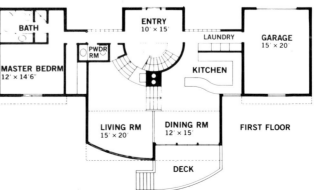

House of light from prizewinning architect Alfredo De Vido, features a series of gables with a frieze of small windows running full-width below, on both south and entry elevations. Entry is flanked by banks of glass blocks. The plan separates family functions, with master bedroom suite at one end, garage/kitchen/service wing at other, two-story living/entry area at center.

3

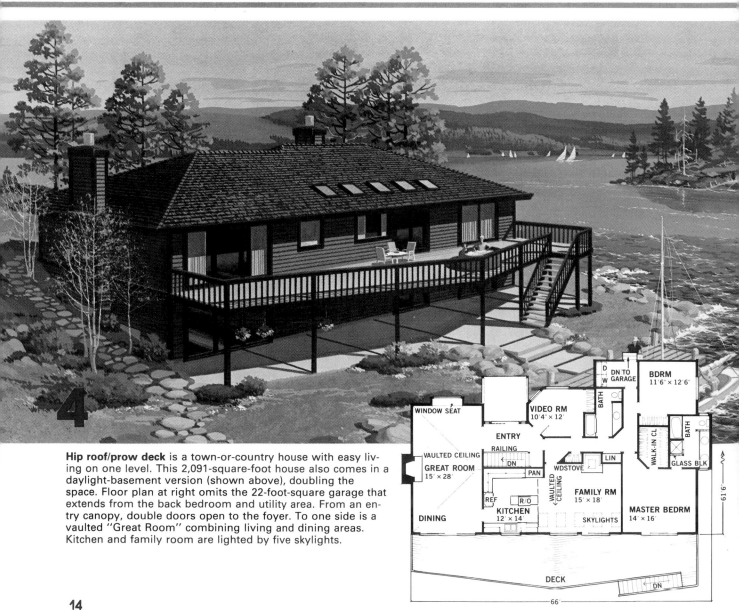

4

Hip roof/prow deck is a town-or-country house with easy living on one level. This 2,091-square-foot house also comes in a daylight-basement version (shown above), doubling the space. Floor plan at right omits the 22-foot-square garage that extends from the back bedroom and utility area. From an entry canopy, double doors open to the foyer. To one side is a vaulted "Great Room" combining living and dining areas. Kitchen and family room are lighted by five skylights.

WINDOW SEAT

VIDEO RM
10'4" × 12'

BDRM
11'6" × 12'6"

DN TO GARAGE

BATH

ENTRY

RAILING

LIN

WALK-IN CL

BATH

GLASS BLK

VAULTED CEILING

GREAT ROOM
15' × 28'

DN

PAN

WDSTOVE

VAULTED CEILING

FAMILY RM
15' × 18'

REF

R/O

DINING

KITCHEN
12' × 14'

SKYLIGHTS

MASTER BEDRM
14' × 16'

16'

DECK

DN

66'

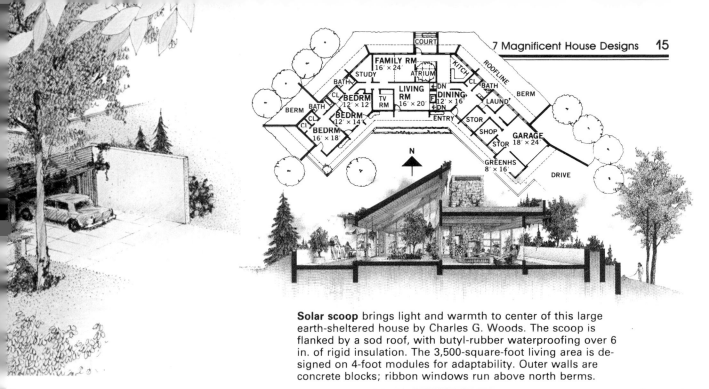

Solar scoop brings light and warmth to center of this large earth-sheltered house by Charles G. Woods. The scoop is flanked by a sod roof, with butyl-rubber waterproofing over 6 in. of rigid insulation. The 3,500-square-foot living area is designed on 4-foot modules for adaptability. Outer walls are concrete blocks; ribbon windows run above north berms.

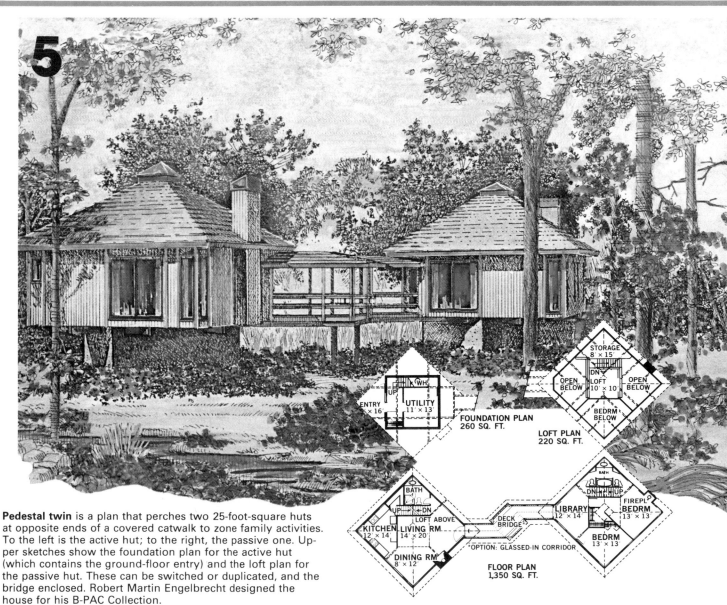

Pedestal twin is a plan that perches two 25-foot-square huts at opposite ends of a covered catwalk to zone family activities. To the left is the active hut; to the right, the passive one. Upper sketches show the foundation plan for the active hut (which contains the ground-floor entry) and the loft plan for the passive hut. These can be switched or duplicated, and the bridge enclosed. Robert Martin Engelbrecht designed the house for his B-PAC Collection.

6

7

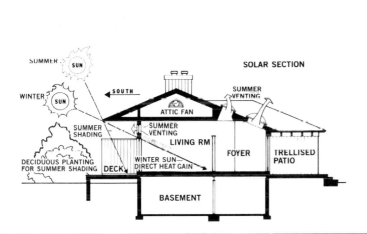

SOLAR SECTION

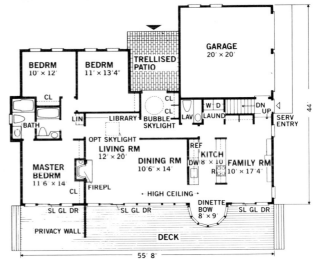

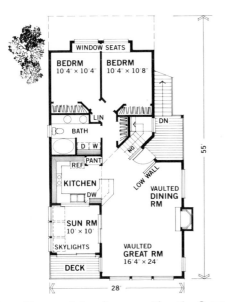

Upstairs cottage switches floors, putting the Great Room and a skylighted sun room upstairs for the best vistas (usually wasted on bedrooms). These rooms feature vaulted ceilings—and the sun room can be converted to a screened porch. Back bedrooms, over the garage, have window seats and are removed from late-night activities.

How to order plans for the house of your choice

1 and **3** Detailed plans for the Chopped Cubes or the Solar Scoop are $150 for one set, $25 for each additional set (for filing permits, financing). Address: Natural Architecture, RD 3, Box 538, Honesdale, PA 18431.

2 House of Light plans are $125 per set, $175 for four sets. Write Alfredo De Vido Associates, 699 Madison Ave., New York, NY 10021.

4 Plans for the Hip Roof/Prow Deck are $250 for a set of four without basement (PS-1064-1A) or $275 with daylight basement (PS-1064-1D). Mirror-reverse plans are available, so is materials list ($30). Write Kenneth E. Gephart AIBD/CSI, 9630 S.W. Eagle Lane, Beaverton, OR 97005.

5 Plans for the Pedestal Twin are $85 a set or $120 for three, from Princeton Plans Press, Box 622, Princeton, NJ 08540. For the B-PAC Collection catalog, send $5.

6 A set of plans for the Janus is $110, $25 for additional sets, or $175 for five sets. Mirror-reverse plans are $15 per set; materials list is $25. Write Homes for Living, Inc., 107-40 Queens Boulevard, Forest Hills, NY 11375.

7 Plans for the Upstairs Cottage are $100 for one set, or $150 for four. Specify plan no. PS541-2A. Materials list is $30; specifications, $20. Write Piercy & Barclay Designers, 7080 S.W. Fir Loop, Tigard, OR 97223.

Please include $8 postage and handling on all plans orders from this portfolio.

1. **Nail 2 × 4s** around the roof's perimeter, then add horizontals 4 feet apart, up to the ridge. There's no need to insulate the roof projection at the gable ends, so to support the bridging steel, add centered horizontals the length of the projection as shown.

2. **Set foil-faced planks** into recesses formed by cleats, over deteriorated shingles.

3. **The manufacturer** cut steel panels to my specifications; most were 26 inches wide. The longest panel was 24 feet (shown in photo), the maximum length that can take expansion and contraction without distorting. The panel was fastened with self-starting, self-tapping, self-sealing screws that have a steel washer and neoprene gasket (see drawing). To drive the screws, use a magnetic 1/4-inch nut driver chucked into an electric drill.

4. **New roof** looks good, and its surface sheds snow. The roofing maker offers preformed gable trim, ridge caps, and valley flashing (see sketch).

re-roofing? add insulation

After 20 years' exposure the asphalt shingles on my vacation house in northern California's Trinity Alps were in poor shape. The house had originally been roofed with a two-inch-thick tongue-and-groove deck, covered with 1/2-inch sheathing. I had nailed on 300-pound shingles directly, with no roofing felt. There was practically no insulation from hot summer sun, and on winter visits I burned a lot of wood to keep cozy. With many of the shingle tabs worn away by repeated snows and heavy rains, it seemed an ideal time to rectify the situation.

The insulating solution shown in my photos only works, of course, over cathedral ceilings. In houses with unheated attics, insulation should stay between the ceiling joists. But for an A-frame or any roof deck with living areas directly below, the installation shown is the best way to go. And if you plan to finish off your attic, you *must* move the insulation from underfoot to overhead. If the time's also ripe for a new roof, as it was in my case, the system shown offers many advantages—including the option of leaving the rafters exposed in your new

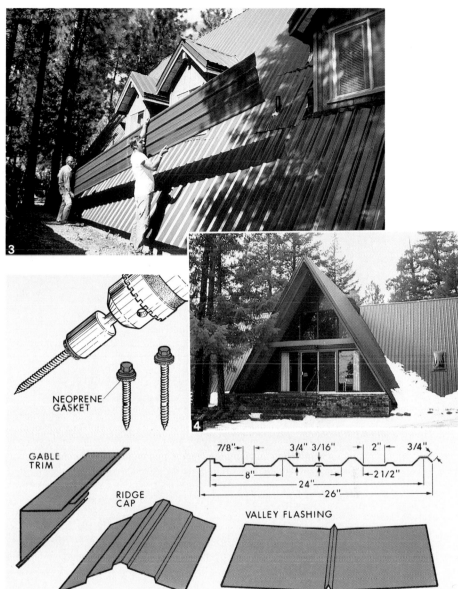

NEOPRENE GASKET

GABLE TRIM

RIDGE CAP

VALLEY FLASHING

DRAWING BY GERHARD RICHTER

vaulted ceiling. My two-story T-shaped A-frame shown here has the rafter beams exposed inside, and I didn't want to lose that look.

For the finished roofing I used enameled steel with a ridge pattern made by Champion Metal Co. It's available in eight colors, including white. I chose chocolate brown.

This roofing could have been applied directly over my deteriorating shingles, but a new roof gave me the chance to add exterior insulation. For this I chose 1½-inch-thick rigid polyisocyanurate foam board, double-faced with aluminum foil. The brand I used was ThermalGard, made by Thermal Systems. Over this went a layer of 30-pound roofing felt, applied in vertical overlapped strips; steel panels were then fastened to the 2 × 4 cleats that framed the foam.

The anchoring system that a local roofer and I devised for the steel saved me 4,200 square feet of plywood for a new roof deck over the foam—plus the cost of the foam on the overhangs (where the roof projects beyond actual living space).

After placing foam board over the roof, as shown above, we nailed on valley flashing before adding the roofing felt. Applying the steel roofing was easy. The two outer ridges of each panel, when overlapped vertically, form a watertight seal. But the method of anchoring the panels is critical: The sheets must be screwed to the 2 × 4s—not nailed. Nails tend to lift with expansion and contraction.

I chose screws colored to match the siding: one inch long for the runs and 1½ inches on the ridge cap. Drive them until the neoprene gasket seats firmly against the metal surface.

I'm well pleased with the performance of the new roof. The interior temperature of my house is 20 to 25 degrees cooler on the occasional 100-degree days in my area. And I enjoy winter visits much more now that I can heat up the house in a jiffy—*by Ken L. Herrington. Drawing by Gerhard Richter.*

Champion Metal Co., 12851 Stockton Blvd., Galt, CA 95632, **Thermal Systems,** 5772 Bolsa Ave., Huntington Beach, CA 92649

solar-powered sunshades

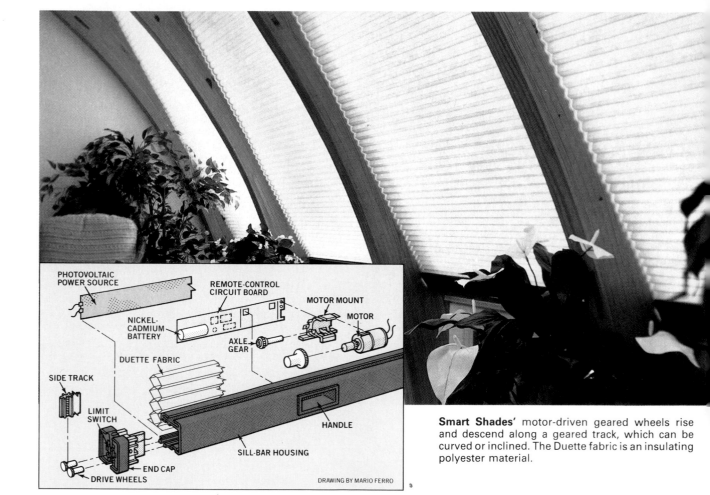

Smart Shades' motor-driven geared wheels rise and descend along a geared track, which can be curved or inclined. The Duette fabric is an insulating polyester material.

When the sun comes up, the shades come down: This is often the daily ritual for homeowners trying to control the buildup of solar heat in their greenhouses or glassed-in porches. Smart Shades, a customfitted window shade from Comfortex Corporation, eliminates that chore by traveling up and down automatically in response to the sun.

Smart Shades' heat-sensing feature uses a thermometer in a glass tube positioned outside the window to monitor changing temperatures. The system "operates very much like the thermostat on an air-conditioning system," explains John Schnebly, chairman and technical director of Comfortex. A microprocessor compares the probe temperature with programmed thresholds to control movement. "When the temperature rises above, say, eighty degrees in the glass plenum outdoors, the shades will come down, even on a hot, cloudy summer day when there is no sunlight. Then in the winter the shades rise once the temperature is above, say, seventy degrees," says Schnebly. "The variable summer and winter modes are set by the installer, but the homeowner can learn to reset them also." A clock timer supplies an alternative automatic operation, one attuned more to lifestyle and needs for privacy than to climate-control. The programmable timer handles as many raisings and lowerings as you need in a day.

Smart Shades are electric-motor-driven; the small drive system fits right into the sill bar (handle). In sunny locations, photovoltaic cells on the outfacing shade charge nickel-cadmium batteries. One sunny day provides enough power to function through 30 cloudy days (60 raisings and lowerings). On a north-facing or shaded window a DC charger powers the batteries. An infrared remote-control unit allows the user to move the shades at will.

Each 3-by-12-foot shade pictured here costs about $700. Comfortex Corporation, Box 728, Cohoes, N.Y. 12047—*by Nancy Negovetich.*

elegant low-cost door

To finish, you sand the prime coat lightly with 320-grit paper, dust, and brush a heavy coat of stain on the panels first, then the frame, stroking with the grain. Using a cloth pad moistened with the stain, wipe off all excess. You may need a 1-inch brush to feather stain out of the corners. When dry, apply a clear top coat. The Conventry is shown here; the Classique is shown in the large photo.

Until I tried it myself, I wouldn't have believed it. The anemic-looking raw surface of a new Masonite Conventry or Classique hardboard-skinned door costing less than one-third the price of a comparable solid oak door could—with a coat of stain and a clear finish—be transformed into a truly elegant-looking interior door.

Masonite doesn't actually make the doors. The company supplies the hardboard face panels—or "skins," as they are called—to door fabricators all over the country, who bond them onto wood rail-and-stile frames. The assembled doors, available in all standard sizes, come in two styles: Conventry, a raised-panel design (4 panels); and Classique, a two-panel door with an arched top panel.

The secret of the effective stain-ability of the new doors is a special off-white primer that has been applied to the deeply oak-grained hardboard surface. All you have to do is apply a heavy-bodied stain—oil-based works better than water-based—and wipe it off.

I found it took a bit of experimenting to apply the right amount of pressure when removing the stain. To achieve the desired effect, leave stain on the surface and make sure your wiping strokes go the full length on each rail, panel, or stile. Barring an extremely close inspection, it's difficult to detect that the finished door is not solid wood.

To stain existing painted door trim to match, try sanding, applying a neutral enamel primer, and then applying the same stain as you used on the new door.

The skin supplier is Masonite Corporation, Specialty Products, One South Wacker Dr., Chicago, IL 60606—*by Phil McCafferty.*

plastic soffits for cabinets

You can spend several hours installing 2 × 4 soffit framing for your new kitchen or bathroom cabinets. Or you can use a new product, Ultra-Soffit prefabricated rigid-foam soffits, to reduce installation time to minutes.

The innovative system, developed by Epsco, Inc. (4080 First Avenue N.E., Suite 105H, Cedar Rapids, Iowa 52402), consists of 4-foot-long L-shaped segments of heavy-walled rigid expanded-polystyrene foam with particleboard fastening strips bonded onto the edges. The Epsco designers have included several rectangular holes in each section to provide convenient access when installing wiring and ductwork. The Ultra-Soffit system fits standard 12-inch cabinets and is designed for either new construction or renovation projects. A carton of two 4-foot soffit lengths retails for about $28.

You mount the soffit segments by simply screwing them to 1 × 2 wood furring strips that have been fastened to the wall and ceiling. One-half-inch gypsum wallboard is then screwed to the face and bottom of the soffit. For 13-inch-deep cabinets, Epsco supplies a special custom shim, or spacer strip, to space the soffit out an inch from the wall.

To provide a soffit above angled corner cabinets, a triangular gusset, or corner piece, is available for about $10. This handy item saves lots of installation time.

The prefabricated foam soffit system can also be used above utility-room cabinets or as a perimeter soffit around a room. Another useful application: Install the lengths vertically to hide pipes or ducts in corners—*by Phil McCafferty. Drawings by Adolph Brotman.*

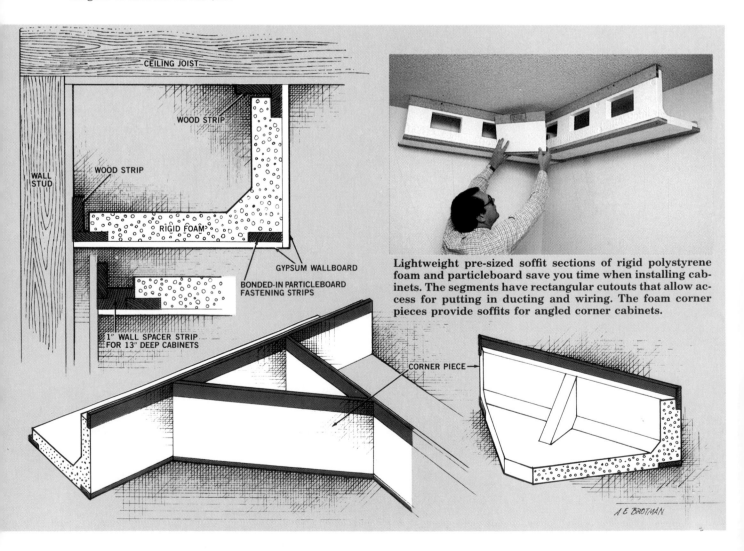

CEILING JOIST

WOOD STRIP

WOOD STRIP

WALL STUD

RIGID FOAM

GYPSUM WALLBOARD

BONDED-IN PARTICLEBOARD FASTENING STRIPS

1" WALL SPACER STRIP FOR 13" DEEP CABINETS

CORNER PIECE

Lightweight pre-sized soffit sections of rigid polystyrene foam and particleboard save you time when installing cabinets. The segments have rectangular cutouts that allow access for putting in ducting and wiring. The foam corner pieces provide soffits for angled corner cabinets.

A E BROTMAN

add a sunspace—fast

Conservatories, sun rooms, greenhouses, solaria. They're all names for the glass-walled rooms, usually aluminum-framed but sometimes made of laminated wood, that have become increasingly popular among homeowners. These structures—with their prefabricated parts, integral insulation, and appealing styling—are economical, attractive additions to any house, new or old.

As an engineer, I'm interested in sunspace technology, so I jumped at a chance to watch Tom Nova of Energy Shield Systems erect a sun room. Nova and two other experienced workers were installing it on a house under construction in Dover, VT, but they'd use the same materials and techniques to put up additions to existing houses.

The glass room that Nova built is a bit larger than the one pictured above; both are made by Sunplace, Inc., of Hinesburg, VT. Four 38-inch-wide bays look out on the yard, and the end walls are two bays deep (or 6 feet 9 inches). The unit cost about $6,000 installed. Work was completed in a day and a half, except for a few finishing details. You can use the same procedure to erect a similar unit.

First, you'll need a foundation. The Dover house has a concrete slab 14 feet long and 7 feet wide, set nine inches lower than the living-room floor. Since no interior wall divides the living room and the step-down sun room, Nova constructed a "splice" by lag-screwing 2 × 4s to the house exterior. The greenhouse rests on 2 × 6 subsills lag-screwed to the slab.

Tack the roof ridge, end-wall framing bars, and sills into place temporarily on the 2 × 4 and 2 × 6 mating surfaces, and readjust them until the dimensions of the greenhouse match the manufacturer's specifications. When all the corners are square, caulk the back sides of the metal beams and lag-screw them down.

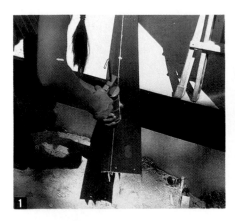

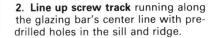

1. When you're sure subsills and attaching surfaces on the house are flat and the corners are square, caulk the back sides of the ridge, end-wall bars, and sills. Lag-screw them into place.

2. Line up screw track running along the glazing bar's center line with predrilled holes in the sill and ridge.

3. End-wall bars have aluminum plugs, called spigots, that attach to glazing bars. Glazing bars slip into a slot in the ridge. Later, glass slips into a similar slot above the glazing bars.

4. Screws fit through predrilled holes in muntins (horizontal beams) and the screw track in glazing and end-wall bars. A wood template ensures proper spacing. Muntins extend over a maximum of three bays.

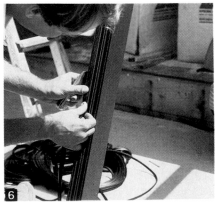

5. Install the top muntin for a 40-inch sliding window. Cut 1-by-2-inch spacer templates according to the manufacturer's instructions.

6. Place multi-finned vinyl gaskets in slots in glazing bars to keep out moisture. Weep channels on either side of the screw track carry leakage or condensation into drain holes in the sill.

7. Apply 1/16-inch double-stick tape to the sill. Just before installing the glass, remove the blue backing. Place the glass panels on the tape to form a seal.

The glazing bars, which are the primary structural parts, go up next. They're hollow 2-by-3-inch rectangular aluminum extrusions. Like the other metal parts, the glazing bars are precut, pre-painted with a baked-on enamel, and pre-drilled at the factory. To assemble them, line up the screw track running along each bar's center line with holes in the sill and ridge. Fit aluminum plugs into the hollow tops of the end-wall bars, and attach them to bottoms of glazing bars.

The muntins (horizontal beams) are the only remaining structural components. Cut wood spacers to the lengths specified in the installation manual, and use them to position the muntins across the glazing bars.

Like most prefabs, the Sunplace glass room uses a "dry glazing" system. The glazing panels are two sheets of tempered 1/8-inch clear glass with a 5/8-inch hermetically sealed air space between them to improve thermal efficiency. Tempering makes the glass so tough that it's safe to walk on the roof panels once they're installed. You can also order the panels with a bronze tint that filters out about 15 percent of the light and heat, or with a Solar Cool coating that reflects about half of the heat transmitted through clear double-paned glass.

You weatherproof the sun room with special gaskets and double-stick tape that press against the glass and keep out moisture. Check the fit of the panels before you remove the blue backing on the sealing tape. It's almost impossible to move the glass once this tape has taken hold. When the glass is in place, secure the glazing-bar caps and snap on the muntin caps. You new glass room is ready to use—*by Jack Horst. Photos by Ben Day. Drawings by Gerhard Richter.*

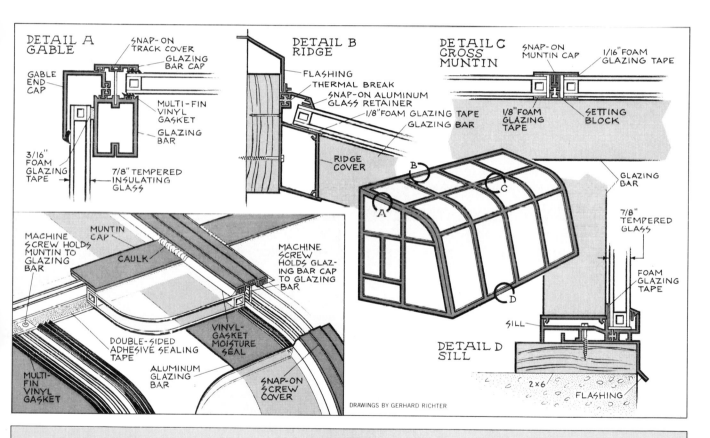

DRAWINGS BY GERHARD RICHTER

Is a sun room right for your house?

Doug Taff, president of Sunplace, Inc., says the majority of the residential glass rooms his company sells are add-ons to existing houses. But a glass room won't satisfy every homeowner's space needs, location, and budget. I asked Taff how an owner should decide if a prefabricated greenhouse is right for his house. Here's his list of the five factors you should consider:

Purpose: How do you plan to use your sunspace? Glass rooms are best suited for "outdoor-type" uses—to house a whirlpool spa or potted plants, for example. They can also be used to add living space to a kitchen or dining room, or to create a sunny family room. But think twice about using a sunspace as your guest bedroom.

Location: Where will you build the sunspace? In the northern states, the ideal location is a sunny spot where you'll get the most heat. In southern regions, you'll want a shady site. The location should also afford some privacy. And you should avoid potential hazards like falling tree branches or icicles.

Aesthetics: A glass room can add to the attractiveness and value of your house, but only if you choose an appropriate unit. Prefabricated sunspaces come in many styles and almost any size. Select one that will blend with your house's architecture and environment.

Cost: The average glass room costs about the same amount as a conventional room addition. You can reduce your expenses by using an existing concrete patio or carport slab as a foundation. Accessories such as ventilating fans, thermal shades, or low-emissivity glass, which allows heat in during the day but retards its escape at night, will increase cost. But you can justify purchasing these extras if they significantly reduce heating bills or increase the overall value of your house.

Dealer reputation: Nationally known sunspace manufacturers choose their dealers carefully and usually stand behind their products. Even so, it is wise to check with several former customers before selecting a dealer. Pick one who guarantees his work, or—if you plan to install the add-on yourself—make sure the dealer agrees to provide plenty of advice and instruction.—J. H.

2 ways to a back room

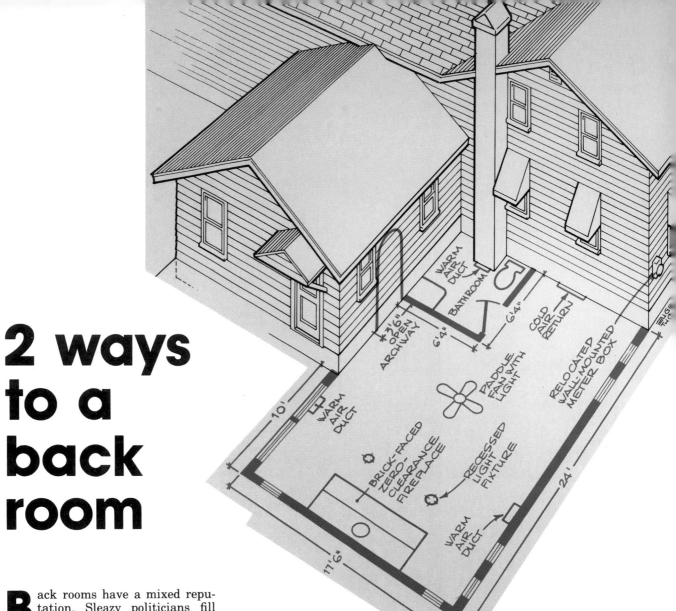

Wasted yard space notched into this small house was annexed for an elegant addition complete with its own bathroom, tied into existing plumbing.

Back rooms have a mixed reputation. Sleazy politicians fill them with cigar smoke. Sultry Marlene Dietrich sings, in her *Destry* saloon: "See what the boys in the back room will have." A similarly dubious quality can plague the back rooms in houses. Tucked beyond traffic lanes, they're often forgotten, stuffed with bulk storage, left to deteriorate.

But nobody is better able to appreciate their potential than the homeowner who doesn't *have* one. So: a toast to that most underrated of spaces—with two examples of back rooms that truly serve their owners, and double as self-contained guest suites. One of them is an imaginative redo of a neglected space. The other is new construction tacked onto a cramped house that lacked any such amenity. Both projects contain details that would be applicable to many other back rooms.

The add-on

Room additions that are energy efficient and appropriate to your neighborhood can bring an investment recovery of more than 100 percent—especially if you tackle much of the work yourself. Adding an extra bathroom can also significantly increase the resale value of a house. Owens-Corning Fiberglas Corporation, a leading manufacturer of building materials, demonstrated these precepts for *Popular Science* by tacking this back room on a Midwestern home, photographing the work of Wayne Dibert and his crew at PTL Home Improvement of Temperance, Michigan.

In designing an add-on, you must first decide how it will tie into the existing house's floor plan. Then determine the number and type of windows you'll want—as well as their placement, which can significantly affect the room's energy efficiency.

The first construction step is, of course, laying the foundation. Unless that's your trade, hire a contractor for this. In the room shown, a monolithic concrete slab was chosen because it's faster and less costly than a perimeter foundation bridged by wooden joists. Before the slab was poured, a four-mil polyethylene vapor barrier was laid over the compacted fill. Energy Shield foam sheathing was placed over the vapor barrier, around the perimeter, and down the inside of the footings (see sketch), before the plumbing and HVAC systems were installed. Dibert used watertight PVC ductwork, propped up so the concrete could be poured around the sides and bottom. The ventilation apparatus was tied into the house's existing system.

BEFORE

Photos show project from start to finish. Studs were conventional 2 × 4s, 16 inches on center and doubled at each window to support doubled 2 × 12 headers. One-inch-thick foam insulating sheathing is nailed on outside before Owens-Corning Fiberglas batts are placed in stud cavities (right). Rafters were 2 × 12s with a single pitch to create a vaulted ceiling. A prefabricated zero-clearance fireplace was built into the end wall.

Once the slab had cured, bottom plates of pressure-treated lumber were anchored to its perimeter and erection of the framing began (see photo and sketch).

To construct the vaulted ceiling, Dibert erected 2 × 12 rafters, 16 inches on center. These are strong enough to support the weight of the waferboard roof deck, the fiberglass-based three-tab shingles, and the interior drywall—in addition to a Michigan snow load. He nailed aluminum drip edge along the eaves edge of the roof, then laid 15-pound felt over the drip edge and roof deck. Lastly, a rake edge was installed over the felt at both gable ends.

Energy Shield insulating sheathing was nailed directly to the outside of the studs—after both outside corners were reinforced with diagonal metal corner bracing. The sheathing must cover the top and bottom plates of the framing.

Venting skylights were installed in the vaulted ceiling to permit the escape of warm air in the summer. For all windows, fixed thermal-pane units were chosen. All stud spaces were packed with R-13 unfaced Owens-Corning Fiberglas batts. Combined with the R-7.2 provided by the sheathing, the walls have an R-value of over 20. Between the rafters, faced R-30 batts were stapled, with about

an inch of airspace left below the roof deck for ventilation.

To prevent moisture from condensing in the insulated wall, a six-mil polyethylene vapor barrier was stapled across the wall studs. Dibert recommends that you leave the barrier intact across electrical outlets until your drywall is up, taped, and painted, to keep moisture and debris out of the boxes. Cut the film only when you're ready to complete wiring hookups.

To finish the interior, molding was installed around the floor, and casings around all windows and doors. Before applying the latter, however, you should stuff all cracks with scraps of fiberglass. To save tedious work, paint

27

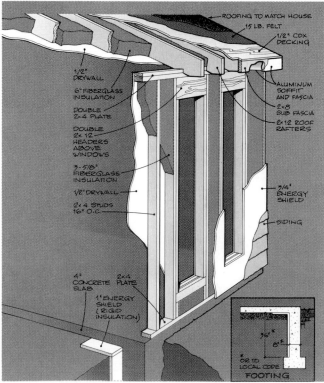

ROOFING TO MATCH HOUSE

15 LB. FELT

1/2" CDX DECKING

1/2" DRYWALL

6" FIBERGLASS INSULATION

DOUBLE 2x4 PLATE

DOUBLE 2x12 HEADERS ABOVE WINDOWS

3-5/8" FIBERGLASS INSULATION

1/2" DRYWALL

2x4 STUDS 16" O.C.

ALUMINUM SOFFIT AND FASCIA

2x8 SUB FASCIA

2x12 ROOF RAFTERS

3/4" ENERGY SHIELD

SIDING

4" CONCRETE SLAB

2x4 PLATE

1" ENERGY SHIELD (RIGID INSULATION)

OZ TO LOCAL CODE

FOOTING

BEFORE

or paper your walls, and paint or stain your molding strips *before* applying the molding.

The ceiling fan used in this project is an energy saver: It keeps heated air from stratifying at the peak of the ceiling during the winter. It also helps move unwanted warm air out through the venting skylights in summer.

As a finishing touch, strip mirrors the same size as the tall, skinny windows were fixed to the walls; wallpaper border strips provide an accent that ties the room together.

The redo

The owners of this modest home in Princeton, New Jersey, had a problem. A new baby required converting a small upstairs guest room into a nursery. Where could guests spend the night—especially since the only bathroom was upstairs? Also, a safe play space was needed for the toddler—somewhere out from under the mother's feet but close enough for constant supervision.

Enter Andy Pressman, AIA, who was invited to the home to see if anything could be done with a long-neglected back room. Pressman is an architectural designer now located in the Midwest (Pressman Associates, 1400 N. Lake Shore Dr., No. 2-L, Chicago, IL 60610); he sketched up a new floor plan and lighting scheme for the

space. And since one wall of the back room partitioned it from the kitchen, he saw that plumbing runs for a new bathroom could be kept fairly short.

Pressman tucked clever storage into the compact bathroom. A medicine chest is built into the back of the linen closet to the right of the bathroom door. Cleaning gear stores under the corner counter, with access doors under the towel rack (see photo). The corner tub is Eljer's Montego; it fits in a space only 37 by 42 inches (Eljer Plumbingware, 3 Gateway Center, Pittsburg, PA 15222).

Pressman first acquired a standard twin-bed mattress to set the dimensions of the bed platform. Built in underneath are simple box drawers, side-mounted on rollerbearing slides to clear the rug by 1½ inches. The 27-inch-wide false fronts project at both sides of each drawer to conceal the slide hardware when they're closed. No pulls are needed because the false fronts also project beyond the bottom of the drawers to provide a finger grip.

There's a tall cupboard built into the corner to the left of the entry door. A counter top butts this cupboard and wraps, in a broad U-shape, around the loose bolsters for the couch, ending in a spacious alcove counter for displaying sculpture. The corner plant shelves are hung on standards and brackets so the spacing can be ad-

justed to plant growth. All shelves, counters, and verticals can be either enameled or surfaced with plastic laminate. The lighting is a combination of inexpensive bare-bulb fixtures mounted behind a fascia board around the perimeter and a dropped soffit into which three "pin" down lights are recessed.

When I checked out the room recently with photographer Greg Sharko, the rest of the house was piled high with packed cartons. Homeowner/sculptor Wendy Kvalheim explained she and her husband had just sold the house and were awaiting the moving van. She told me the renovation of the back room had cost about $12,000, not including the bathroom tiling (which was done directly over mortar-based backer board, in this case Wonder-Board, made by Modulars Inc., Hamilton, Ohio).

"This back room raised our selling price at least that amount," Kvalheim told me. "Prospective buyers zeroed in on this room as a real plus. If they'd seen it as it was before, it would have been a turnoff. I can tell you one thing," she added, as Greg signaled that he was through shooting so she could begin packing her sculpture, "it's the one aspect of this house we'll miss the most"—*by Al Lees. Drawings by Eugene Thompson. Photos by Greg Sharko.*

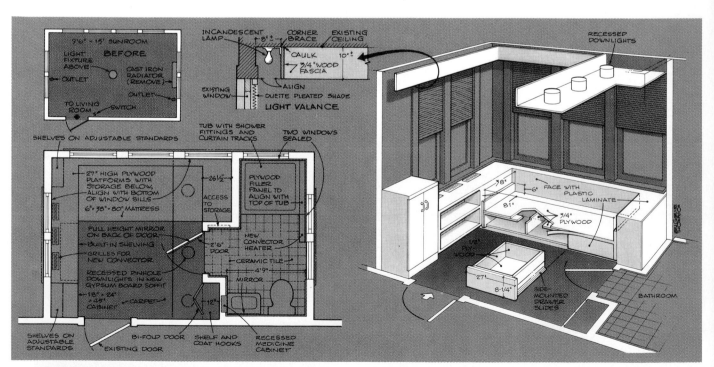

Existing room's many windows limited remodeling. Since a bathroom was needed, two corner windows were sealed so blinds left in place (to match adjacent windows) would not collect dust. Bathroom is seen, far left, through an open door, with the vanity side reflected in the mirror. Note the light sof-

fit above the door. Floor plan shows how built-in shelf counters and storage bed made the best use of space. Three plywood drawers move on metal slides mounted near the bottom of their sides. The mattress is 38 by 80 inches—standard size for a twin bed.

bedroom/home-office suite

Nondescript one-story house was transformed by a two-room addition and a handsome redwood deck. The new wing was spliced onto the wall at the right.

Often the key to staying put—bringing your current home in line with family needs instead of resorting to the disruption of moving to a larger house—is a room addition. But before you start to tear out a wall for a tack-on, give serious thought to what such a project can contribute toward your living space. The three homeowners whose add-ons are featured in the next pages came up with *multi-purpose* additions: In each case, the new space provided a dual function—and quickly became an essential part of the home.

The first project, shown here, met the needs of an expanding family while adding eye appeal and outdoor living to the back of an ordinary single-story house. Tacked onto a rear wall where two windows gave light (but little privacy) to two cramped bedrooms, this addition created a spacious master-bedroom suite; one of the old bedrooms was converted to a nursery, the other became a guest room.

Because the exterior wall became an interior partition, those existing windows were removed and their holes filled in with studs covered with wallboard. Their positions were not duplicated in the new end wall, because it was thrust closer to the lot line and large windows here would have violated privacy. Instead, the family used two skylights and a glazed corner that gives onto the new deck. New windows to those existing bedrooms were cut into the walls just

Home office is partitioned from sleeping area so reading at desk will not disturb someone who has retired for the night.

Double-faced fireplace pierces the wall between the study area and spacious master bath with its twin vanity counter.

Compartmented bathroom allows dual use and has skylight and frosted window.

tion (which tends to remain around 55°F) to help heat and cool the living space above. There are vents in the stem wall that open automatically in summer but remain closed to retain the soil's heat during the winter. The earth is covered with a vapor barrier to prevent moisture buildup.

Note in the foundation section that the builder chose to use a permanent all-weather wood foundation of pressure-treated lumber and plywood. The only concrete is in the footing. He also chose batts of mineral wool for insulation; this could as well have been rigid plastic foam plank.

At five locations in the stem wall, the builder inserted Energy-Saver foundation vents. They're equipped with a bimetal coil that operates louvers as the temperature rises and falls; the louvers close fully at about 40°F and open at 70. Within this range, the coil continues to expand and contract, ensuring the correct amount of constant ventilation to lessen any chance of condensation on the underside of floors cooled by air conditioning. These vents are easy for a novice builder to install.

Once the insulated stem walls are erected, joists are dropped in place, supported on the house end by galvanized hangers nailed to a ledger that has been lag-screwed into the framing of the existing wall. In the Sturd-I-Floor system photo, note the staggered blocking that stiffens the framing.

To increase the R-value of the insulation to R-24, all exterior wall framing was done with 2 × 6 studs. These cavities were filled with blown-in insulation. Netting was stapled across the interior edges of the studs after all wiring and rough plumbing was in, then a hose was inserted into each cavity and fluff insulation was pumped in up to the top plate.

The photos show the unique effect of the interior soffit built "under the eaves" of the cathedral ceiling (it's shown as shaded areas on the floor plan). A similar effect is carried across the partition between the bed/study and master bath, creating a plant shelf. The soffit permits recessed lighting around the perimeter.

Access to the whirlpool tub's pump is through an outdoor hatch. The redwood deck covers the existing patio slab (with planks nailed to sleepers), but extends far beyond it. Here, it is conventionally supported on concrete piers. All the lumber in the deck is Construction Common and Construction Heart grade redwood—*by Al Lees. Drawings by Carl DeGroote.*

around both corners from the filled-in windows (see floor plan).

No floor insulation

This addition was not built on a poured-concrete slab. Instead, it was done on a new system, called PIRF (for perimeter-insulated raised floor). This is a new approach to crawl-space construction, designed both to reduce building costs and to upgrade energy performance. Insulation is applied only to the inside of the perimeter stem walls; *none* is placed between the floor joists. This permits the thermal mass of the earth within the founda-

1. Trowel concrete footing for the all-wood foundation. Anchor bolts will be added to receive the treated mud sill.

2. Sturd-I-Floor system: Lay subfloor of ¾-inch tongue-and-groove plywood underlayment over adhesive.

3. Nail plywood sheathing over 2 × 6 framing for new walls (gap was a goof, closed before Tyvek was stapled on).

4. Nail APA-rated plywood lap siding through the Tyvek (which decreases air infiltration); paint to match house.

5. With ceiling insulation in place, cut drywall to fit between overhead beams and attach with drywall screws.

6. Apply asphalt shingles to align with those on adjacent roof (in background). Pneumatic stapler speeds this job.

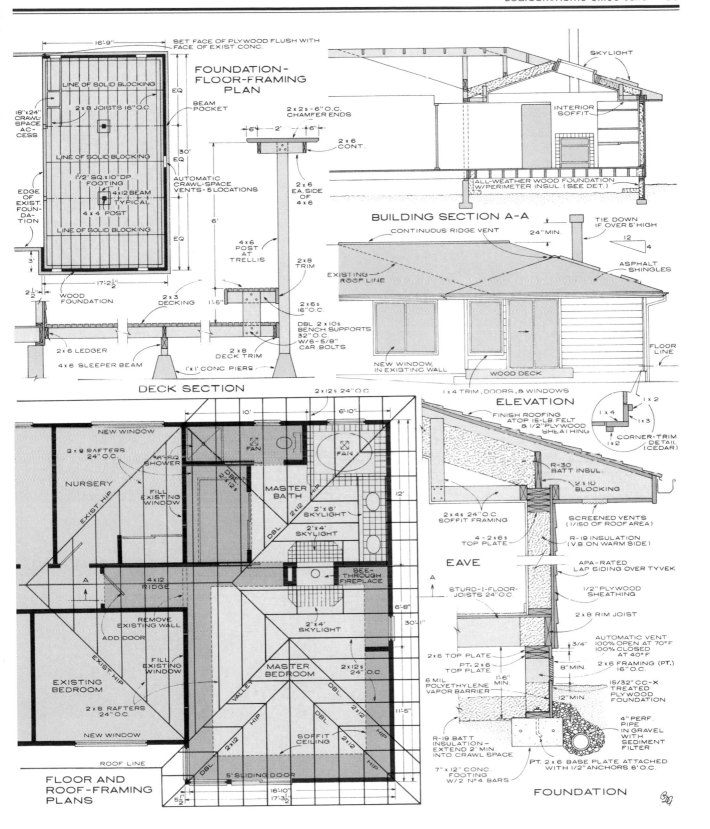

FOUNDATION-FLOOR-FRAMING PLAN

BUILDING SECTION A-A

DECK SECTION

ELEVATION

EAVE

FOUNDATION

FLOOR AND ROOF-FRAMING PLANS

THE FOLLOWING WERE SELECTED FOR PARTICIPATION IN THIS PROJECT:

Photographer: Bob Strode, Tacoma WA; architect: William Kreager, AIA, and interior designer: Cynthia Mennella—both with Mithun-Bowman-Emrich Group, P.S., 2000 112th Ave. N.E., Bellevue WA 98004; builder: Dale Enterprises, Tacoma WA; furnishings: JCPenney Co.; finishes: Parker Paint Mfg. Co., Box 11047, Tacoma WA; windows: Vinyl Building Products, 1 Raritan Rd., Oakland NJ 07436; skylights: Paeco, Inc., 59 E. Newman Springs Rd., Shrewsbury NJ 07701; counter-top laminate: Ralph Wilson Plastics Co., Wilsonart Division, Box 6110, Temple TX 76503-6110; deck material: California Redwood Assn., 591 Redwood Hwy., Suite 3100, Mill Valley CA 94941; automatic foundation vents: Underworld Energy Systems, Box 450, Clayton CA 94517; plumbing fixtures, faucets: Eljer Plumbingware, 901 10th St., Plano TX 75074; ceramic tile: American Olean Tile Co., 1000 Cannon Ave., Lansdale PA 19446; construction tools: (circular saw, miter saw, cordless drill, sander, power screwdriver) Skil Corp., 4801 W. Peterson Ave., Chicago IL 60646; (pneumatic nailer, stapler, air compressor) Stanley-Bostitch, East Greenwich RI 02818; (table saw, sawbuck) Delta International Machinery Corp., 246 Alpha Dr., Pittsburgh PA 15238; landscaping: Emerald Turfgrass Farms, 13826 16th St. E., Sumner WA 98390

FOR FURTHER GUIDANCE ON THIS PROJECT:
• Two videotapes are offered to readers: Tape 1—"Add-A-Room" follows project from start to finish.
Tape 2—"Remodeling Decision" offers advice from experts and instruction on how to work with professionals in planning, designing, and building. Each tape is $9.95 in U.S. funds, plus $2.95 for shipping (whether ordering one or both tapes): Send check to InstructoVision, 9800 Bayard Ave. N.W., Seattle WA 98117; for Visa or MasterCard orders, call (800) 541-4100. Specify VHS or Beta.
• *Add a Room: A Practical Guide to Expanding Your Home* by Paul Bianchina is published by Tab Books (Box 40, Blue Ridge Summit PA 17214) and priced at $17.95.
• For free booklets on the All-Weather Wood Foundation and PIRF systems, write American Plywood Assn., Box 11700, Tacoma WA 98411.

raise your floor

Nancy and Dann rejoiced in their first house, despite its modest size—until Nancy's college roommate phoned from a distant city proposing a week's visit in the fall. Though Nancy welcomed the chance to entertain Donna and to meet her new husband, Ken, she abruptly realized that a house that was adequate for herself and Dann offered no hospitality for guests. Not only was there no extra bedroom, there was not even space to store another bed. True, the living room needed a couch, but Nancy didn't want to settle for a sofa bed.

Fortunately, the announced visit was several weeks off, and Dann had been planning major work on their home's skinny living room, where furniture groupings were awkward. He hoped to create a dining area off the small kitchen.

The characters are fictional, but the situation is typical of the problem I designed this innovative project to solve. My solution, as the drawings show, raises the floor of the dining area 2 feet so that a full-size bed could be stored underneath. This meant rebuilding most of the non-load-bearing partition along the kitchen, and the addition of two sets of steps to turn the corner from the living room into the kitchen. But elevating the dining area with a platform added architectural distinction as well as badly needed storage space. And the pass-through from the kitchen can also double as a serving shelf.

I asked Louisa Cowan of Armstrong World Industries' Design Center to refine the concept, and she came up with the idea of putting the guest bed on lockable casters so that it could be left (during the day) protruding far enough from the platform to serve as a bolstered couch. Cowan chose materials for the floor and ceiling and mocked up a prototype of the setting at the Design Center.

To resume the scenario: When Donna and Ken arrived, they were treated to their own guest space—an area that quickly converted from living room to bedroom by simply rolling the bed forward from under the platform and drawing vertical blinds across the dining room.

In the morning Nancy could proceed with breakfast preparation, placing food on the pass-through and even setting the table without disturbing the privacy of her guests. And the guests could then restore the living room to its main function by simply rolling the bed back into its couch position and replacing the bolsters.

The guests were grateful for restful sleep on a real bed rather than a compromise fold-out sofa. And because the dining room's sheet vinyl flooring seals all joints in the plywood platform, there's no sift-through of floor debris onto the bed below. The same sheet vinyl used on the living room floor ensures easier rolling of the bed casters than carpeting would, and it won't develop a wear pattern. To link the two areas, vinyl flooring was also applied to the stair treads.

The privacy blinds are attractive in themselves, and they offer a bonus function: After dinner, they can be drawn to screen table clutter from view. Even when guests aren't spending the night, this lets the hosts postpone cleanup so they can join their guests in the living room for coffee. On the other hand, *before* a dinner party the open blinds offer an almost theatrical display of the decorated table. And to permit ready access to the "stage," the blinds at the top of the stair tuck neatly into a wall recess next to the sliding pocket door.

Construction of the platform was started by attaching level 2×6s to all three walls of the dining area, with their top edges $23^{1}/_{4}$ inches above the existing floor all around. (We were working from a level floor; in actual houses ledger heights might have to be adjusted to compensate for floor sag.) When $^{3}/_{4}$-inch plywood is fastened on top, it brings the platform height to 2 feet. These ledgers should be tied into existing wall framing wherever possible by driving 5-inch-long lag screws into studs. Then, to create the open edge of the platform, two 6×6 posts were erected from floor to ceiling and framed out to create the opening of the bed recess. It's a good idea to lay out this location on the living-room floor with masking tape so you'll be certain the couch will be positioned exactly where you want it.

Rebuilt kitchen partition features pocket door, recess for blinds.

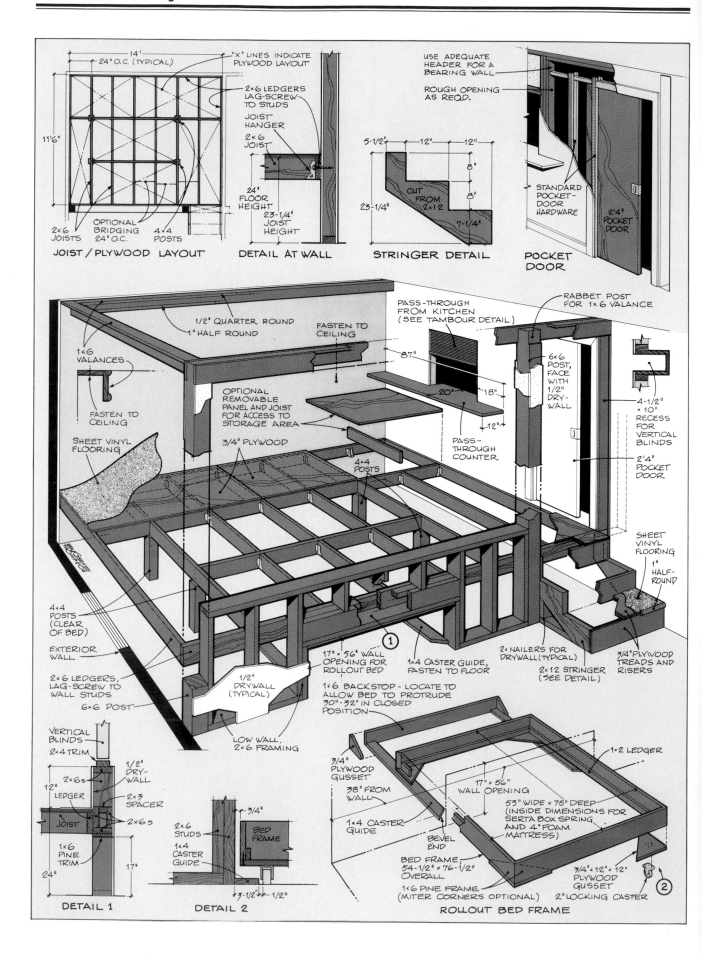

JOIST / PLYWOOD LAYOUT

14'
24" O.C. (TYPICAL)
"X" LINES INDICATE PLYWOOD LAYOUT
2×6 LEDGERS LAG-SCREW TO STUDS
JOIST HANGER
2×6 JOIST
11'6"
24" FLOOR HEIGHT
23-1/4" JOIST HEIGHT
2×6 JOISTS
OPTIONAL BRIDGING 24" O.C.
4×4 POSTS

DETAIL AT WALL

STRINGER DETAIL

5-1/2"   12"   12"
8"
CUT FROM 2×12
8"
23-1/4"
7-1/4"

POCKET DOOR

USE ADEQUATE HEADER FOR A BEARING WALL
ROUGH OPENING AS REQD.
STANDARD POCKET-DOOR HARDWARE
2'4" POCKET DOOR

1/2" QUARTER ROUND
1" HALF ROUND
FASTEN TO CEILING
PASS-THROUGH FROM KITCHEN (SEE TAMBOUR DETAIL)
RABBET POST FOR 1×6 VALANCE
1×6 VALANCES
FASTEN TO CEILING
87"
6×6 POST, FACE WITH 1/2" DRYWALL
SHEET VINYL FLOORING
OPTIONAL REMOVABLE PANEL AND JOIST FOR ACCESS TO STORAGE AREA
3/4" PLYWOOD
20"   18"
PASS-THROUGH COUNTER
12"
4-1/2" × 10" RECESS FOR VERTICAL BLINDS
4×4 POSTS
2'4" POCKET DOOR
4×4 POSTS (CLEAR OF BED)
EXTERIOR WALL
2×6 LEDGERS, LAG-SCREW TO WALL STUDS
6×6 POST
1/2" DRYWALL (TYPICAL)
LOW WALL, 2×6 FRAMING
17" × 56" WALL OPENING FOR ROLLOUT BED
1×4 CASTER GUIDE, FASTEN TO FLOOR
1×6 BACKSTOP - LOCATE TO ALLOW BED TO PROTRUDE 30"-32" IN CLOSED POSITION
2× NAILERS FOR DRYWALL (TYPICAL)
2×12 STRINGER (SEE DETAIL)
SHEET VINYL FLOORING
1" HALF-ROUND
3/4" PLYWOOD TREADS AND RISERS
①

DETAIL 1

VERTICAL BLINDS
2×4 TRIM
1/2" DRY-WALL
12"
2×6s
LEDGER
2×3 SPACER
JOIST
2×6s
1×6 PINE TRIM
24"
17"

DETAIL 2

3/4"
2×6 STUDS
1×4 CASTER GUIDE
BED FRAME
3-1/2"   1/2"

ROLLOUT BED FRAME

3/4" PLYWOOD GUSSET
38" FROM WALL
1×4 CASTER GUIDE
BEVEL END
BED FRAME 54-1/2" × 76-1/2" OVERALL
1×6 PINE FRAME (MITER CORNERS OPTIONAL)
2" LOCKING CASTER
17" × 56" WALL OPENING
53" WIDE × 75" DEEP (INSIDE DIMENSIONS FOR SERTA BOX SPRING AND 4" FOAM MATTRESS)
1×2 LEDGER
3/4" × 12" × 12" PLYWOOD GUSSET
②

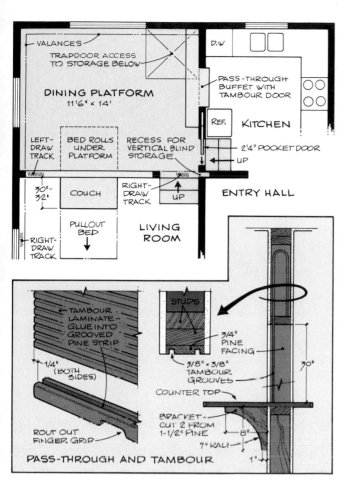

LEFT-DRAW TRACK — VALANCES — TRAPDOOR ACCESS TO STORAGE BELOW — DINING PLATFORM 11'6" × 14' — D.W — PASS-THROUGH BUFFET WITH TAMBOUR DOOR — KITCHEN — REF. — BED ROLLS UNDER PLATFORM — RECESS FOR VERTICAL BLIND STORAGE — 2'4" POCKET DOOR — UP — 30"-32" — COUCH — RIGHT-DRAW TRACK — UP — ENTRY HALL — RIGHT-DRAW TRACK — PULLOUT BED — LIVING ROOM

PASS-THROUGH AND TAMBOUR — TAMBOUR LAMINATE — GLUE INTO GROOVED PINE STRIP — 1/4" (BOTH SIDES) — ROUT OUT FINGER GRIP — STUDS — 3/4" PINE FACING — 3/8" × 3/8" TAMBOUR GROOVES — COUNTER TOP — BRACKET — CUT 2 FROM 1-1/2" PINE — 30" — 8" — 7" RAD. — 1"

Product specifications

The following manufacturers were selected for participation in this project:

Armstrong World
Industries, Inc.
Liberty & Charlotte Sts.
Lancaster PA 17604

Ceiling tile
Pattern: Willow Square 12 x 12 tiles
Color: Beige

Floor covering
Pattern: Timespan San Xavier,
No. 67782
Color: Taupe

Benjamin Moore & Co.
51 Chestnut Ridge Rd.
Montvale NJ 07013

Wall paint
Dining-room walls: GN-77
Living-room walls: GN-76

Chapman Mfg. Co.
481 W. Main St.
Avon MA 02322

Table lamps

Gilliam Furniture, Inc.
820 Cochran St., Box 1610
Statesville NC 28677

Furniture (upholstered)
Armchairs, No. 345

Louver Drape, Inc.
1100 Colorado Ave.
Santa Monica CA 90401

Vertical blinds
Pattern: Mountain Shadows
Clear-Edge Louver Groover

Thomasville Furniture
Industries
401 E. Main St., Box 339
Thomasville NC 27360

Furniture (wood)
Dining room: Prestige Collection
Living room: Country Collection

West Point-Pepperell, Inc.
Consumer Products Div.
1221 Ave. of the Americas
New York NY 10020

Bedding

DESIGN BY LOUISA COWAN, A.S.I.D.; PHOTOS BY CARL SHUMAN;
DRAWINGS BY EUGENE THOMPSON

A 2 × 6 band joist was bolted across these posts at the same height as the wall ledgers. The space between the right-hand post and the kitchen partition was also bridged by a plywood riser to support the extra piece of plywood that extends the floor here. Next, metal joist hangers were nailed on and the 2 × 6 joists laid in, as shown in the perspective sketch. The pattern is determined by how you wish to position your 4-by-8-foot sheets of plywood, because each joint between sheets must fall along support framing.

At this point, you'll have to determine how much access to the storage you'll want. By rolling the bed all the way forward, we could reach areas surrounding the bed recess, but the right-rear corner of the platform remained inaccessible. The sketches show one option for reaching this area: Leave a floor panel loose so it can be lifted. By choosing a vinyl flooring with a grid design (such as the Armstrong Timespan San Xavier shown) you can cut along grid lines so that a "trapdoor" can be created without disrupting the pattern.

The flooring was easy to install, on both the platform and the living-room floor. Unlike most sheet vinyl, Armstrong's Interflex flooring doesn't have to be cemented down all over. You just fasten it around the edges.

Before constructing the bed cart, you should obtain the box spring to dimension the cart to fit. Under each corner gusset we mounted a flat-plate caster. The front pair have lever locks. The mattress itself was fully upholstered, and a matching pleated skirt was tacked around the cart. The bed assembly was positioned against the open end of the platform to check the recess framing before applying drywall. We upholstered 8-inch-diameter cylinders of foam rubber to create 26-inch-long bolsters. For the headboard (which remains stationary as the bed is rolled under it so that it also serves as the back of the sofa), a 16-by-56-inch slab of 4-inch foam was upholstered.

In rebuilding the kitchen partition, we not only framed in the pass-through (with a pull-down tambour door to hide the kitchen from diners) and hung a door panel on a pocket track, but also built in a tall, skinny recess into which the stacked vanes of the vertical blinds tuck so that the full width of the stair entry is left open.

One of Louisa Cowan's clever design touches is the complex two-tone effect she achieves with the wall-paint colors she selected for the two rooms. Look carefully at the photos, and you'll see that a dark field of color with light trim is used in the living room; the walls in the smaller dining area are painted the lighter tone while the darker one is used on the trim. The trim moldings are lengths of 3/4-inch quarter-round (against the ceilings) with 1-inch half-rounds along the bottom edge of all cornices. To tie the rooms together, this treatment is carried along the right-hand walls, where no cornice boards are needed. You'll save yourself tedious masking chores if you paint all the moldings before you apply them.

Will a platform work in your house? Probably, if the ceilings are *at least* 8½ feet high. even where head room will be tight, a platform makes special sense in a dining area. Unlike a kitchen or living room, this area's function keeps you seated, so a 6½-to-7-foot ceiling here will feel cramped only to extra-tall people. *Popular Science* has another type of storage platform (with roll-out carts) under construction for a future issue—by Al Lees. Photos by Carl Shuman. Drawings by Eugene Thompson.

bathrooms: 2 DIY approaches

add-on master bath

Entire 7½-by-11½-foot second-story bathroom is captured by the camera's fish-eye lens.

What's one of the most cost-effective home-improvement projects the average homeowner can take on? You guessed it: adding a second bathroom (according to the National Association of the Remodeling Industry). Whether you do the work yourself or hire it out, your house will increase in value more than the cost of the job.

That was one reason I added a bath to the plan when I contemplated my roof-raising project. The other was convenience. With the added living space on the second level, an accompanying bathroom seemed logical. Besides, my wife Marion and I felt the need to spoil ourselves a bit with a spacious bath off our equally spacious and airy master bedroom.

The result, which includes a fiberglass whirlpool tub, water-saving toilet, and built-in laundry chute, is shown here. My father and I did all the work, and most of it, as you'll see, was pretty easy. But first we did have to clear one major hurdle: the plumbing.

Whenever you add a bathroom, especially on the second floor, the plumbing can trip you up unless you're lucky and can place the fixtures near existing waste and supply lines. I was partially fortunate: An interior partition gave me a clear shot from upstairs to the basement mains. With the toilet and lavatory on the same wall as the new roughed-in plumbing, there were no problems with hookup.

Magnetic catches on the fiberglass whirlpool tub's removable front panel make for easy servicing (above); a removable panel built into the tub-side wall of the large linen closet shown below right also provides access to the pump (see drawing). Flush door of laundry-chute cabinet (above right) is fitted with spring hinges; 7½-in. cavity opens to 11½-in.-sq. chute just below floor.

But the tub on the opposite side of the room was anything but problem-free.

I could have installed the plumbing for the tub under the floor; however, the outside wall supports a cantilevered deck with doubled joists extending 5 feet into the house. Therefore, the bathroom floor is supported by *triple* 2×6s every 16 inches. Threading 12 feet of waste and supply lines through this mass of lumber would mean a lot of hard work and reinforcement of the joists.

I had a number of other alternatives, but the best seemed to be to double the outside wall. I would lose 3½ inches of floor space, but a bathroom this size could afford that. What would I gain? Double the insulation on the outside wall, a generous insulated cavity for plumbing, extra space for a laundry chute, a shelf at the south-facing window, and a clean, finished look. The only compromise I had to

make was raising the tub/shower by 8 inches so it would drain properly.

The fiberglass whirlpool tub/shower and enclosure from Sears, Roebuck and Co. couldn't have been easier to install. The whirlpool plumbing is already assembled on the tub: Just drop the tub into a prepared cavity, hook it to the drain, and connect and wire up the whirlpool pump. The no-caulk fiberglass enclosure is just as easy. It comes with complete instructions and will take a reasonably handy homeowner just a few hours to install.

Look out below!

With any second-floor bathroom, installing a laundry chute is a great idea, if possible. As with plumbing, happenstance plays a large part in planning one: You must have a clear pathway to the laundry room, and it has to coincide with a convenient spot in your bathroom. My 11½-inch-

square chute extends from the bathroom through a first-floor closet directly to the laundry area in the basement. I built a 4¾-inch-deep oak-plywood cabinet lined with ¼-inch hardboard, so a 7½-inch space funnels into the 11½-inch chute.

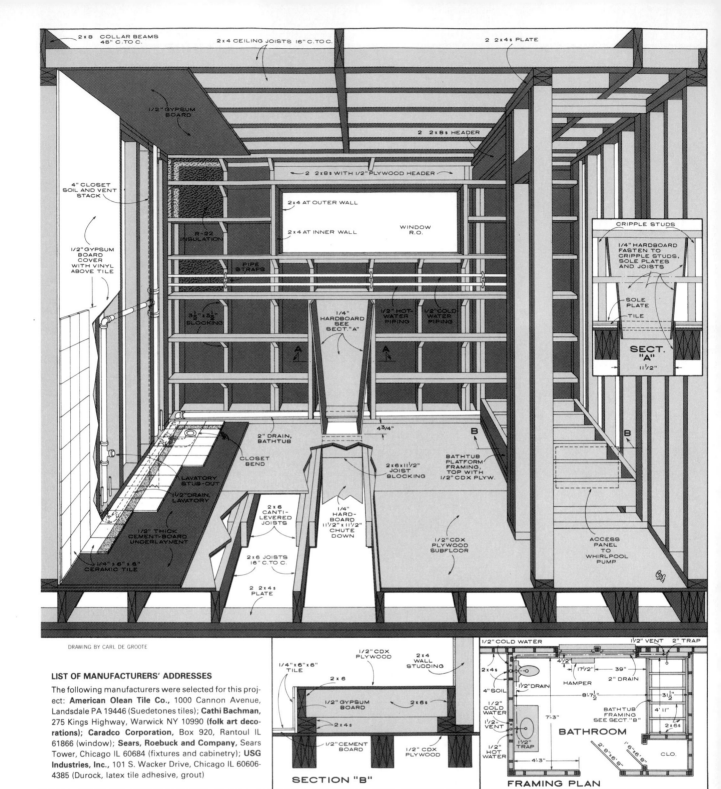

2 x 8 COLLAR BEAMS 48" C. TO C.

2 x 4 CEILING JOISTS 16" C. TO C.

2 2 x 4s PLATE

1/2" GYPSUM BOARD

4" CLOSET SOIL AND VENT STACK

2 2 x 8s HEADER

2 2 x 8s WITH 1/2" PLYWOOD HEADER

2 x 4 AT OUTER WALL

2 x 4 AT INNER WALL

WINDOW R.O.

1/2" GYPSUM BOARD COVER WITH VINYL ABOVE TILE

R-22 INSULATION

PIPE STRAPS

1/4" HARDBOARD SEE SECT. "A"

1/2" HOT-WATER PIPING

1/2" COLD WATER PIPING

CRIPPLE STUDS

1/4" HARDBOARD FASTEN TO CRIPPLE STUDS, SOLE PLATES AND JOISTS

SOLE PLATE

TILE

3 1/2" x 3 1/2" BLOCKING

A

A

SECT. "A" 11 1/2"

2" DRAIN, BATHTUB

CLOSET BEND

LAVATORY STUB-OUT

1/2" DRAIN, LAVATORY

1/2" THICK CEMENT-BOARD UNDERLAYMENT

1/4" x 6" x 6" CERAMIC TILE

2 x 6 CANTI-LEVERED JOISTS

2 x 6 JOISTS 16" C. TO C.

2 2 x 4s PLATE

4 3/4"

1/4" HARD-BOARD 11 1/2" x 11 1/2" CHUTE DOWN

2 x 6 x 11 1/2" JOIST BLOCKING

B

B

BATHTUB PLATFORM FRAMING, TOP WITH 1/2" CDX PLYW.

1/2" CDX PLYWOOD SUBFLOOR

ACCESS PANEL TO WHIRLPOOL PUMP

DRAWING BY CARL DE GROOTE

LIST OF MANUFACTURERS' ADDRESSES

The following manufacturers were selected for this project: **American Olean Tile Co.**, 1000 Cannon Avenue, Landsdale PA 19446 (Suedetones tiles); **Cathi Bachman**, 275 Kings Highway, Warwick NY 10990 (**folk art decorations**); **Caradco Corporation**, Box 920, Rantoul IL 61866 (window); **Sears, Roebuck and Company**, Sears Tower, Chicago IL 60684 (fixtures and cabinetry); **USG Industries, Inc.**, 101 S. Wacker Drive, Chicago IL 60606-4385 (Durock, latex tile adhesive, grout)

1/2" CDX PLYWOOD

2 x 4 WALL STUDDING

1/4" x 6" x 6" TILE

2 x 6

1/2" GYPSUM BOARD

2 x 6s

2 x 4s

1/2" CEMENT BOARD

1/2" CDX PLYWOOD

SECTION "B"

1/2" COLD WATER

1/2" VENT 2" TRAP

2 x 4s

4" SOIL

1/2" DRAIN

1/2" COLD WATER

1/2" VENT

1/2" TRAP

1/2" HOT WATER

4 1/2"

HAMPER

17 1/2"

39"

2" DRAIN

8-7 1/2"

7-3"

4-3"

3 1/2"

4' 11"

2 x 6s

BATHTUB FRAMING SEE SECT. "B"

BATHROOM

CLO.

2' 6"x 6' 9"

6"x 6' 9"

FRAMING PLAN

I used oak as a major design element, and this, along with the modern-looking tub, the low-boy water-saving toilet (also from Sears), and original folk art decorations by Cathi Bachman, creates a Country Contemporary atmosphere. To complement all the oak cabinetry, I used 6-by-6-inch ivory-colored tiles from American Olean's new line, Suedetones. By using the same tiles on the floor and walls, I achieved a wraparound effect. The Cadet Blue accent stripe in the floor is echoed by the wallpaper border.

The floor tiles were installed over USG Industries' Durock tile backer board with a latex adhesive that's easy to work with. The portland cement-mortar-based Durock provides a strong bond for tile, and although it's intended for water-soaked areas like tiled-in tub surrounds, this is a good secondary application—no need to worry about water that inevitably finds its way to the floor. When you install ceramic tiles, I recommend renting a power tile saw. You can make almost any cut easily with this handy tool, and you'll find that it saves a lot of time.

I also advocate adding a second bath. You can't go wrong with the investment, and if you have just one bathroom, especially in a two-story house, you don't realize the convenience you're missing—*by Timothy O. Bakke. Photos by Greg Sharko. Drawings by Carl De Groote.*

all-wood bathroom

When Bruce and Claudia Dwyer decided on a wood look for their new bathroom, they had an advantage: Bruce is a professional builder in Laguna Beach, California, and he's used redwood in bathrooms before.

As a professional, Bruce knew that redwood was the best choice because of its dimensional stability,, easy workability, and natural resistance to rot. The walls and the cathedral ceiling were paneled with 1 × 6 clear-grade boards. Redwood boards were also used to construct the long light fixture.

But the most unusual feature is the laminated counter top. Dwyer started gluing up counter and table slabs from scraps of redwood tongue-and-groove siding left over after a job. Here's how he outlines the process:

1. Rip the scrap lengths to an appropriate width. Subsequent planing and sanding will remove about 1/2-inch of material, so if you want a 1 1/2 inch-thick counter top, rip the boards to 2 inches.

2. Select the best board edges by appearance. Mark them so it will be easy later to tell which edge goes up.

3. Apply waterproof glue to both mating surfaces, then join them. If the boards have both a smooth and a saw-textured face, don't place two sawn faces together.

4. Stack the boards and apply pressure with bar clamps 2 feet on center. Wipe excess glue from the joints. Let the assembly set overnight.

5. Plane and sand the upper surface to a level face. Dwyer has this done on a 24-inch-wide power planer at a professional woodworking shop, but it can be done with a hand plane.

6. Make cutouts for the vanities.

7. Apply multiple coats of a clear polyurethane varnish or alkyd-resin sealer to form a protective surface impervious to water. Seal all edges and the undersurface, too. Remember that those creamy sapwood streaks that add such striking patterns are *not* naturally resistant to decay. But a thorough coating protects the entire slab. Dwyer has never had one delaminate in service—*by Al Lees. Drawing by Eugene Thompson.*

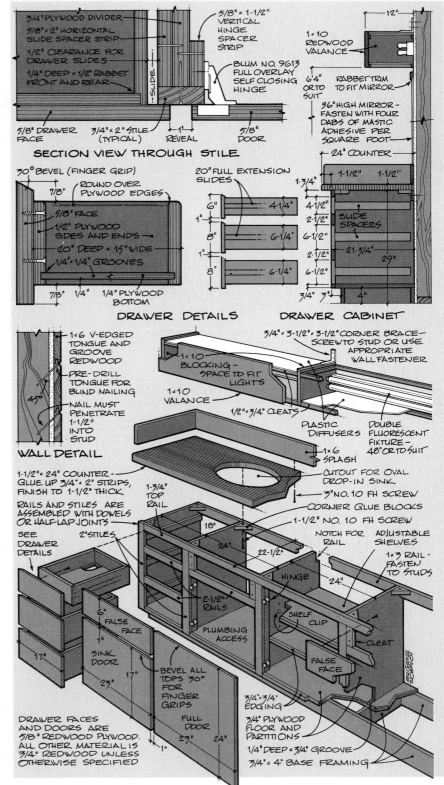

mail-order mantels

PHOTOGRAPHED FOR POPULAR SCIENCE BY FOTO-GRAPHICS, INDIANAPOLIS

Magnificent mantels (previous page, top): Stratford mantelpiece in oak frames marble facing on this new 42-inch prefab fireplace by Majestic. Above: Dressy mantel makes a special contribution to a "converted" fireplace—one that's been fitted with a more efficient wood-stove insert. Shown here is Lopi's Flawless Performance Model X, which comes with a metal surround. Original fireplace was framed in rustic glazed tile; by adding the wood mantel, decorated with a combination of moldings and sporting a wide display shelf, the fireplace was made to dominate the room even though the firebox is reduced. Other photos show the range of custom mantels made by Newport Mantel & Panel Company: Directly below is an oak mantel deep enough to have a built-in bookshelf. The homeowner mixed mahogany and walnut stains to get this traditional dark-red effect. This style costs about $850 but can be ordered without the bookcase. Previous page, bottom right, is a much simpler design, a mantel shelf of crown moldings supported on 4½-inch-thick corbels of solid wood. It could be stained instead of painted and costs about $450. On left is a mantel style that will be at home in either traditional or modern room settings. As shown, about $550.

We decided to give our home a Christmas present. Our starkly plain fireplace just didn't look festive, and its lack of a mantel shelf left no place for holiday greens and candles. The addition of a custom-built mantel made a dramatic improvement to our living room. It provided a focal point for our yule decor, and after the holidays the shelf will be an ideal home for our heirloom clock.

Most new homes come without fireplace mantels since these are usually added later to complement the furniture. Mantels come in a wide range of types and styles, as the photos on these pages show.

"Carved" mantels are actually assembled from various solid moldings to form the intricate shapes. The large top molding is commonly called a cornice, or *crown molding,* which, along with other smaller moldings, casings, panels, and flutings, form the complete mantel. Decorative wood carvings are often attached to the front of the mantel, or the front panels may be carved or routed with designs or initials. Mantels may also be designed with legs, to frame and provide a pleasing surround of the fireplace, and the legs may be plain or fancy with edge detailing and fluting.

The large size of some of the crown moldings and the angles involved require the use of specialized saws and jigs to make accurate cuts. Newport Mantel & Panel Company, the builder of our mantel, makes each one to the specifications of the buyer. The company does custom carving on fireplaces and panels of the mantel, and will build all styles from traditional to contemporary. Newport Mantel often works from photos or magazine clippings and the homeowners' measurements to provide custom service (see address at end of article). The mantels are available finished or unfinished, to any stage of completion, and are shipped via UPS with complete instructions for installation by the customer. We've drawn on these instructions for the assembly sketches on the next page.

Add a firebox or fireplace insert

Don't have a fireplace? You can still give your home this touch of yuletide cheer. A custom mantel will do wonders for a simulated fireplace. Or you can build a steel firebox into an existing room—and get heat-circulating efficiency as a bonus. Several manufacturers of such units offer customized surrounds, including choices of mantel designs. The steel fireplace in our lead photo is Majestic's Warm Majic II—a new model that features a 42-inch firebox opening. As shown it has a marble surround and hearth extension, available from the Majestic dealer. This comes in slabs, with a quick-setting adhesive; you glue the slabs across the gap between the prefab unit and the rough framing. The wooden mantel then goes on top of this surround. Made of choice hardwood, Majestic mantels are offered in three styles, including the classically ornate Stratford shown in our photo, and come with directions for easy installation.

Or perhaps you have an outdated fireplace that's too much of an energy waster to use—even at Christmas. The best option here is to seal it off with an efficient woodstove-type insert, such as the Lopi Model X in our photo.

Attaching mantels to brick and masonry is as simple as the sketches indicate. A support board (1 × 3 pine as shown)—or three support boards if legs are planned—is attached to the brick surface using 2½-inch No. 10 wood screws placed in each of the dowels. Pre-drill through the pine support board and into the wood dowels using the proper size bit. The predrill bit should allow the screw to enter the wood without danger of splitting, yet hold tenaciously by allowing the threads of the screw to cut into

Mail-order mantels arrive ready for mounting

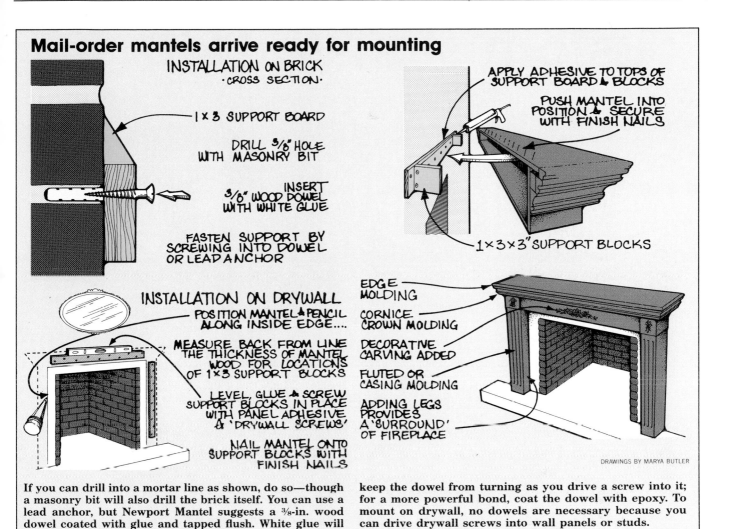

INSTALLATION ON BRICK
·CROSS SECTION·

1 × 3 SUPPORT BOARD

DRILL 3/8" HOLE WITH MASONRY BIT

INSERT 3/8" WOOD DOWEL WITH WHITE GLUE

FASTEN SUPPORT BY SCREWING INTO DOWEL OR LEAD ANCHOR

APPLY ADHESIVE TO TOPS OF SUPPORT BOARD & BLOCKS

PUSH MANTEL INTO POSITION & SECURE WITH FINISH NAILS

1 × 3 × 3" SUPPORT BLOCKS

INSTALLATION ON DRYWALL

POSITION MANTEL & PENCIL ALONG INSIDE EDGE....

MEASURE BACK FROM LINE THE THICKNESS OF MANTEL WOOD FOR LOCATIONS OF 1 × 3 SUPPORT BLOCKS

LEVEL, GLUE & SCREW SUPPORT BLOCKS IN PLACE WITH PANEL ADHESIVE & 'DRYWALL SCREWS'

NAIL MANTEL ONTO SUPPORT BLOCKS WITH FINISH NAILS

EDGE MOLDING

CORNICE CROWN MOLDING

DECORATIVE CARVING ADDED

FLUTED OR CASING MOLDING

ADDING LEGS PROVIDES A 'SURROUND' OF FIREPLACE

DRAWINGS BY MARYA BUTLER

If you can drill into a mortar line as shown, do so—though a masonry bit will also drill the brick itself. You can use a lead anchor, but Newport Mantel suggests a 3/8-in. wood dowel coated with glue and tapped flush. White glue will keep the dowel from turning as you drive a screw into it; for a more powerful bond, coat the dowel with epoxy. To mount on drywall, no dowels are necessary because you can drive drywall screws into wall panels or studs.

the wood their full depth. As the screw enters, the dowel will expand slightly and wedge itself ever tighter in the hole. Put screws at 6-inch to 1-foot intervals.

Attached to the support boards are 3-inch 1 × 3 pine blocks (or adjust size as needed), which will fit inside and under the mantel to support and provide alignment from the backside. The support blocks are best screwed to the support board from the rear, before fastening it in place on the wall. Blocking, or a doubler, is also placed between these pine blocks to add additional strength. One pine support block at either end of the mantel top is usually sufficient. For mantel legs the same system is recommended, with at least one block at the top and bottom of each leg. Newport Mantel will supply needed support boards and blocks if requested by the homeowner.

The mantel shelf or top is normally separate from any legs and may or may not be attached to smaller support knees or corbels. Panel adhesive is also used to provide additional attachment to the wall, and is spread on the backside of the mantel shelf just before it is placed on the support board and pushed into place against the wall.

When the mantel shelf is in place, drive several No. 5 finish nails down at an angle through the mantel top and into the support board. These finish nails are usually countersunk slightly below the surface, and the holes are filled with a putty stick or wax pencil. Do finishing before the mantel is installed, final detailing and touch-up afterward.

Installation on drywall

Attaching a mantel to a flat drywall surface is even simpler. Pine 1 × 3 supports for the mantel top (and legs if applicable) are attached to the drywall using self-tapping drywall screws and panel adhesive. Once the adhesive sets, nail the mantel shelf and legs in place using No. 5 finish nails as before. For additional support, wall studs may be used by driving long drywall screws through the support boards and into the studs. Very long drywall screws may need to be waxed or soaped to allow them to be driven easily into solid wood. The same techniques may be used on wood-paneled walls.

Caution and good sense should be used to provide recommended adequate safety clearances in all stove and fireplace installations. Local building codes may be the best source of information about flammable materials around a fireplace or a wood-burning fireplace insert—*by Paul and Marya Butler. Drawing by Marya Butler.*

ADDRESSES OF SOURCES
Custom-built mantels: Newport Mantel & Panel Co., 2140 Newport Boulevard, Newport Beach CA 92663; **Fireplace insert stoves:** Consolidated Dutchwest, Box 1019, Plymouth MA 02360; LOPI International, 10850 117th Place N.E., Kirkland WA 98030; **Surround facings and mantels for prefab fireplaces:** Majestic, 1000 E. Market Street, Huntington IN 46750

custom stair-rail kit

Before and after: Typical 1950s wrought-iron stair rail pales next to rich wood version.

If you're like many homeowners, for you there's no substitute for real wood. Wood conveys the feeling of warmth, comfort, and substance.

Like many other families, we live in a suburban tract house built in the 1950s. That meant our home was loaded with a variety of wood substitutes, including a 50s-modern black iron railing that ran up the stairway from the front hall foyer to the second floor.

We were able to live with the iron railing during our first few years in our home. It was when we decided to replace the worn stairway carpeting that we discovered the oak parquet flooring on the landing and the real oak stair treads that lay hidden beneath. With the real wood now revealed in all its glory, the transformation continued when we covered the stairway wall with a rustic tan, burlap-like paneling. Finally, it was time to seriously consider a wood railing. The problem with these impressive railings is that they also require some impressively difficult cuts and intricate millwork. Hardly the type of home remodeling project for us. We consider our DIY skills above-average, but certainly not on the professional level.

A step-by-step kit

Our search for a solution ended when we decided on a Rail Easy pre-assembled adjustable rail system by Morgan Products Ltd. (601 Oregon Street, Oshkosh, WI 54903-2446). Made of hemlock, which can be stained, painted or varnished, Rail Easy can be used for open or partially-open stairway applications. The system would also work well as a room divider or balcony rail.

The key component of the Rail Easy System is the adjustable rail section. The hand rail fastens to the newel with a unique key lock and shoulder screw attachment, and can accommodate stair slopes of 33 to 45 degrees. The pre-assembled section comes with a hand rail and a shoe rail connected by balusters approximately 6 inches apart

from each other. Fillets are provided for a convenient, time-saving method of putting the finishing touches on the project.

Available in lengths of 3, 4, 5, 6, and 7 feet, one adjustable rail section will accommodate a variety of straight runs and partially-open stairs, in addition to some L-shaped and U-shaped staircases. Other components in the Rail Easy system include starting newels, landing newels, and half-wall newels. All come in attractive designs, as we saw firsthand, and each eliminates the need for all that intricate carpentry work my wife and I were leery about. Morgan also provides a cutting guide, which clamps on each side of the hand rail and shoe rail. We found it a big help in making accurate cuts at the ends of the rail section.

No special tools are needed to put in the Rail Easy system. Hammer, saw, nail set, and chisel are your main requirements, though a power miter saw comes in especially handy for trimming the fillets of wood trim pieces around the newels.

Deciding rail height

The first step in our project was to determine the height of the rail. We decided on 38 inches, a little higher than the manufacturer's recommendations because our family is fully grown.

Since we were working with an L-shaped stairway, we cut the landing newel first to proper length. Following the manufacturer's directions, we added $4^3/_4$ inches to the height of the bottom riser, which was 8 inches. The total, $12^3/_4$ inches, was trimmed off the bottom of the newel.

We then lined up the size and location of the notch to be made in the nosing of the bottom tread. The center point of the newel base determines the area to be notched out. From the center line, we measured $1^{11}/_{16}$ inches to either side of the cutout area. Then we measured the overhang on the nosing, from the front of the nosing to the riser, and marked our cutting points on the same lines.

1. Key component in Rail Easy system, the adjustable rail section, is unloaded from a sturdy shipping crate ready for the homeowner's installation.

2. Center point of newel base determines area to be notched out of the bottom-tread nosing.

3. Basic cut for the area to be notched out is made with a saw.

4. Landing newel is anchored to the riser with four wood screws. Be sure key lock in newel faces up stairway.

5. An ordinary level is used to make sure the half-wall newel is plumb with the stairs.

6. Four finishing nails anchor the half-wall newel to the wall.

7. Rail section is cut to length with the help of a cutting guide, which assures that the angle is plumb with the balusters.

8. A level lets you check that the balusters are plumb with the stairs before the rail section is cut to proper length.

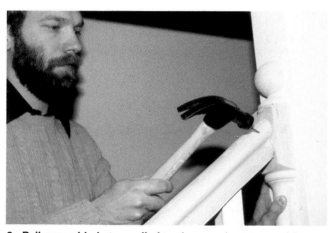

9. Rail assembly is toe-nailed to the newels at top and bottom of stairs.

10. Rail is also toe-nailed at top and bottom of the half-wall newel.

11. Handy template helps you determine location of the shoulder screw.

We made our basic cuts with a saw, and then cleaned up the notch area with a sharp chisel. The newel was inserted flush into the notch, and then checked to be sure it was plumb.

We then anchored the newel to the riser by countersinking four wood screws, making sure that the key lock in the newel was facing up the stairway. Wood plugs that come with the system covered the screws neatly.

Handling the measurements

The next step was to cut the rail section to proper length. Our advice is to enlist a third pair of hands at this point. Our neighbor, a former carpenter, proved invaluable help. In addition to his expertise with wood, his presence on the job made it easier to handle the rail while we made our measurements.

We set the assembly on the treads so that the rail passed the landing newel post. A half-wall newel was held against the wall at the top of the stairs. The assembly was adjusted until the balusters were plumb. We made sure the end balusters were equal distance from the ends of the rail. When the balusters were plumb, we marked the ends of the hand rail and shoe rail with a pencil where they passed the landing newel. We did the same at the other end where the two rails met the half-wall newel. These marks indicated where our cuts had to be made.

Before making any cuts, however, we moved upstairs to determine the height of the half-wall newel. That was done by holding the newel, prior to trimming, against the wall. Making sure our 38-inch rail height was correct for the entire length, we marked the wall at the height where the top of the hand rail met the half-wall newel. Then we trimmed the bottom of the newel and attached it to the wall with finishing nails.

Our next step was to attach the cutting guide to the rail for making our cuts. One edge was aligned with the marks on the rails, and the bolts were tightened. We followed the same process at the other end of the rails, making our cuts only after checking that the guides were plumb with the balusters.

The shoulder screw was then drilled into the end of the rail for the key lock. A rail template that comes with the system provided a convenient way to determine the screw location. It was important to line up the template with the bottom of the rail. We then inserted the screw as far as it would go.

With the rail placed in the key lock, the assembly was then attached by toe-nailing the hand rail and shoe rail to the newels at the top and bottom of the stairs.

Installing the short run

We followed much the same procedure for installing a short 12-inch run of rail from the landing to first step. In most projects, the rail would have been extend to the floor. We elected to put a starting newel on the first step because both elements are wood. Since the floor at the bottom of the steps was covered with vinyl tile, we felt it would not be compatible with the wood newel. Our main concern was to provide a solid anchor for the newel. We did it by using the metal anchor plate that comes with the system—and was designed to do just what we hoped it would.

The anchor plate was placed against the base of the newel by counterboring four interior screw holes facing out. The newel with attached anchor plate was then secured to the step using a second set of holes in the four corners of the plate. The exposed edges of the anchor plate were covered with quarter-round pieces of wood trim, carefully cut with a miter saw at the corners for a professional-looking appearance. We accommodated the thickness of the anchor plate by cutting dados in the quarter rounds.

The result? Our Rail Easy system was an ideal complement to the oak stairs and wall. Our real-wood stair rail looks as if it's custom-made, yet our material costs amounted to approximately $500. Total installation time came to eight hours, with three of us involved in the project.

If it's true that first impressions make lasting ones, our front foyer fits the role almost perfectly. The last step in converting our foyer to an all-wood motif will be the floor. Then, if my wife has her way, we'll start looking at the fireplace mantels and entry-door trim Morgan also makes —*by John and Ruth Stover.*

12. Shoulder screw goes into the keylock of the landing newel.

13. Fillets are measured at one end for cutting to proper length.

14. Small finishing nails securely anchor the fillets into the shoe rail.

15. Hemlock stains beautifully for a professional looking, warm appearance.

back-door lattice

Handsome patio lattice lets you see out—but obscures the view in.

BEFORE

After extending existing slab and lag-screwing 4 × 4s to the house, this home-owner erects a lattice frame.

Ample bench stores firewood and keeps it drier. It's also handy for removing boots before entering the house.

A private sunny space for refreshments . . . a windbreak . . . a blind to conceal those items that accumulate near the back door: barbecue grill, firewood, trash cans. A handsome finishing touch to the rear of the house . . . *and* a project to let me work with a great new panel material—a plastic lattice that looks better than wood lath and never needs painting.

These were my goals in designing and building this entry upgrade. In my case, the door opened into the family room, but the structure can be adapted to any side or rear door, swinging or sliding, that opens into a kitchen, utility room, or stair hall. For my house, I tucked the framing under a second-story overhang, but you could as easily cleat it to a straight wall or run it under a roof soffit.

For the "roof" of the structure, I nailed on pre-painted 2 × 2s, spaced one foot apart. This gives a trellis effect and also lets you hang planter baskets inside. Though the top and sides remain largely open, the wind (which used to whistle around this corner) is noticeably diffused these days thanks to this addition.

Because you're near the openings when you're inside, you can see out; but when looking in from outside at a greater distance, detail is obscured.

Vinyl lattice would seem to be the answer for anyone who's ever worked with wood lath. The vinyl comes in 4-by-8-foot and 2-foot-10-inch-by-8-foot panels in nine colors that never need repainting. Because the foamed polyvinyl-chloride (PVC) strips are chemically welded together, there are no nails or staples to rust out. The maker, Cross Industries (5262 Peachtree Road, Atlanta, GA 30341), supplies the panels in the rectangular pattern I used and also in the traditional diagonal pattern where the strips run at a 45-degree angle to the panel edges.

Easy to work

This tough material won't rot, and it's of no interest to termites. I found it easy to saw with a fine-toothed blade, and easy to nail—even close to an edge—without predrilling.

PVC lattice does cost nearly three times more than wood lattice, but the maker figures that by the time you sand, paint, repaint, and replace rotted lath, the smooth maintenance-free PVC should cost you *less* than wood over the life of the project.

Start your entry structure by assembling a frame of treated 4 × 4s to enclose the desired area, pre-dadoing the posts for the 2 × 4s that will form the bottom rail of the frame for the lattice panels. I designed my frame to take full sheets of lattice wherever possible. In fact, I cut only two sheets—the ones closest to the walls at each end—to take up the odd dimensions.

Add joists at the top to strengthen the structure and provide support for the 2 × 2 top strips, which are far easier to prime and paint *before* they're nailed in place. (If you prefer actual shelter for your space, you could fasten sheets of plastic patio cover to these 2 × 2s.)

Instructions come with the lattice to show how panels should be installed to allow for expansion and contraction. A sketch below shows how I secured the panels within the frames. As an alternative, you can buy PVC angles and channels from Cross.

It's a good idea to prime and paint the entire frame before mounting any panels. And if you use pressure-treated wood for all frame parts, repainting the frame is the only future maintenance you'll ever face.

Another diagram details the construction of the woodbin bench. I used much the same construction to build the planters that flank the door—*by Phil McCafferty. Drawing by Eugene Thompson.*

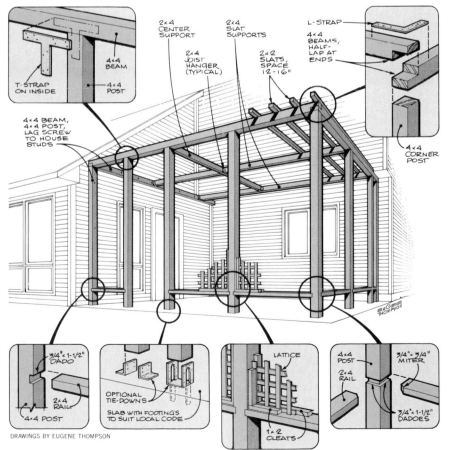

DRAWINGS BY EUGENE THOMPSON

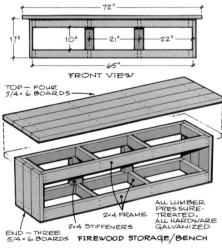

kitchen/great room

FAMILY ROOM 15'x20'

NEW KITCHEN 14'x25'

REF DW SINK

OLD KITCHEN

NEW ENTRY

LEGEND

■ — EXISTING CONSTRUCTION

■ — MODIFIED CONSTRUCTION

□ — NEW CONSTRUCTION

CLO CL CLO

BATH

Ilmar Junge had a unique family problem. Even when he and his wife, Anda, and their two teen-age sons were all at home relaxing, he felt a lack of togetherness. The Junges weren't experiencing communication problems or a widening generation gap. What they had was a design problem: Their Glendale, Wisconsin, home had a cramped kitchen with no dining table and lacked any central gathering place.

"Our home is an old farmhouse with lots of small rooms," says Junge. "In fact, there were too many, and it gave our two sons a feeling of being cut off from family activities. The family wanted a space where we could all be together, and we also needed space for multiple cooks, as the whole family contributes to meal preparation."

Junge, an architect with his own design firm in Milwaukee, consulted with Anda and then drew up a set of plans for a new kitchen/family room addition that created a spacious "great room" to accommodate all the family's needs. The design required the removal of portions of the existing south and west walls of the original kitchen, a small back porch on the south, plus a small second-level room above the kitchen. This provided open space that extended to the apex of the house roof—a height of 20 feet. Also, the wall removal exposed an interior stairway leading to the second level.

After the demolition phase was completed, a 14-by-25-foot addition was built to the south to house the new kitchen, and a 15-by-20 foot addition was made to the west to contain the new family room. This created the spacious new great room desired by the family.

Although the rooms are open to one another, each is clearly defined visually. This was accomplished by elevating the kitchen floor 6 inches above the family room's and using different floor coverings in each. Armstrong World Industries Solarian inlaid vinyl covers the kitchen floor; carpeting graces the family room. There's also a unique ceiling treatment in each room: The kitchen has a cathedral ceiling that soars to 20 feet at the apex; below is a maze of beams and ductwork around a structural support column all "boxed in" with 1/2-inch-thick drywall. Together with a dropped ceiling above the dining area, the design updates the kitchen, giving it an open, geometric appeal.

The family room has a portion of its ceiling sloped in two different directions, and a centrally placed skylight lets the sun stream into both rooms. A second skylight was installed near the roof apex above the kitchen to allow daylight to flood the newly exposed stairway.

During remodeling, a portion of the old kitchen was retained as a pantry area and storage closet along the north wall. A small snack bar and a work counter are opposite. The area between the wall and the work counter serves as an aisle that leads into the kitchen, past the stairway, then continues on behind a new free-standing cooking island into the sunken family room. The dining area fronts the cooking island and is furnished with a pedestal table and teakwood chairs. Besides creating a large, airy cooking and dining space, the kitchen renovation also gave the Junges a wealth of storage space. The cooking island is flanked by cabinets, and natural-finish oak cabinets custom-built by Wood-Mode Cabinetry of Kreamer, Pennsylvania, line the east wall, which also houses a double sink, trash compactor, built-in dishwasher, and refrigerator. Sliding glass doors in the south kitchen wall open to a small patio.

The family room has a casual ambiance; expandable seating units front the fireplace, which is located against the west wall. For an interesting touch, a brass trunk is used as a coffee table. The fireplace is flanked on the left by glass doors leading to a pool patio and on the right by a picture window.

Junge will attest that major renovations like this one can require endurance. "I'd say the kitchen renovation took about six months," he estimates. "We lived in the house throughout the remodeling and did most of our cooking on a hot plate during that time."

But the whole family agrees that the inconvenience was worth the final outcome, which was 650 square feet of new living space. This space, with its combination of plants, distinctive ceiling treatments, strategically placed skylights, and attractive new cabinets and furnishings, has resulted in the creation of the sleek new great room that Ilmar Junge had envisioned for his family—*by George Lyons. Drawings by Carl De Groote.*

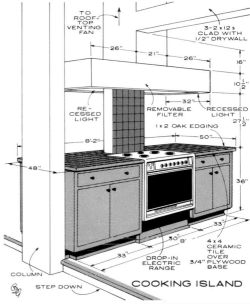

TO ROOF TOP VENTING FAN

3-2 x 12s CLAD WITH 1/2" DRYWALL

26"   21"   26"   16"

10 1/2"

RE-CESSED LIGHT

32"
REMOVABLE FILTER

RECESSED LIGHT

27 1/2"

1 x 2 OAK EDGING

8'-2"   50"

48"

36"

33"

COLUMN

30"   8'

DROP-IN ELECTRIC RANGE

4 x 4 CERAMIC TILE OVER 3/4" PLYWOOD BASE

33"

STEP DOWN

COOKING ISLAND

Architectural designer Ilmar Junge (shown with sons Andrei and Robert) created this airy new kitchen for the family home by leaving much of the ceiling area open and boxing in support columns and vents with 1/2-inch drywall. The vinyl-covered kitchen floor is 6 inches higher than the carpeted slab-on-grade floor of the family room beyond (left). The 45-foot-deep addition is dominated by a massive cooking island built next to one of the support columns. Its ceramic-tiled counter top surrounds an electric range; the hood above contains an exhaust vent and down lights. Storage cabinets flank the range and are tucked at both ends and in back (above). Stairway at right was part of the existing two-story house.

garden bar/sun room

Some great home improvements grow from modest intentions. This lovely addition began as a simple wish—by homeowners Robert and Karen Benz—for a sheltered area for outdoor dining. They'd inherited a barren concrete patio outside the kitchen of their Wisconsin house, and their first thought was to erect a lightweight frame to create a screened room large enough for a dining table.

But when they consulted architect Bill Winters of Milwaukee's Junge & Associates, they realized that such a shelter would only be usable for—at most—four months of their climate's year. So the screened room evolved into a fully winterized addition that's not only comfortable year-round, but complements the existing architecture far better than a screened room would have.

New concrete was poured atop and beyond the existing patio, resulting in an eight-inch slab on grade. When the new pour had cured, plywood underlayment was nailed over 1×2 sleepers, and the walls were framed to create a giant window bay.

Roof framing is tricky

Two box beams project from the original exterior wall of the house to rest

Garden was redesigned to create vistas from the new wing and its small side deck. A path of spar dust, bordered by rocks and stone lanterns, leads to the deck and to doors that give direct access to the garden room at left or to an original entry hall of the house. Stepping stones are provided for wet weather. Low-voltage lighting makes the garden appealing by night, as well. The sun room measures roughly 17 by 22 feet and is sided with vertical 1 × 10 rough-sawn cedar. All windows are operable casements for ventilation, and there are skylights on both sides of the main ridge. Inside, a built-in wet bar and free-standing fireplace offer hospitality; the room is furnished for entertaining. Folding doors hide bar when it's not in use. Brick wall and hearth are flanked by walls of windows.

on the full-height brick wall behind the fireplace. The section detail shows how these beams are clad to create a top trough into which fluorescent fixtures fit to provide indirect lighting bounced off the faceted cathedral ceiling above. As the color overlay on the floor plan indicates, the roof framing is somewhat complex, especially where it ties into the existing structure. Specifics differ with each situation; so unless you're comfortable with opening the main roof deck to pass new framing members through for nailing to existing rafters, it's best to call on the services of a professional builder to engineer the roof supports. You could then take over to apply the plywood deck and the asphalt shingles. Shingling is a labor-intensive chore on a faceted roof such as this, with much angle trimming. This makes it a practical, money-saving do-it-yourself job.

The only hint that those angled facia boards conceal the gutter system is the downspout at the far left in the exterior photo. The runoff can be diverted to catch basins for watering the garden during dry spells.

Note that the bar corner is boxed in with its own dropped ceiling. The flat "shelf" above is ideal for house plants, because it's under a large skylight.

With all its interior baffles (the faceted ceiling is faced with drywall and has fiberglass insulation above), the space is acoustically alive—ideal for listening to music. These homeowners have speakers tucked into end tables and hung on the wall. Hi-fi gear is concealed in the closet beside the bar.

This built-in bar makes the addition an ideal space for entertaining. Hosts never have to leave their guests to rustle up refreshments. The undercounter refrigerator keeps ice, mixers, and fresh fruit at hand, while the Kohler Gimlet bar sink eases preparation and cleanup. In fact, you can just stash used glassware on the sink counter and close the folding doors, leaving dishwashing for after guests have gone.

Let's party

Because this new wing was spliced onto the existing kitchen, it is handy to serve dinner here, as well. All the windows are operable and equipped with interior screens; and in hot weather, they swing wide for the next best thing to the alfresco dining originally intended. In summer the deck adds another 200 square feet of space for large parties. Spotlights under the eaves keep the area festive after the sun sets.

The decking is pressure-treated 2 × 4s, spaced ¼ inch apart for drainage. The outer edge of the deck is projected from the 45-degree angled wall of the garden room. This creates a deck area large enough to accommodate a small wrought-iron table and chair set, and because the structure bridges a corner of the house, it's easy to hang the joists from ledgers lagscrewed to the two walls of the house. Only two posts were needed to support the outer edge. For more space, of course, you could build the deck square—*by Al Lees. Photos by George Lyons. Drawings by Carl De Groote.*

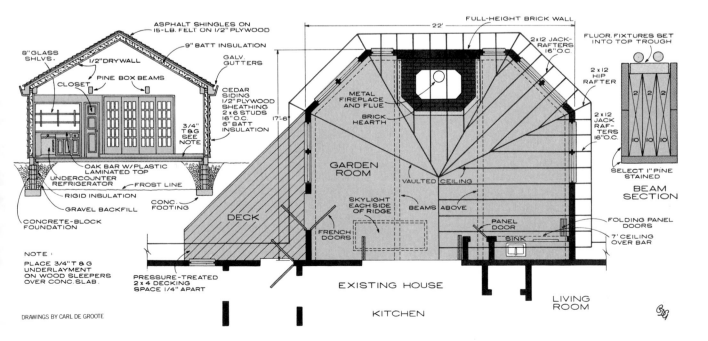

DRAWINGS BY CARL DE GROOTE

warp-resistant entry door

Luxurious wood entry door not only improves a home's appearance, it can also save on energy bills—for a long, long time!
Original door was typical aluminum-frame type that leaked air and looked boring.

Upgrading your home can start with a most natural place: the front door. An appealing entry-door system not only welcomes visitors, it can be a true home-design element. But with the multitude of door styles on the market, the trick is finding one that is attractive, energy-efficient, and durable. You also want it to be easy to install.

These thoughts ran through my mind as I considered replacing our front door. A sturdy, insulated steel model, I never was quite comfortable with it. The sound it made when it opened or closed reminded me more of a factory than a home. What I really wanted was a custom wood door, but I found it hard to justify the extra cost, especially with what I'd heard about the tendency of wood doors to warp, split, leak air, and require constant maintenance. Yet the wood door I wound up buying was attractive, as well as uniquely constructed and energy efficient.

A high-tech sandwich

The Pella Entry Door system is $1^7/8$ inches thick, compared with most doors' standard $1^3/4$-inch thickness. And each door—stile, rail and raised panel—is made out of a solid wood core sandwiched between sheets of aluminum. A special adhesive bonds the aluminum to two more layers of wood—an inner wood layer and an outer layer of oak. The aluminum keeps moisture away from the core to reduce warping, while the wood layers are bonded at right angles to each other to prevent splitting. Called Warpguard construction, Pella claims the system assures a strong, stable, and weather-tight door. In fact, the company devoted nearly four years of research and testing to perfecting the design.

To protect the wood further, two coats of end-grain sealant are applied at the factory. The exterior door surface is then covered with a clear compound that screens out

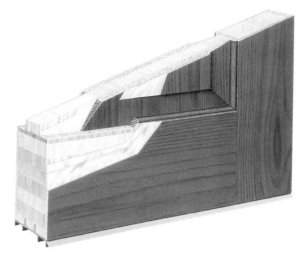

Solid wood core is sandwiched between sheets of aluminum—which are, in turn, covered by two more layers of wood for added warp resistance.

the ultraviolet rays that turn wood gray. The last coat is a clear sealer. According to Pella, the three-step process can provide up to double the life of ordinary paint and stain finishes.

Would this new door keep cool air in during summer—and *out* in winter? Here, too, I was impressed by the permanently flexible weatherstripping that acts as a double seal around the door's sides and top (Fig. 1). An adjustable sill prevents air leakage below the door. The weatherstrip is also coated to provide for smooth opening and closing. My wife and I chose a traditional single door with optional sidelights for our home, although we could have also chosen from available contemporary styles and double-door models. Transoms are also available.

1

2

3 ▼

4 ▼

5

7

6 ▼

Where to begin

Since this was my first door installation, I learned a lot quickly. Before I bought the door, I measured over the existing frame to get an idea of the rough opening. Had the opening been too wide to accept the 33½-inch-wide door, I had two options: add a sidelight to the opening, or frame out the opening and conceal the framing with a wide molding.

My job was simplified considerably because the opening looked to be about right, and by the fact that Pella shipped the door prehung (Fig. 2), with sidelights, jamb extensions, brickmold, and sill nose already attached to the frame. I assembled my tools—a bar for prying out the existing frame, flat- and Phillips-head screwdrivers, a tape, a level, a caulking gun, and a plumb bob—and got to work.

After removing the trim, my first job was to remove the existing door and frame (Figs. 3 and 4). I used a reciprocating saw for the job, cutting through the nails securing the frame to the studs. The opening was about ¼ inch larger on the sides and ½ inch larger on the top than the door frame itself. Once the sill was removed, I checked the opening for plumb squareness and continued.

I began installing the new sill by applying a bead of urethane sealant to the floor (Fig. 5). After removing the skid plate from the bottom of the door frame, I placed it carefully atop the urethane sealant (Fig. 6). Then I applied urethane sealant to the full length of the polyurethane backer rod along the sill and along the brickmold around the entire unit, as shown in figure 7.

Being careful not to disturb the sealant, we set the sill into the door opening and tilted the Pella door into place (Fig. 8). Note: Be sure *not* to slide the sill across the floor, or you'll disturb the sealant. After making sure the hinge jamb was plumb, I tacked it within 6 inches of the top of the door to hold the jamb in place.

Once we confirmed that the sill was straight and level, I applied a dab of silicone sealant to each of the screw holes in the aluminum sill. Then I drove the No. 8 × 2-inch stainless-steel mounting screws through the sill into the floor, and placed support blocking under the sill nose. That completed the sill installation.

To secure the hinge jamb I placed shims between the frame and studs at each hinge. On the outside, I nailed through the jamb and shims into the studding, being care-

8

ful not to nail through the jamb extension. I then removed the wood bracing and packing shims on the interior and carefully opened the door to remove the packing shim from the bottom weatherstrip.

Four-by-four butt hinges were secured to the wall by driving the long hinge screws through the one open hole available and into the studs. I double-checked the hinge jamb for bow, then adjusted the shims. Next, I adjusted the lock jamb. Closing the door carefully to avoid damaging the weatherstripping, I adjusted the jamb to meet the door evenly, so the door would make contact with the weatherstrip along its entire length. Once the jamb was adjusted, I tacked it in place.

The lock jamb was then shimmed just above the lock strike. Note: Be especially careful that the jamb is straight, and that there's an even gap between door and jamb from top to bottom. Next, I opened the door and nailed through the lock jamb and shims into the studs. After swinging the door to make sure it operated properly, I shimmed and nailed the lock jamb at the top, center, and bottom on the exterior, again being careful not to nail through the jamb extension.

To complete the installation, I used galvanized nails to nail through the brickmold into the studs, and applied urethane sealant between brickmold and siding. Our door is not protected by a soffit, so we installed a head flashing. We then checked the bottom weatherstrip. Our interior floor is slightly uneven, so we found a slight gap between threshold and weatherstrip. Tightening the threshold's adjusting screws was all it took to convert the problem (Fig. 9).

9

Installing a double door

Suppose classic double doors are what you really have in mind. As a Pella representative demonstrated, putting in their double-door system is just as straightforward.

First, plumb both jambs and tack them both in place. Then, shim the hinge jamb of the inactive door (the one you'll keep closed most of the time) and nail through the shims into the studding. Once interior wood bracing and packing shims are removed from the door, the inactive door jamb is secured to the wall.

After checking the straightness of the inactive door jamb, secure the frame head by: 1) shimming between frame and header at the flushbolt strike; 2) checking that the frame head is straight; and 3) nailing through head and shims into the header.

10

11

Carefully close and lock the inactive door, checking for even clearances and making sure that the flushbolts engage the strikes. Now carefully close the active door. It must make even contact with the weatherstrip on both the astragal and the head. If it doesn't, adjust the hinge jamb until the active door fits evenly.

Now place the shims between the active door jamb and the studs, open the door, and drive the long hinge screws through the hinges and shims into the studding. Close the door and check for even clearances, again, adjusting the shims as necessary. Nail the active door jamb at three places on the top, bottom and, center on the exterior. Finish off the installation of the double doors as you would the single door.

Whether you install a single- or double-door system, you can order the Pella door prebored for a 2$\frac{1}{8}$-inch-diameter lockface and deadbolt with a 1-inch cross-bored hole for the lockset.

The single-door installation took about six hours. Most of that time was well-spent checking and double-checking to make sure the jambs were straight and the opening was square. Otherwise, you could waste the money you've saved by installing the door yourself.

Pella Entry Door systems come in seven different styles and more than 30 configurations. They're available at Pella Window Stores around the country—*by Steve Rudner. Photos by Richard Foertsch.*

Manufacturers and consultants
Entry door by Rolscreen Company, 102 Main street, Pella, IA 50219; contracting consultancy by Craig Bunton, Alternatives in Home Design & Remodeling, Park Ridge, IL.

basement on a budget

Remodeled basement/family room features prefinished hardboard paneling, vinyl wallcovering, and real wood parquet floor.

The warmth of wood helps make this newly renovated family room an inviting place for informal gatherings and entertaining.

The home, located in Illinois' Twin Cities area, was bought with its 250-square-foot basement left unfinished. That not only reduced the initial purchase price for the young couple, it also allowed them the option of custom designing the area to match their needs and personal tastes.

More and more builders now offer this finish-it-yourself option. In most cases, only basic plumbing and minimal electrical work are roughed in. Occasionally an adjoining second bath is part of the "unfinished" package, although that was not the case in this home.

With help from local interior designer Susan Moore, the couple developed a plan that would meet their needs and those of their two children. Total cost of the materials used in this DIY project was a little over $3,000. That included construction of a custom storage cabinet by a cabinetmaker friend. The same family room project would have cost $8,500-plus if done by a professional contractor.

The owners selected materials that were easy to install and—with an eye toward their children—easy to maintain. Main elements of this design therefore include a tongue-and-groove wood parquet floor, prefinished hardboard paneling, and vinyl wallcovering. The couple combined the paneling and vinyl wallcovering in a classic wainscot treatment along the outside walls. Both flooring and paneling give the look and feeling of solid wood, at a fraction of the cost.

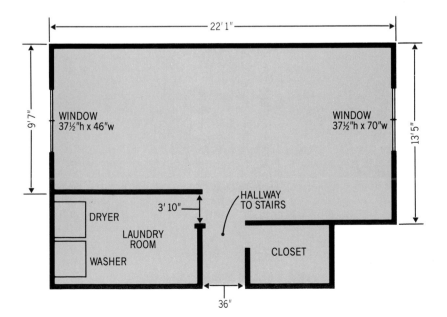

22' 1"

9' 7"

13' 5"

WINDOW
37½"h x 46"w

WINDOW
37½"h x 70"w

DRYER

3' 10"

HALLWAY
TO STAIRS

LAUNDRY
ROOM

CLOSET

WASHER

36"

"Before" view above shows section where custom-built oak cabinet was placed (right). Unfinished basement came with cement floors, and cement block made up the lower 39 inches of the walls. Batt insulation and vapor barrier on upper portions of the walls were included with purchase.

Opposite end of unfinished basement was transformed into the cozy conversation area at right.

Wainscoting and wallboard

The wainscot treatment was a natural, given the existing wall design. The bottom 39 inches of the exterior walls was cement block (below ground level). Above that was standard wood framing, which was insulated and covered with a vapor barrier. The top of the cement block was built out slightly from the framed wall above and provided a perfect point for a chair rail.

Masonite's Barnstable hardboard paneling was glued and nailed over 2 × 2s attached to the cement blocks beneath the chair rail. Next, the couple applied the paneling over a polyethylene vapor barrier and styrofoam insulation along the entire outside wall.

The paneling looks like naturally weathered wood planks and, according to the manufacturer, is durable and easy to clean. Like all hardboard paneling products, it's made from compressed wood fibers bound together under intense heat and pressure. The result is a tough, dimensionally stable material that has already withstood several barrages from the owners' six-year-old son.

Sheetrock-brand gypsum panels were applied to the wood studs on the upper half of the wall and later covered with a patterned vinyl wallcovering from Color Tile. The couple used two oak moldings for the chair rail separating the paneling and the vinyl wallcovering, one on top of the 4-inch built-out cement block lower wall, the other on the side, over the top edge of the paneling.

The ceiling was sprayed with a textured paint, coordinated to match an adjoining hallway. Two ceiling vents extended down from existing ductwork provide heat for the room. The owner also wired in additional electricity to accommodate two wall-space heaters should they be needed.

Putting down the floor

The wood parquet floor tiles, also from Color Tile, were applied directly over the existing cement floor. Since the home is situated well above the local water table, water

With 2X2s applied over vapor barrier, the owner applied styrene-foam insulation to framed-out section along lower 39 inches of wall.

When using a circular saw to cut wall panels, be sure to cut from the *back*. If using a hand saw, cut from the *front* to keep rough edge of cut at back. When cutting for height, deduct one-half inch from your wall-height measurement.

Before gluing, clean all studs with a wire brush for a tight bond. Trim applicator end of cartridge for a one-eighth-inch bead. Apply a continuous strip of adhesive at panel joints and to top and bottom of panel edges. Place 3-inch beads 6 inches apart on studs.

Place a level on edge of first panel to check true plumb. Then install successive panels, applying a one-eighth-inch continuous bead of glue at panel joints and at top and bottom edges. *Remember:* First panel establishes vertical alignment for all panels that follow.

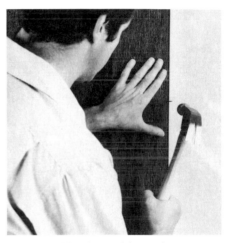

Hold panel in place with a color-coordinated nail at the top corner. Then nail 4 inches apart along panel edges.

proofing was not required. Instead, the owners put a primer coat over the cement and applied the parquet tiles over that. Installing parquet flooring isn't difficult, but it is a two-person job; one applies the adhesive, the other lays the tiles in place. Oak base molding was chosen to match the oak chair rail, and was nailed over the parquet gaps along all wall edges.

A separate laundry room was framed out to accommodate a solid oak cabinet custom-built by a local cabinetmaker. A built-out seating area was also framed out along one wall, in back of the game table.

More to come . . .

Ultimately the owners plan to add a bathroom on the lower level. The bath will be located between the laundry room and a bedroom (not shown on the floor plan), since the water and sewer lines are easily accessible at that point.

New furnishings provided the finishing touch to the new family room. The result is a useful, easy-to-maintain family entertainment room. Best of all, by doing much of the work themselves and choosing the right materials, the owners wound up paying about half of what they would have had the builder done the job—*by Allan Charnish.*

Nails on intermediate studs should be 8 inches apart.

powder-room pair

1

2

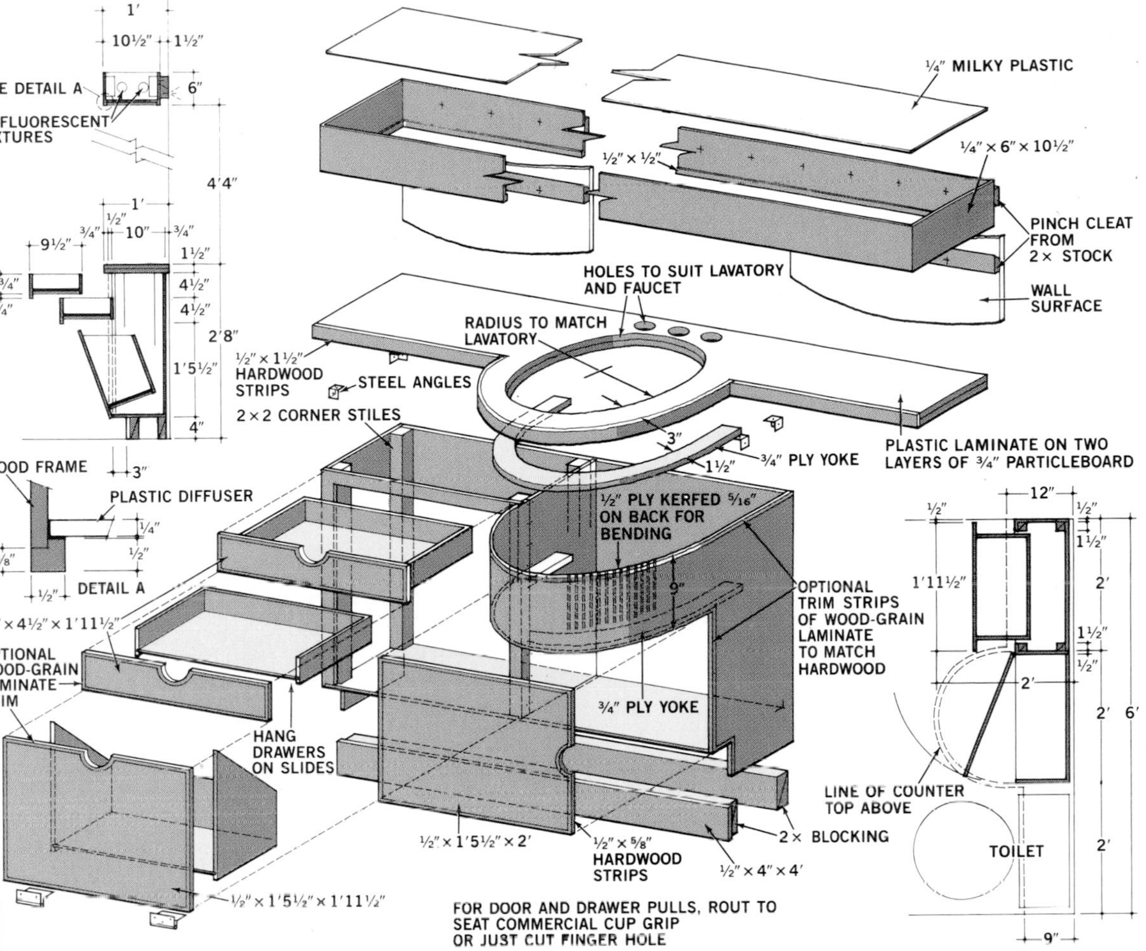

1′
10½″
1½″
SEE DETAIL A
6″
5′ FLUORESCENT FIXTURES
4′4″
1′
½″
¾″
10″
¾″
9½″
1½″
3¾″
¾″
4½″
4½″
2′8″
1′5½″
4″
3″
WOOD FRAME
PLASTIC DIFFUSER
¼″
⅜″
½″
½″
DETAIL A
¼″ MILKY PLASTIC
¼″ × 6″ × 10½″
½″ × ½″
PINCH CLEAT FROM 2× STOCK
WALL SURFACE
HOLES TO SUIT LAVATORY AND FAUCET
RADIUS TO MATCH LAVATORY
½″ × 1½″ HARDWOOD STRIPS
STEEL ANGLES
2×2 CORNER STILES
3″
1½″
¾″ PLY YOKE
PLASTIC LAMINATE ON TWO LAYERS OF ¾″ PARTICLEBOARD
½″ PLY KERFED 5/16″ ON BACK FOR BENDING
9″
OPTIONAL TRIM STRIPS OF WOOD-GRAIN LAMINATE TO MATCH HARDWOOD
½″ × 4½″ × 1′11½″
OPTIONAL WOOD-GRAIN LAMINATE TRIM
¾″ PLY YOKE
HANG DRAWERS ON SLIDES
½″ × 1′5½″ × 2′
½″ × ⅝″ HARDWOOD STRIPS
2× BLOCKING
½″ × 4″ × 4′
½″ × 1′5½″ × 1′11½″
FOR DOOR AND DRAWER PULLS, ROUT TO SEAT COMMERCIAL CUP GRIP OR JUST CUT FINGER HOLE
12″
½″
½″
1½″
1′11½″
2′
1½″
½″
2′
2′
6′
LINE OF COUNTER TOP ABOVE
TOILET
2′
9″

1

2

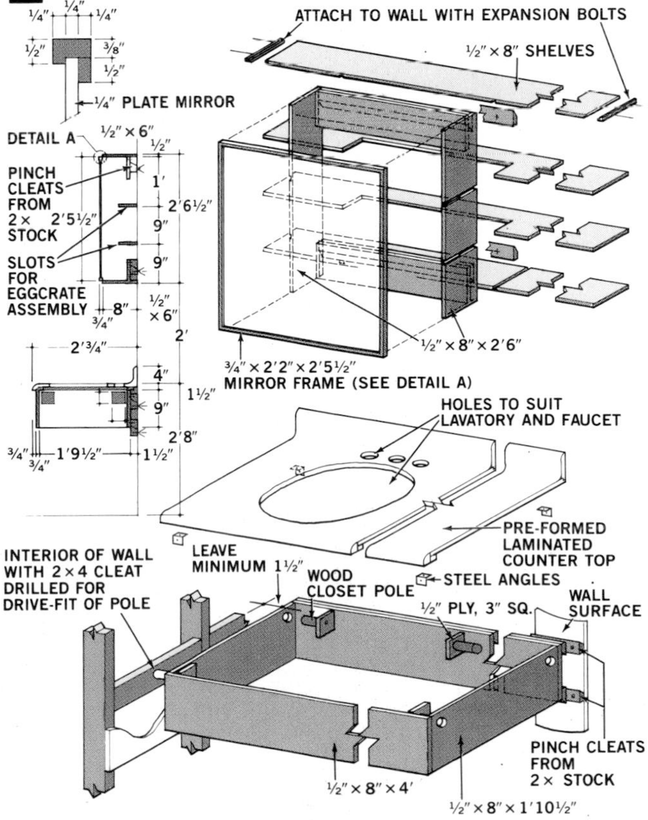

¼″
¼″
¼″
½″
⅜″
½″
¼″ PLATE MIRROR
DETAIL A
½″ × 6″
½″
PINCH CLEATS FROM 2× STOCK
1′
2′6½″
2′5½″
9″
SLOTS FOR EGGCRATE ASSEMBLY
9″
8″
¾″
½″ × 6″
2′
2′¾″
4″
1½″
9″
2′8″
¾″
1′9½″
1½″
¾″
ATTACH TO WALL WITH EXPANSION BOLTS
½″ × 8″ SHELVES
½″ × 8″ × 2′6″
¾″ × 2′2″ × 2′5½″ MIRROR FRAME (SEE DETAIL A)
HOLES TO SUIT LAVATORY AND FAUCET
PRE-FORMED LAMINATED COUNTER TOP
INTERIOR OF WALL WITH 2×4 CLEAT DRILLED FOR DRIVE-FIT OF POLE
LEAVE MINIMUM 1½″
WOOD CLOSET POLE
STEEL ANGLES
½″ PLY, 3″ SQ.
WALL SURFACE
PINCH CLEATS FROM 2× STOCK
½″ × 8″ × 4′
½″ × 8″ × 1′10½″

A visitor wants to freshen up, but you're reluctant to send him to your cluttered upstairs bathroom where soggy towels and oozing tubes of toothpaste abound. You long for a powder room where your guest could find some fresh hand towels and a spotless lavatory. If you're willing to sacrifice a downstairs walk-in closet or a small room, here are two ways to add a powder room.

A standard bathroom requires an area at least 7½ feet long, but a half-bath can easily fit into a space only 4½ by 6 feet long. The first design (top drawing and photo) requires 6 feet of floor space along one wall where the vanity and toilet are located.

The curved surface around the lavatory provides a transition between the left and right portions of the counter top, concealing the difference in their widths. On the right, the narrow counter extends over the toilet tank, at a height that still lets you remove the lid. On the left are the vanity's drawers—the bottom one is a tip-out bin. The lavatory protrudes from the wall, but the drawers are set back, freeing more floor space in the room. The cabinetry in the photo was customized in a professional shop, but the drawing suggests a home-shop approximation.

The second design (bottom drawing)—a simple lavatory counter—can be built in a smaller area, to any length desired. The counter "floats" between the walls to avoid caulked seams at each end. You can build-in a medicine cabinet behind the mirror, hinging the framed panel.

Both vanities are faced with plastic laminate—*by Dawn Stover. Drawings by Mike Hardiman.*

through-the-wall cabinets

By banishing a bulky china cabinet (top photo) and replacing it with sleek recessed cabinets and serving counter, floor space for the dinette set was opened up.

With a cramped dining area just off their kitchen, the owners of this home wanted more space around the table. A headline in *Popular Science* caught their eye: "Need More Floor Space for Cabinets? Shove 'Em Through the Wall!" In the article, a dining room was enlarged by recessing china cabinets so their fronts were flush with the existing wall.

The homeowners eyed their giant hutch and calculated it ate up 10 square feet of floor space. Why not bump it through the wall into the adjacent garage?

But as they pondered their options, they realized they weren't that fond of their outsized period piece. While they were at it, why not build new Scandinavian-style cabinets and a handy serving counter? You can judge the result. With an approximately $700 investment in materials, the homeowners built an addition that's been estimated as adding more than $1,800 to the value of their home. And the old hutch? They donated it to charity and earned a tax deduction.

The new cabinets feature laminate surfaces for easy cleaning, natural-oak accent trim, display areas with adjustable half-shelves, a lighted counter top, concealed hinges, and generous storage space in the drawers and cupboards.

Inspect the wall to be cut away. Turn off your electricity and water if any cables or plumbing runs must be rerouted. You should add a temporary header across the new opening before cutting away existing studs and sole plate with a reciprocating saw.

If you're notching into an unfinished unheated area such as a garage, you can minimize the mess by stapling polyethylene across the gap and working from the back. You'll most likely need an elevated platform to bring a garage floor up to the level of the finished floor inside the house. Don't forget to insulate the floor, walls, and ceiling of the alcove you create. (If you are bumping the cabinets into an adjacent living space, the back wall requires some special treatment.)

Construct the upper and lower cabinets of plywood. (Check the materials list on next page.) To cut required dadoes, use a router equipped with a 3/4-inch straight-face bit and make a T-square-type straightedge to guide the tool. Cut rabbets with a rabbeting bit equipped with a pilot guide.

After assembling with glue, dowels, and finishing nails, paint the cavities of both cabinets to suit; the back of the display cabinet should be the same color as your room's walls. Do not cut the oak door and drawer trim to length until you have laminated the particleboard core. Cut the laminate in oversized strips and apply to all edges first. When the adhesive has set, rout the laminate flush with a trimming bit. Use a flat file to square inside rounded corners.

Install the upper cabinet with countersunk wood screws into the alcove studs. Drill holes for shelf pins and install the adjustable shelves. Then

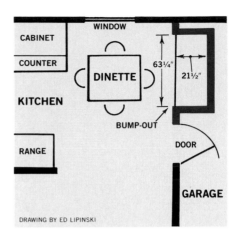

apply the backsplash tile with an adhesive before installing the lower cabinet.

All doors are mounted with European-style hinges available at specialty hardware stores and through mail-order catalogs. Drill the recesses for these hinges with a 1 3/8-inch Forstner bit. For best alignment, attach pulls after doors are hung—*by Al Gutierrez. Lead photo by Brantley Photography.*

PARTICIPATING MANUFACTURERS
The following manufacturers participated in this project: **Glazecraft flooring tile,** adhesive: Armstrong World Industries, Box 3001, Lancaster PA 17604; **new steel panel door to garage, lumber:** Knox Lumber Co. (subsidiary of Payless Cashways), 801 Transfer Road, St. Paul MN 55104; **power tools:** Wen Products, 5810 Northwest Highway, Chicago IL 60631; **sheetrock panel, Durabond wallboard joint compound:** USG Corporation, 101 South Wacker Drive, Chicago IL 60606-4385; **stain:** Minwax Company, 102 Chestnut Ridge Plaza, Montvale NJ 07645; **Wilsonart laminate, adhesive:** Ralph Wilson Plastics Co., Box 6110, Temple TX 76503.

Use a hammer to remove the drywall and sheathing from garage-side of kitchen wall.

Once you've removed drywall and sheathing, cut the lower wall and sole plates. Wear eye goggles when using power tools.

Frame in the cabinet bump-out from the garage side of the wall. Insert subfloor and underlayment to bring the extended flooring up to kitchen's level. Be sure to insulate floor.

Trim laminate with a router equipped with a trimming bit and pilot guide.

Cut dadoes with a router equipped with a straight-faced bit guided against a straightedge.

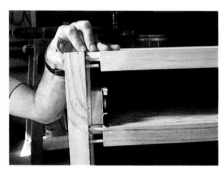

Attach stiles and rails to lower cabinet with dowel pins, glue, and nails.

Laminate stiles and rails by first laying center-rail laminate strip, then stile strips, then rail strips.

Cut rabbets into the oak display doors with a rabbeting bit stocked with a piloting guide.

Attach doors with these European-style hinges. Predrill hinge recess with 1 ³⁄₈-inch Forstner bit.

Install fluorescent lighting units and light shield per manufacturer's instructions.

If you redo the floor, loosen old tile with a heat gun; then removed softened tile with a putty knife.

Detailed plans, step-by-step photography, and instructions are available from Jonathan Press, PO Box 19, Cannon Falls, MN 55009 ($7.95 postpaid).

MATERIALS LIST

ITEM	QUANTITY
12-ft. 2 × 6 pine	1
10-ft. 2 × 4 pine	24
³⁄₄-in. A-B plywood	3 4 × 8-ft sheets
¹⁄₂-in. oak plywood	4 × 4-ft. sheet
⁵⁄₈-in. particleboard	4 × 8-ft. sheet
¹⁄₄-in. plywood	2 4 × 8-ft. sheets
6-ft. 1 × 4 pine	1
8-ft. 1 × 3 oak	9
8-ft. 1 × 2 oak	8

Oak pulls	16
Hidden hinges	24
16-in. drawer slides	4 sets
¹⁄₈ × 11⁵⁄₈ × 19³⁄₄-in. Plexiglas	4 pieces
¹⁄₁₆-in. × 4 ft. × 8 ft. Wilsonart laminate (Light Beige 1531-6)	3 sheets
Lokweld 270 contact adhesive	2 qts.
USG Sheetrock (4 × 8 ft.)	7 sheets
No. 10 × 2¹⁄₂-in. flathead wood screws	30
No. 10 × 1¹⁄₈-in. flathead wood screws	6
No. 8 × 1¹⁄₄-in. flathead wood screws	16
No. 8 × 3-in. flathead wood screws	6

9-in. Armstrong Glazecraft floor tile (Ginger 54416) with 1-qt. Armstrong S-140 Glazecraft wall tile adhesive	17 tiles
Miniwax Polyshade stain (Antique Walnut 340/450)	1 qt.

Miscellaneous items: 16d common nails; 4d and 8d galvanized finishing nails; 1¹⁄₄-in. brads; subflooring and underlayment; matching floor tile with adhesive; ¹⁄₄ × 2-in. dowel pins; insulation and vapor barrier; wallboard nails and tape; Durabond wallboard joint compound; fluorescent lighting; corner channel and caulk

elegant alcove built-ins

Most of us don't live in custom houses designed by imaginative architects to meet our personal needs. So our rooms tend to be boxes, without much distinction. But we needn't settle for that. Take your pick of this pair of built-ins that will perk up a plain room.

Every home should have a privacy nook, away from major traffic lanes and distractions, where a reader can curl up with a book or magazine. Your home may already have the setting: an underused clothes closet, perhaps in the guest room or den. If not, you can *create* an alcove by building a false wall in front of an existing partition. As shown in a plan view you can gain flanking closets as a bonus—with access from either side.

The most economical way to proceed if you're starting from scratch is to buy the cushions and bolsters first, so you won't have to have them made specially to fit.

The couch features a storage base—four box drawers large enough to store bedding, family games, and gift wrapping. This assembly sits on a recessed base of 2×4s, assembled with 10d finishing nails and glue. Simple butt joints are used throughout, so you need no special tools for routing or mitering.

Reading alcove can be created along any partition by building out a false wall—or by building it into an existing closet. Shelf and drawers are assembled with simple butt joints. Shelf slips over wall cleats (top photo).

Serving Alcove can be created in a corner of any family room by building in this peninsula bar. Tie the structure into the room by facing it with matching prefinished panels—wood-veneer wainscot, patterned panels above.

Serving alcove

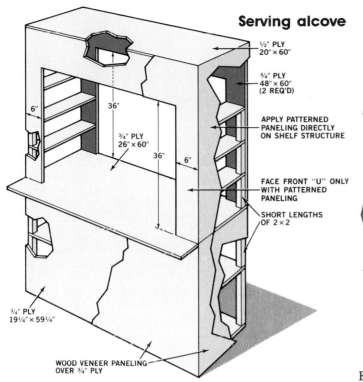

½" PLY
20" × 60"

¾" PLY
48" × 60"
(2 REQ'D)

APPLY PATTERNED
PANELING DIRECTLY
ON SHELF STRUCTURE

¾" PLY
26" × 60"

36"

36"

6"

6"

FACE FRONT "U" ONLY
WITH PATTERNED
PANELING

SHORT LENGTHS
OF 2 × 2

¾" PLY
19¼" × 59¼"

WOOD VENEER PANELING
OVER ¾" PLY

APPLY PAINTED CORNER MOLDING
AND OTHER TRIM AFTER ASSEMBLY

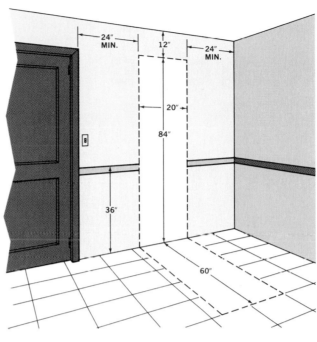

24"
MIN.

12"

24"
MIN.

20"

84"

36"

60"

Reading alcove

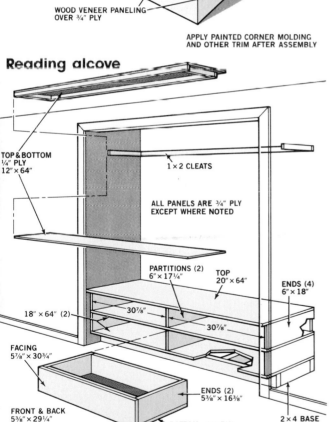

TOP & BOTTOM
¼" PLY
12" × 64"

1 × 2 CLEATS

ALL PANELS ARE ¾" PLY
EXCEPT WHERE NOTED

PARTITIONS (2)
6" × 17¼"

TOP
20" × 64"

ENDS (4)
6" × 18"

18" × 64" (2)

30⅞"

30⅞"

FACING
5⅞" × 30¾"

ENDS (2)
5⅜" × 16⅜"

FRONT & BACK
5⅜" × 29¼"

BOTTOM—½" PLY
16⅜" × 30¾"

2 × 4 BASE
15" × 64"

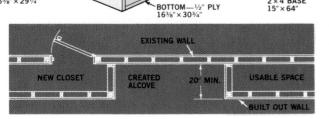

EXISTING WALL

NEW CLOSET

CREATED
ALCOVE

20" MIN.

USABLE SPACE

BUILT OUT WALL

Even the drawers are assembled from six lapping parts, with no need for grooving. (Be sure to make them sufficiently undersized to avoid binding, and apply paste wax to bottoms and sides before inserting them in their recesses.) Install drawer pulls of your choice.

The bookshelf is assembled like a box beam. After you complete the walls of the alcove, fasten 1 × 2 cleats to the back wall and 11¼ inches out along both side walls. Then assemble the two "skins" of ¼-inch plywood to a 1 × 2 frame. Note that although the front strip of this frame is flush with the edge, the other three members are recessed ¾ inch. This creates channels to take the wall cleats. Putty any voids in the exposed front, then sand smooth and paint the assembly. To mount, spread all channels with glue and push them back onto the cleats, securing them with a few brads while the glue sets. Remove any glue drips with a moist cloth. Wire in an end-wall lamp, place the cushions and bolsters, and settle in for a good read.

The peninsula bar that creates the serving alcove was designed by Michael Cannarozzi to add interest and convenience to a family room. It's great for mixing individual drink orders—soft or hard—and creates storage for glasses, mixers, and snack items. You could even build in a bar fridge or ice maker under the counter.

Assembly (mostly from ¾-inch plywood) is straightforward, beginning with the counter, which is an open-backed box with a center shelf. It's a good idea to stiffen all four joints with 2 × 2 glue blocks above and below the shelf. The easiest way to create the upper shelf unit is to cut the U-shaped front and back from single sheets of ¾-inch ply. The left-hand shelves can be cleated to the wall.

Though the counter top is only ¾-inch ply, the edge is bulked up with chair-rail molding. The designer has tied the counter into its corner by running a chair rail around the room at the same height.

For other ideas and installation techniques, send a stamped, self-addressed envelope to Plywood Paneling Council-PS, 1633 Broadway, New York, NY 10019—*by Al Lees. Drawings by Mario Ferro.*

shrewd storage with trundle platforms

Before (above): Author-builder contemplates unpartitioned space and plans future construction (dotted lines). Bed/wardrobe divider supports right side of platform. As final phase of project, living-room floor was raised nearly 30 inches to store tall items on two trundle carts (far right)—but to fit your room, platform can be lower, carts narrower. Carts roll under and are hidden behind snap-on closure panels of ¾-inch waferboard. Access to platform is by two removable step units—one at front (photo right), other out of sight at far end of partition.

Problem: A large unpartitioned space offered no storage—and no privacy for sleeping areas. This project supplies practical concealed storage for bulky items while adding rather theatrical distinction to open space.

Before you build a storage platform into any room in your home, you'll probably apply for a building permit. Even if that's not required for an indoor improvement in your community, check local codes for any restrictions concerning ceiling height over a living area. The Uniform Building Code calls for a minimum of 7½ feet, except for kitchens, bathrooms, and halls, where the ceiling may be as low as 7 feet. If your living room has a soaring cathedral ceiling, you can tuck a storage platform under the high end, leaving floor space for pulling out the trundles at the lower end.

Since I built my under-30-inch-high platform into a city apartment with 10½-foot ceilings, height codes didn't apply. However, building codes did call for noncombustible construction materials, so all the lumber and panels used were treated with the fire-retarding Dricon system from Koppers.

The Dricon treatment doesn't discolor the wood, so I was able to leave my band joists and support posts exposed without any finish. The lumber and plywood is as easy to work as untreated materials, though heavier to lift. I did all my cutting with a Black & Decker Piranha blade with 18 carbide teeth, mounted in my portable circular saw.

I set my platform as high as existing window sills and trim permitted and drew a level line on the three supporting walls, an inch below the finished height. In older buildings you'll doubtless find a non-level floor; keep your ledger lines level around the room. Fasten good, straight 2×6s along the side walls with their top edges flush with your lines.

The type of fastener you use depends, of course, on the wall structure. My back wall was brick, so I drove lag screws through the 2×4 and into lead shields. For the hollow wall I used both Molly and toggle bolts.

All joists are nailed into Teco metal hangers; there's enough "give" to these hangers to take a joist at a slight angle. (As the drawing shows, one corner of my room was not square.)

Knowing I was working with pressure-treated wood, Teco supplied galvanized nails with the hangers—though Dricon isn't supposed to affect metal the way earlier fire-treatment chemicals did. Anyway, be sure to use Teco's special nails when purchasing your hangers: They're heavier gauge and shorter than standard nails and have blunt points to reduce splitting.

Installing a platform gave me a special bonus. As the "before" photo shows, the room had two exposed radiators connected with unsightly pipes. One radiator was short enough to frame the platform above it, leaving an opening I'd later bridge with industrial grating—steel bars painted black, ordered in two pieces for easier access to radiator controls.

The other unit stood higher than the platform, so I simply framed around it. To direct the heat upward (so as not to bake items stored under the platform), I enclosed the radiators with hoppers formed of 1/4-inch-ply panels, attached to the platform joists and floor cleats with screws for emergency removal. I then stapled on a lining of foil-faced Reflectix bubble-pack insulation. I found that one 2-by-25-foot roll lined both radiator cavities, with material to spare.

I finished off my platform with a commercial carpet and pad and nailed a painted molding along the exposed front edge.

Construction of the trundle carts couldn't be simpler. Assembly must be sturdy, though, since the carts must carry a good deal of weight. I fastened all joints in the 2×4 frame with 1/4-inch lag screws 4 inches long. Be sure to place any bowed 2×4 with its bow *up*. This avoids sagging against the floor later, when weight is applied.

Once the frame is assembled, flip it over and apply the 3/4-inch-ply panels

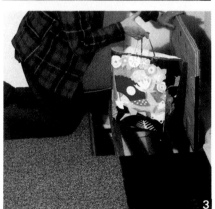

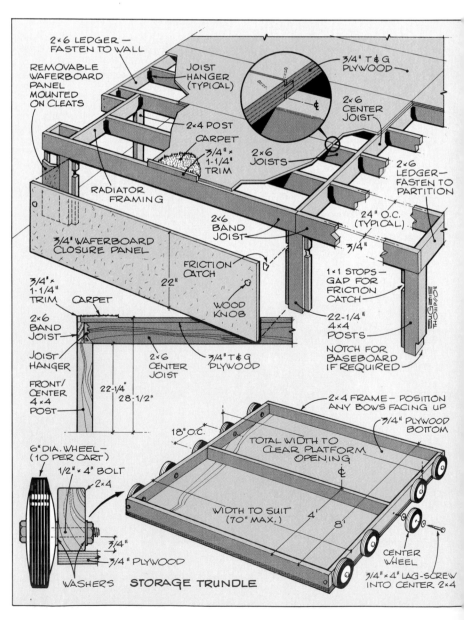

to the bottom edge using construction adhesive (it should be a type—such as Liquid Nails—recommended for treated wood). Now countersink flat-head No. 10 screws, 3 inches long, every 18 inches around the perimeter and along both sides of the "seam."

I could have mounted the platforms on fixed, flat-plate casters, but this would have risked wear tracks on my hardwood floor. So I decided to go with side-mounted rubber-tire wheels. The best I found were made by Power Lawnmower Parts Inc. They're marked 6″×1.5″ and are sold under the Kwik-Fix label in hardware stores and home centers. Half-inch-diameter machine bolts make ideal axles for these wheels. To pass through the 1³/₈-inch-thick hub and the 2×4 frame, these bolts should be 4 inches long. I bought hex-head machine bolts, threaded at the nut end only; a

smooth shank won't cut up the hub bushing. At the center position, 5-inch-long ¹/₂-inch lag screws serve as frame fasteners and axles.

I first tried three wheels per side—for a total of six per cart. But when I loaded the carts with heavy cartons they wouldn't budge. Additional wheels distributed the axle weight more evenly, solving the problem.

For the closure panels, I ripped a 4-by-8-foot sheet of ³/₄-inch-waferboard to sizes that fit within the platform's support frame. I chose a quality sheet of Louisiana-Pacific's Waferwood and found the panels so dimensionally stable and free of warp that no back frame was necessary. I just sanded the cut edges and applied a matte varnish to faces and all edges.

A wooden knob near each top corner provides a grip for easy handling. The panels just set against stop-cleats

Closure panels have finger knobs for easy removal (1); they're held in place by friction catches. Since carts are not as deep as platform, access to storage along back wall is by means of removable stair treads (2) at one corner and trap door (3) at other. Note grate in foreground. If radiator stands taller than platform (4), frame around it; add hopper and line with insulation.

nailed on the side posts—cleats that are gapped for mounting a spring-loaded roller catch.

A word about the steps: Since my platform is about 29 inches high (it varies because it's built level over a sloping floor), my two-step stairs have treads spaced more than 9½ inches apart. That's a deeper step than most people are used to (women guests in tight skirts have objected). But my platform height didn't warrant adding a third tread—which would have made the front unit cumbersome to move. This unit must be lifted to one side for access to the storage. I've also found it handy around the apartment as a step stool. The treads project at each side to serve as finger grips.

To avoid marring the top surface of the hardwood treads, I assembled the unit with three metal angles on the underside of each tread, fastened to

the sides and riser. I glued and nailed the risers to the sides and drove several screws up through the back edge of the bottom tread into the top riser. I notched a rear cross-brace into the sides, fastening it with glue and finishing nails. All this makes a sturdy, lightweight step. To match the closure panels it sets against, I chose waferboard for my risers; I bought commercial treads at my lumberyard.

To support the loose treads beyond the partition, I lag-screwed Teco stair angles to each wall and trimmed the treads to a snug fit that prevents them from shifting when stepped on. Yet they're easy to lift free for access to items stored behind them, as I'm demonstrating in the photo.

Just visible above my head in that photo is the bottom of a partly raised pleated shade. When this stair access is closed, the shade drops onto the

tread I'm lifting and "seals" the partition between the rooms. It's Hunter Douglas's remarkable Duette double-fabric shade with honeycomb air spaces. It's used here as a privacy screen and an air barrier, and is particularly effective when only the space on one side of this partition is to be air conditioned—*by Al Lees. Photos by David Stubbs. Drawings by Eugene Thompson.*

SOURCES FOR MATERIALS
Foil insulation: Reflectix Inc., Box 108, Markleville IN 46056; **industrial grating;** J. C. MacElroy Company, 91 Ether Road, W. Piscataway NJ 08854; **joist hangers (22 No. A-28) and step supports (4):** Teco, 5530 Wisconsin Avenue, Chevy Chase MD 20815; **pleated shade (Duette):** Hunter Douglas Inc., 601 Alter Street, Broomfield CO 00020; **waferboard:** Louisiana-Pacific Corporation, 111 S.W. Fifth Avenue, Portland OR 97204; **wall paint (Regal AquaPearl China White):** Benjamin Moore & Company, 51 Chestnut Ridge Road, Montvale NJ 07045; **wheels (20 No. SBW-6C):** Power Lawnmower Parts Inc., 1920 Lyell Avenue, Rochester NY 14606.

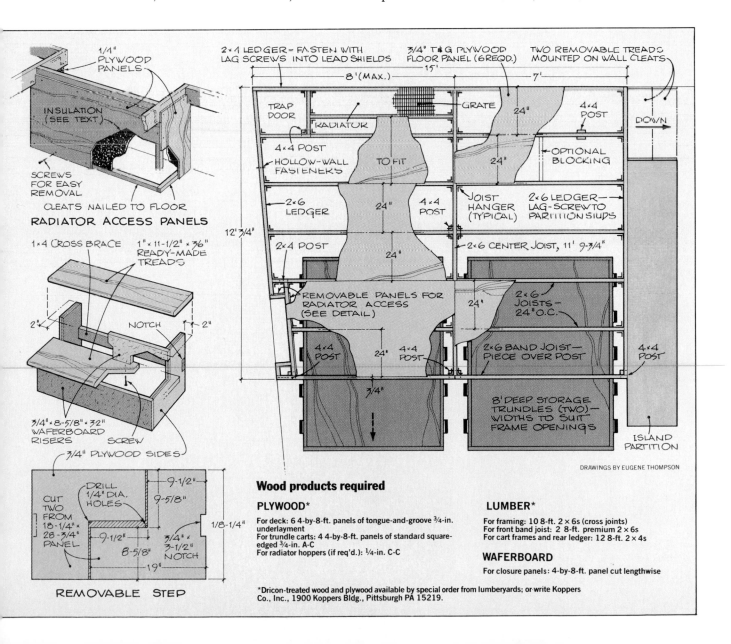

DRAWINGS BY EUGENE THOMPSON

Wood products required

PLYWOOD*

For deck: 6 4-by-8-ft. panels of tongue-and-groove ¾-in. underlayment
For trundle carts: 4 4-by-8-ft. panels of standard square-edged ¾-in. A-C
For radiator hoppers (if req'd.): ¼-in. C-C

LUMBER*

For framing: 10 8-ft. 2 × 6s (cross joints)
For front band joist: 2 8-ft. premium 2 × 6s
For cart frames and rear ledger: 12 8-ft. 2 × 4s

WAFERBOARD

For closure panels: 4-by-8-ft. panel cut lengthwise

*Dricon-treated wood and plywood available by special order from lumberyards; or write Koppers Co., Inc., 1900 Koppers Bldg., Pittsburgh PA 15219.

build in a video corner

Does the "before" photo look familiar? You've seen many family rooms like this—perhaps you're harboring one in your own home: dark and crowded, with dated wood paneling and a beamed ceiling. And the entertainment center shoved into a corner makes for uncomfortable group viewing of television and awkward wiring of properly spaced stereo speakers.

When my wife and I decided to update our electronic gear, we felt it was also time to update our setting for home entertainment. Because this room shares a wall with our kitchen, we decided to add a refreshment pass-through while we were at it—a long, low slot above the counter backsplash with a ledge that lets us serve family and friends directly from the kitchen without loading up clumsy trays. The long counter below this pass-through is ideal for spreading out a self-serve buffet. The new built-ins have made casual entertaining easy. Even cleanup is speeded because all counters are faced with wipe-clean plastic laminate, and dinnerware can be collected on the pass-through ledge for access to the sink.

We housed all our electronic gear in a 6-foot-high, 2½-foot-wide cabinet angled across the corner. The TV was placed on a shelf 8 inches above the floor, which let us tuck a drawer underneath to stash a viewing guide, magazines, and newspapers. The VCR is on an open shelf immediately above the TV; the stereo tuner and tape deck are on separate shelves above the VCR and closed from view by two doors—with space to spare for video games and compact discs. By positioning this cabinet in the corner, we left access space behind for electrical hookups, with no wires showing.

The electronics cabinet is flanked by 15-inch-wide units with closed storage below the open shelves above. All cabinets are made of ¾-inch furniture-grade flakeboard; the 4-inch-radius rounded corner on the "floating" cabinet is created by gluing a full-height preformed molding (which you can buy from most cabinet shops) between the end panel and the front frame. Plastic-laminate surfacing will conceal all the construction joints to present a seamless surface. European-style hinges and touch latches complete this look by leaving no hardware exposed.

We applied wallpaper directly over the paneling after spackling the grooves, sanding smooth, and brushing on an appropriate primer to which wallpaper would stick. We minimized the impact of the ceiling beams by painting them off-white—*by Marc Brett. Drawings by Mario Ferro.*

ADDRESSES OF SOURCES
Cabinetry: Styline Products, Inc., 4185 Merrick Road, Massapequa NY 11758; **Stereo speakers (Model TSW 410)**: Teledyne Acoustic Research, 330 Turnpike Street, Canton MA 02021

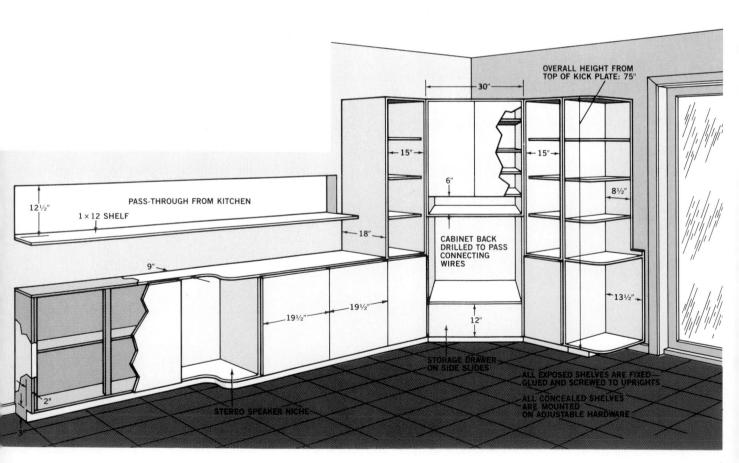

BEFORE

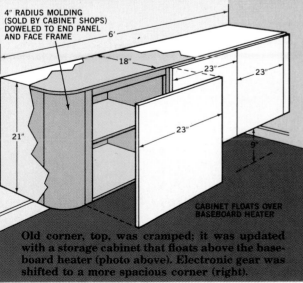

4" RADIUS MOLDING
(SOLD BY CABINET SHOPS)
DOWELED TO END PANEL
AND FACE FRAME

6'

18"

23"

23"

23"

21"

9"

CABINET FLOATS OVER
BASEBOARD HEATER

Old corner, top, was cramped; it was updated
with a storage cabinet that floats above the base-
board heater (photo above). Electronic gear was
shifted to a more spacious corner (right).

end tables for VHS cassettes

I built a pair of these tables for my daughter-in-law. Her problem: how to properly store a steadily-increasing hoard of video cassettes. Now each of her tables will store more than 40 cassettes, or a few cassettes and the family's board games. They also serve handsomely as end or lamp tables.

I originally designed the tables to be built in ponderosa pine, stained dark, and I think this would be my personal preference. But I wound up building them of Honduras mahogany to match other pieces in the room. The tops are tiled. That not only adds the sparkle of variety to the room's decor, it makes the tables pretty well kid-proof. As you may know, teenagers tend to build little finish-destroying compost heaps with abandoned foodstuffs and spilled soft drinks beside their favorite chairs. Of course, you can make the tops of an equally stain-resistant solid material if you prefer.

When I went to the tile store I was pleased to find that you can buy tile cheap as remnants or discontinued stock. I got 8-inch-square, hand-decorated Italian tiles for a small fraction of their regular price. Those pictured were originally priced at $64.50 per set; I paid a buck a tile.

I also learned that tiles come in various sizes. They measure out to be $1/8$-inch smaller than their nominal size in order to allow for a grout line. You can choose from several sizes, three of which are included in the chart for cutting the table elements (see drawing inset).

In the drawings, Detail No. 2, please note that the $5/16$ dimension may vary according to the thickness of the tile you buy. Also, be sure all your tiles are the same thickness. The first batch I bought varied as much as $1/8$ inch from tile to tile and from side to side of the same tile. I had to return them to the store and they ground the little lugs off the backs.

Attractive end table also stores VCR tapes. Drawers can accommodate 40 video tapes and—by pulling out partitions—can also be used for miscellaneous storage.

Dark wood in drawer faces and light wood in sides gives these optional dovetailed drawers a striking appearance. Stain the faces *before* you cut the dovetails.

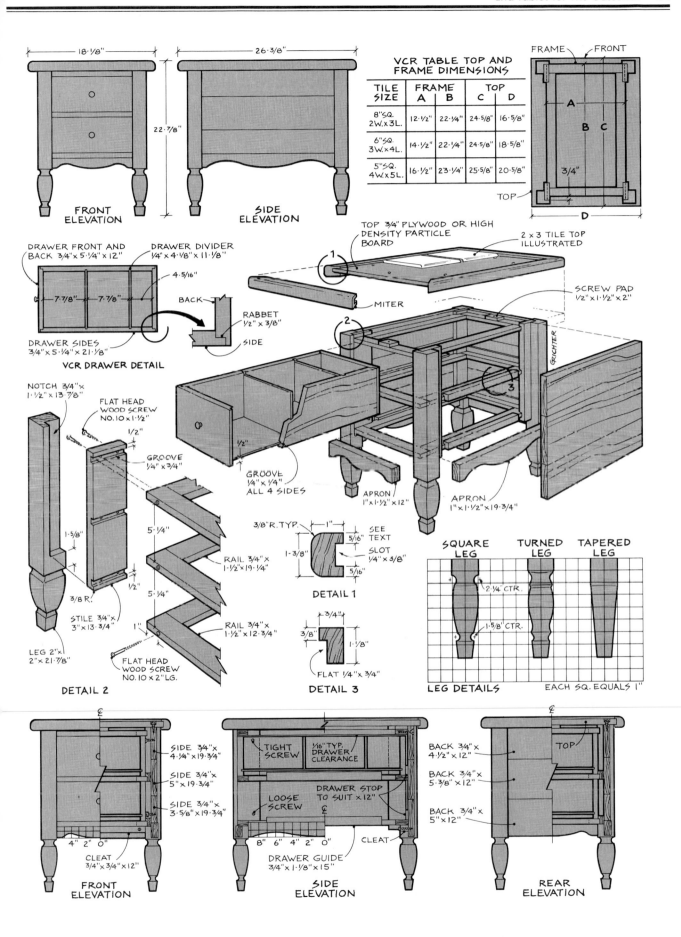

VCR TABLE TOP AND FRAME DIMENSIONS

TILE SIZE	FRAME A	B	TOP C	D
8"SQ. 2W.x3L.	12·1/2"	22·1/4"	24·5/8"	16·5/8"
6"SQ. 3W.x4L.	14·1/2"	22·1/4"	24·5/8"	18·5/8"
5"SQ. 4W.x5L.	16·1/2"	23·1/4"	25·5/8"	20·5/8"

FRONT ELEVATION
18·1/8"
22·7/8"

SIDE ELEVATION
26·3/8"

FRAME   FRONT
A
B C
3/4"
TOP
D

DRAWER FRONT AND BACK 3/4"x 5·1/4"x 12"
DRAWER DIVIDER 1/4"x 4·1/8"x 11·1/8"
4·5/16"
7·7/8" 7·7/8"
DRAWER SIDES 3/4"x 5·1/4"x 21·1/8"
VCR DRAWER DETAIL
BACK
RABBET 1/2" x 3/8"
SIDE

TOP 3/4" PLYWOOD OR HIGH DENSITY PARTICLE BOARD
1
2 x 3 TILE TOP ILLUSTRATED
MITER
2
SCREW PAD 1/2" x 1·1/2" x 2"
RICHTER
3

NOTCH 3/4" x 1·1/2" x 13·7/8"
FLAT HEAD WOOD SCREW NO.10 x 1·1/2"
1/2"
GROOVE 1/4" x 3/4"
1·5/8"
3/8 R.
STILE 3/4"x 3" x 13·3/4"
LEG 2"x 2" x 21·7/8"
FLAT HEAD WOOD SCREW NO.10 x 2"LG.
DETAIL 2
5·1/4"
5·1/4"
RAIL 3/4" x 1·1/2"x 19·1/4"
1"
RAIL 3/4" x 1·1/2"x 12·3/4"

GROOVE 1/4" x 1/4" ALL 4 SIDES
1/2"
APRON 1"x1·1/2"x 12"
APRON 1"x1·1/2"x 19·3/4"

3/8"R.TYP.
1"
5/16"
SEE TEXT
1·3/8"
SLOT 1/4"x 3/8"
5/16"
DETAIL 1

3/4"
3/8"
1·1/8"
FLAT 1/4"x 3/4"
DETAIL 3

SQUARE LEG   TURNED LEG   TAPERED LEG
2·1/4" CTR.
1·5/8" CTR.
LEG DETAILS   EACH SQ. EQUALS 1"

FRONT ELEVATION
4" 2" 0"
CLEAT 3/4"x 3/4"x12"

SIDE 3/4"x 4·1/4"x19·3/4"
SIDE 3/4"x 5"x 19·3/4"
SIDE 3/4"x 3·5/8"x19·3/4"

TIGHT SCREW
1/16" TYP. DRAWER CLEARANCE
LOOSE SCREW
DRAWER STOP TO SUIT x 12"
CLEAT
8" 6" 4" 2" 0"
DRAWER GUIDE 3/4"x 1·1/8"x 15"
SIDE ELEVATION

BACK 3/4"x 4·1/2"x 12"
BACK 3/4"x 5·3/8" x12"
BACK 3/4"x 5"x12"
TOP
REAR ELEVATION

1. For a perfect radius on bottom corners of stiles, or frame supports, round them with a cutter of the same radius as the cutter you will use to make pocket in legs.

2. Use a dado head to cut grooves in the frame supports to accept the frames. It's best to use a stop on the fence of the radial arm saw, or bank the parts against the fence of the table saw.

3. Frames must all lie perfectly flat without rocking. This means you check your saw and jointer for squareness *before* cutting, and clamp the work down to a flat surface as you drill for and drive the screws.

4. If carcase is out of square when you drill for and drive the assembly screws, it will stay that way forever. Check for squareness as you assemble. Five screws were used for the front stile, or frame support, three in the rear.

Where to begin

Your first building job, after you've chosen your tile, is to cut the plywood for the top. Then you put it away in the room the table will occupy until the very last operation. You do this because such materials are often shipped rather wet and are stored under adverse conditions. By making the top last, you give the material a chance to stabilize. (Remember, tile stays the same size and is brittle. Wood, even plywood, may change with humidity and you don't want the tile to crack after the job is done).

Now you can build the carcase. The piece is designed for maximum dimensional stability and is quite simple to build. Just be sure to cut each of the pieces with the end of the stock against a stop, rather than marking the pieces individually. That way you'll get similar pieces all exactly the same size. And that will help assure squareness in the finished job.

The frame supports, or stiles, are marked for cutting the grooves with a pencil line at one end. They are assembled that way to make sure that the location of the center groove is the same on all four. Now you are sure that all four legs will touch the floor at the same time and that a drawer that is built square will fit right. Special care is needed because the drawers don't have a lip and any error in squareness will show.

The corners of the supports will fit into pockets routed in the legs. To clear the radius left by the router you can cut off the bottom, outside corners of the supports at $7/16$ inch × 45 degrees, or you can do it the nice way: If you've cut the pocket with a $3/4$-inch diameter router, stack the four supports and rout the bottom corner with a $3/8$-inch radius-rounding cutter. You get a perfect fit, easily.

Frames and legs

The frames are made from $3/4 × 1^1/2$ stock. Note that the 2-inch screws that hold the pieces together are offset an inch from the outside edge to provide room for $1^1/2 × 10$ screws that hold the frames into the frame support grooves. Only one screw is needed at each corner of the frames; the grooves will keep the parts in line after assembly.

You have to watch it here. When you assemble the frames make sure they will lie flat on the bench without rocking. This is best accomplished first by dressing the sides perfectly square, then by clamping them down when you drill for the screws. Then, when you assemble the frames into the frame supports, check to make sure the assembly is square as you install each piece. The 20 screws you drive through the supports will maintain squareness until you get back and sides on—though the carcase assembly will be rigid with just the screws holding it.

When you have the carcase assembled, you can add those little L-shaped drawer side guides. Check with a straight-edge to make sure they line up with the inside edge of the frame supports.

The legs come next. If you can't get stock in your chosen material to give you 2-by-2-inch blanks you will have to glue up. Try to choose wood that will give you a good match in grain and color. Note that you will be working with left and right legs as soon as you start to cut the frame support pockets. Lay your blanks on the bench and select the grain so you will have flat grain on the front; it doesn't look good to mix flat and edge grain on the same side. Put the best-looking legs in front.

You'll have to pocket the legs for the frame supports, and that takes a little template work. Of course, you can avoid the template if you use a router table or a side guide on the router. I don't care for the side-guide method because, since there isn't enough surface for the base plate, the router isn't stable. That means you're not assured of a nice flat bottom in the cut.

A simple template for the pocket with a template follower on the router was well worthwhile in rabbeting the eight legs I made. If you set up to rabbet two legs at once, as I did, you had better have a base on your router at least 7½ inches in diameter so it can span the opening in the template and give you support on two sides.

Before I bought my big router I made a supplementary 8-inch base from ¼-inch plastic. It installs in minutes and is often useful to extend my 5-inch-diameter router base.

When the rabbeting is done, you can start finishing the leg ends. As the drawing shows, there are three style options, all of which can be turned on the lathe. If you don't have access to a lathe you can make what a buddy of mine calls "square turnings." These were popular many years ago, but the style was too labor-intensive to compete with lathe turning. I think square turnings look rather special—and a bit nicer. Others who have seen Mary Ann's tables agree with me.

Square-turning the legs

You should have a drill press and a band saw to do square turning easily and well. If you have neither lathe, drill press, nor band saw, the simple tapered-leg option will look very good on this piece, harmonizing well with the general design.

To make the square turned leg begin by drilling four holes; the top two are an inch in diameter and the lower two are ¾ inch. These are cut best with bits that will cut part of a circle and leave you with a finish inside the hole that scarcely needs sanding. That means you'll need bits that will cut on the end, such as Forstner or Milwaukee bits, Power Bore, or even spur-type bits. It rules out twist drills, auger bits, and spade bits, which tend to drift in the hole and/or leave a ragged surface behind.

You'll have to clamp a board to the drill-press table because the bit will go right through the piece. Since my little bitty drill press has a small table, I extended it with a piece of three-quarter plywood fastened to the drill-press table with carriage bolts and wing nuts. The setup often comes in handy, as its long overhang makes for easy clamping of guides, stops, and the like.

I cut a piece of 2 × 4 scrap to the thickness of a leg. That was clamped to the table as a guide for the leg blanks and, since part of each hole is in the guide, it stabilizes the bit against side movement during the cut. The result is a smoother finish. The center of the top, 1-inch hole, is located in the guide. The bottom hole center is in the part.

5. You may have to glue up the leg stock to get the 2-inch-square you need. Use plenty of clamps and moderate pressure. Try to match grain and color as well as you can.

6. Use a template follower on your router for the leg pockets. By making the guide opening double-width plus ¾-inch, you can get two legs at once and be sure you have lefts and rights as required. Just tack on a center strip and clamp leg blanks against it.

7. Clamp a piece of ¾-inch plywood to the drill press table to keep drill from striking metal. The wood also makes it easier to attach jigs and fixtures such as in this setup for drilling the holes to start the square legs.

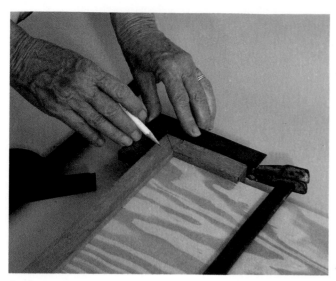

8. An accurate way to mark miters for the top frame: Cut off a couple of short pieces and clamp them to the top, up against the piece to be cut. Using a square mark a line for the length, then a 45-degree line for the cut. Cut pieces 1/32 to 1/16 inch long to avoid corner gaps.

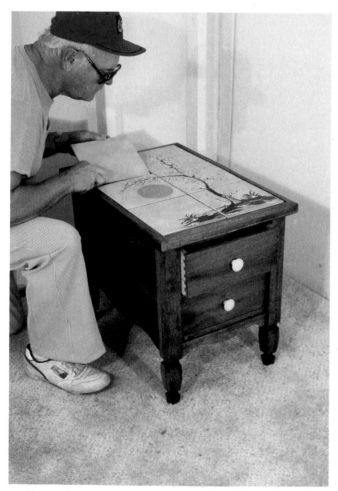

9. About 1/32-inch of tile should stick up above the surface of the top for proper grouting.

When you have the holes located properly, clamp a stop to the table so that every hole is located right and the legs are all alike.

I had made a test leg blank from soft pine so that a possible error in setup would not destroy one of my finished legs. The test blank was carefully laid out, sawn and sanded to the final contour, on two sides only. It is the pattern for all the legs.

Of course, when you saw off two sides of a leg to make the contour, you will saw off any guide marks you made for the other sides. I just laid my dummy leg up against the new leg and carefully marked the piece again. I took out the saw blade marks with a rasp, a Surform file, and a strip of 80-grit paper glued to a narrow strip of wood. I finished first with 100-, then with 150-grit on a vibrator sander.

Fasten the finished front legs onto the frame first using a couple of wood screws and a bead or two of glue. (You'll put the rear legs on when you apply the side and end panels. Then you can pull the legs up tight to the panels and eliminate any gaps).

Side and back panels, drawers

Side and back panels are glued up from the materials you selected. They are fastened on from the inside with wood screws through the frame supports. Now—especially if you bought your material from your friendly local lumberyard instead of a hardwood specialty house—you're smart to mount the sides with "floating construction." The screw holes at the top are drilled for a tight fit, but those at bottom are drilled 1/8-inch oversize; then you countersink for the screw head and a washer. The loose fit of the screw allows the wood to drift a little with humidity changes instead of cracking or buckling. (Failure to do this is often why some furniture requires a matchbook under one leg).

Get the blank for the top out now and make sure the corners are precisely square. The trim has mitered corners. If you cut the groove in the trim so it gives you a nice easy fit, you can glue it on; otherwise, you'll have to fasten it with screws and plug the counterbores. Space the groove so that about 1/32 inch of tile will be above the surface or your grouting will look funny. The drawings show the tops screwed down to the carcase. Actually, I merely set the tops on to check fit and appearance without fastening them down. They haven't been fastened yet—truly floating construction!

There are a dozen ways of making drawers and you can choose your own from any standard text. Our drawings show rabetted corners because that's about as simple as drawer construction can get. If you have a dovetailing fixture, I suggest that you use it. I stained the drawer fronts before cutting my dovetails and used plain varnished-pine drawer sides. The contrast between light and dark makes the drawer look real expensive and classy.

I finished the job with an overall sanding with 150 grit. I stained, then applied two coats of a lacquer-type sanding sealer, sanding after each coat. Final finish was two coats of polyurethane varnish, with the first varnish coat lightly rubbed with steel wool. Incidentally, make very sure both sides of the top are sealed well, or each will expand and contract with humidity at different rates.

When I made the first rough sketches of the cabinets, I asked my wife if she wanted me to build her one. She said no—until she saw Mary Ann's finished cabinets. I have now been instructed to build two more. Thus is careful workmanship rewarded—*by Cy Wedlake. Drawing by Gerhard Richter.*

space-saving staggered stairs

My first sight of a Lapeyre stair was a jolt. With stringers twice as steep as those for conventional steps, it looked like a cross between a staircase and a ladder.

But once I'd gone up and down it, I saw that it made sense. Who needs a full-width tread for each step? You don't put both feet on each tread—unless you're very young or very old. For most of us, half the stairway is wasted every time we use it, and the necessity of spacing out all those full treads extends a stairway far into a room.

By adding a third stringer at the center and clipping each tread in half, a Lapeyre stair can stack steps much more compactly. The unexpected bonus is safety. Though you're climbing the same height, you're covering less ground; you're likely to maintain a good grip on both railings. Dashing up and down stairs—the cause of most tumbles—is discouraged. And your footing is surer since each foot travels a straight, direct path, with less slip vector.

Your first impulse when confronted with a stair rising at 56 degrees (instead of the usual 35) is to think you can't carry anything up or down. In fact, since your feet needn't arc around the skipped tread of a conventional stair, each foot comes down more solidly in the center of its tread; your balance is better maintained. Though you'll normally grip the handrails (as in the photo), you can climb or descend with both hands full. Carrying on a Lapeyre is far easier than carrying on a spiral stair.

Each stair is custom-fabricated to the customer's order, then is shipped ready to assemble, with full instructions. Heights range from 2 feet ($320) to 12½ feet ($610 with a fir handrail assembly; $940 in oak). For more information, write Lapeyre Stair, Box 50699, New Orleans, LA 70150. The company also makes 68-degree stairs in aluminum and steel stairs in both 56- and 68-degree models—but these are mostly for industrial and marine applications. Lapeyre started with aluminum stairs, welded into one unit with cast treads; they're light and corrosion-resistant, ideal for outdoor exposures. Later the company added the steel line, which is adaptable to virtually any situation; these units are finished in a standard gray primer or an industrial yellow—or they can be hot-dip galvanized.

The wooden stairs are the newest addition, bringing the Lapeyre concept, at last, into the home. Stringers and treads are dovetailed and glued for the strength and finished look of fine furniture. They're shipped smoothly sanded for finishing to match your room decor—*by Al Lees. Drawings by Hugo Salhuana.*

DRAWING BY HUGO SALHUANA

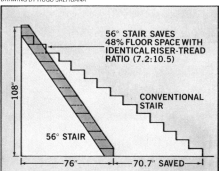

56° STAIR SAVES 48% FLOOR SPACE WITH IDENTICAL RISER-TREAD RATIO (7.2:10.5)

CONVENTIONAL STAIR

56° STAIR

108"

76" — 70.7" SAVED

Custom-built Lapeyre stair in photo gives access to a loft. The homeowner wished to cover as little of the window wall as possible. A 9-foot-tall conventional stair would extend over 12 feet into the room, as diagram indicates.

5 award-winning decks

Are the deck designs on these six pages the shrewdest in America? When the California Redwood Association and I set up the parameters for this national design competition we deliberately kept the qualifications as broad as it was practical to make them. For those homeowners who'd be building a deck especially for the contest, we didn't want to inhibit creativity. And where professional contractors were concerned, we wished to avoid making them fear that their more innovative projects were too far-out to qualify. So except for requiring that redwood be the dominant material, we asked only one thing: that the deck solve at least one difficult problem—taming an unbuildable site, providing built-in storage, concealing an eye-sore, etc.

The response was spectacular, and we're proud of the five winning designs. We were able to inspect and rephotograph the three top winners and were delighted with the workmanship. The first two decks were designed and built by professionals; the third was designed and built entirely by the homeowners.

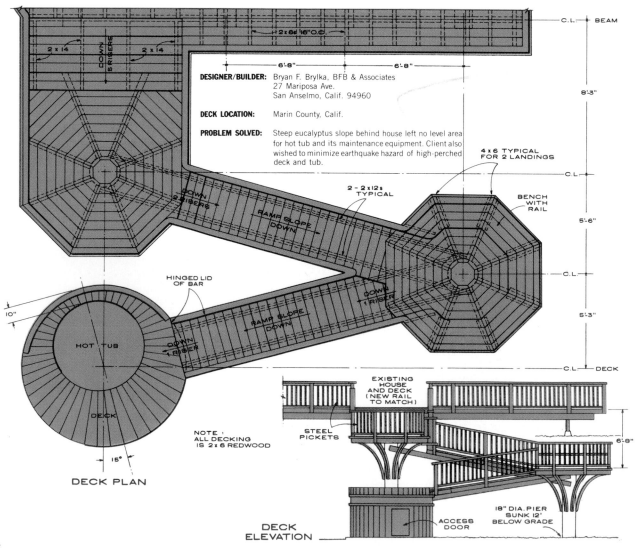

DESIGNER/BUILDER: Bryan F. Brylka, BFB & Associates
27 Mariposa Ave.
San Anselmo, Calif. 94960

DECK LOCATION: Marin County, Calif.

PROBLEM SOLVED: Steep eucalyptus slope behind house left no level area for hot tub and its maintenance equipment. Client also wished to minimize earthquake hazard of high-perched deck and tub.

DECK PLAN

DECK ELEVATION

PHOTOS BY TOM RIDER

Both octagonal pods are supported on concrete piers by boom-erang braces laminated from strips of redwood and fir. Ramps, platforms, and rails are finished with Cuprinol Heavy Duty Deck Stain in chestnut brown. Bottom section of lower ramp hinges up to reveal a bar.

PHOTOS BY TOM RIDER

Glass-paneled railing doesn't hide the view. Curved top rails are pieced. Substructure was engineered by Bob Martin.

PHOTOS BY ERNEST BRAUN

Stained gray to match the house siding, this deck covers the entire backyard. Raised portion gives the look of an in-ground pool. Hinged corner gives access to filter.

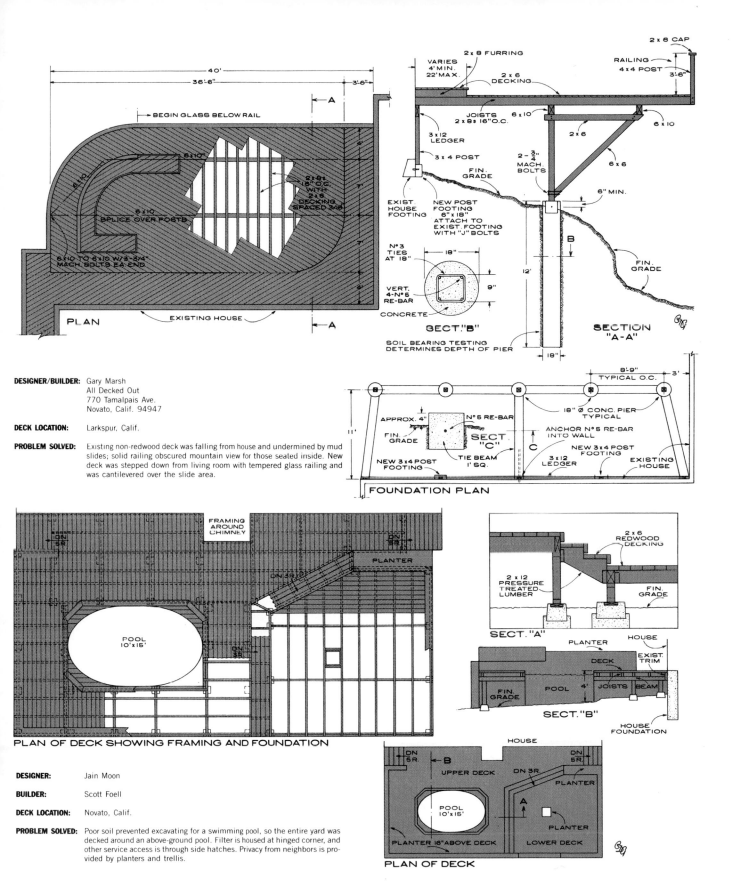

DESIGNER/BUILDER: Gary Marsh
All Decked Out
770 Tamalpais Ave.
Novato, Calif. 94947

DECK LOCATION: Larkspur, Calif.

PROBLEM SOLVED: Existing non-redwood deck was falling from house and undermined by mud slides; solid railing obscured mountain view for those seated inside. New deck was stepped down from living room with tempered glass railing and was cantilevered over the slide area.

PLAN OF DECK SHOWING FRAMING AND FOUNDATION

DESIGNER: Jain Moon

BUILDER: Scott Foell

DECK LOCATION: Novato, Calif.

PROBLEM SOLVED: Poor soil prevented excavating for a swimming pool, so the entire yard was decked around an above-ground pool. Filter is housed at hinged corner, and other service access is through side hatches. Privacy from neighbors is provided by planters and trellis.

● The top prizewinner is the work of a creative young designer/contractor, Bryan Brylka, for a house that perches at the crest of a steep forested hillside. It's a strikingly original solution, combining deck spaces with access to hot tub far below. The "spokes" that radiate from the tub across the surrounding redwood deck are quarter-inch Plexiglas acrylic plastic strips laminated between the planks. Though they are sanded flush with the deck surface (which is then sealed with multiple coats of clear epoxy), the strips project an inch below the deck's underside, where a light source illuminates them as well as the water in the tub.

● For his project, Gary Marsh of All Decked Out inherited an existing deteriorating deck with underpinnings

Winnowing down hundreds of entries to the final selections wasn't easy. In this task, *Popular Science* Home & Shop Editor Al Lees (at right) and CRA's publicity manager, Charlene Draheim (center), were joined by Christopher Grover, CRA's promotion manager. Entries came from 32 states, with greatest representation from California, followed by Colorado and Montana. The prairie states also scored high, with the lightest participation from the East Coast. Al and Charlene report that the final judging was excruciating. "But the joy expressed by the winners when we phoned them," says Charlene, "eased our pain."

Free-form lakeside deck in Maine has bench laminated from redwood strips.

Triple-prow deck floats off a Pennsylvania hill. Section at right has spa sunk into it. Unique railing ties it all together.

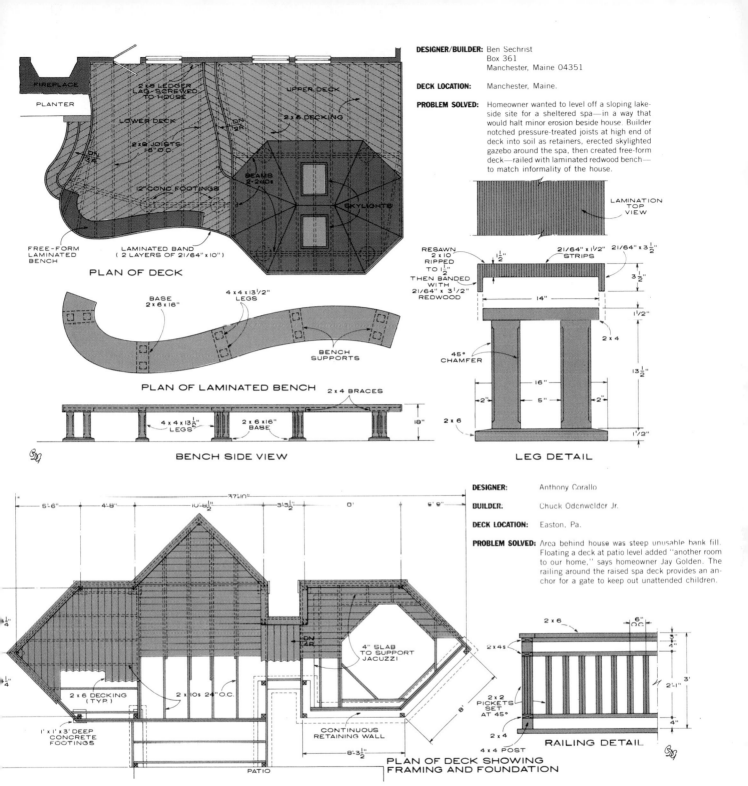

FIREPLACE

PLANTER

2 x 8 LEDGER LAG-SCREWED TO HOUSE

UPPER DECK

LOWER DECK

2 x 6 DECKING

2 x 8 JOISTS 16" O.C.

DN 2R

DN 3R

BEAMS 2-2x10s

12" CONC FOOTINGS

SKYLIGHTS

FREE-FORM LAMINATED BENCH

LAMINATED BAND (2 LAYERS OF 21/64"x10")

PLAN OF DECK

BASE 2 x 6 x 16"

4 x 4 x 13½" LEGS

BENCH SUPPORTS

PLAN OF LAMINATED BENCH

2 x 4 BRACES

4 x 4 x 13½" LEGS

2 x 6 x 16" BASE

18"

BENCH SIDE VIEW

LAMINATION TOP VIEW

RESAWN 2 x 10 RIPPED TO 1½" THEN BANDED WITH 21/64" x 3½" REDWOOD

1½"

21/64" x 1½" 21/64" x 3½" STRIPS

3½"

14"

1½"

2 x 4

45° CHAMFER

16"

13½"

2" 5" 2"

2 x 6

1½"

LEG DETAIL

DESIGNER/BUILDER: Ben Sechrist
Box 361
Manchester, Maine 04351

DECK LOCATION: Manchester, Maine.

PROBLEM SOLVED: Homeowner wanted to level off a sloping lakeside site for a sheltered spa—in a way that would halt minor erosion beside house. Builder notched pressure-treated joists at high end of deck into soil as retainers, erected skylighted gazebo around the spa, then created free-form deck—railed with laminated redwood bench—to match informality of the house.

DESIGNER: Anthony Corallo

BUILDER: Chuck Odenwelder Jr.

DECK LOCATION: Easton, Pa.

PROBLEM SOLVED: Area behind house was steep unusable bank fill. Floating a deck at patio level added "another room to our home," says homeowner Jay Golden. The railing around the raised spa deck provides an anchor for a gate to keep out unattended children.

37'10"

5'6" 4'8" 10'8½" 3'5½" 0' 6'9"

DN 4R

4" SLAB TO SUPPORT JACUZZI

2 x 6 DECKING (TYP.)

2 x 10s 24" O.C.

1' x 1' x 3' DEEP CONCRETE FOOTINGS

CONTINUOUS RETAINING WALL

8'3½"

PATIO

PLAN OF DECK SHOWING FRAMING AND FOUNDATION

2 x 6

6" O.C.

2 x 4s

2 x 2 PICKETS SET AT 45°

2 x 4

4 x 4 POST

3'

2'1"

4"

RAILING DETAIL

weakened by a landslide. For the replacement deck, a bracing system had to be developed to support a center-point beam over which the deck could cantilever. Even with these piers set well back from the edge of the cliff, the engineer drilled 32 feet deep to reach stable soil, then tied the piers and the house foundation together.

● When Jain Moon designed a platform deck around her above-ground pool, this raised the "backyard" 4 feet and compromised the privacy pro-vided by existing fences. So Moon and builder Scott Foell included trellised planters at the deck perimeter. For the trellis top, 4-foot 2 × 4s were cut in half at a 30-degree angle to slant down on both sides of the double beam.

● Maine builder Ben Sechrist's client wanted an underused yard leveled so that a shed sunspace with a hot tub inside could be added to the house. Ben proposed instead an open deck with a gazebo at one end to shelter the hot tub. This took the form of a stretched octagon. Skylights on both long sides of the steep roof flank a vented cupola. All openings are screened against lakeside insects.

● The Golden project in Pennsylvania used (like the other four) redwood decking and railings supported on framing of pressure-treated lumber. Deck boards were fastened with hot-dipped galvanized nails; all bolts were stainless steel—*by Al Lees. Drawings by Carl DeGroote.*

backyard retreat

What could be better than drinking cool lemonade and relaxing in an airy backyard gazebo that also offers a bit of privacy from close neighbors? Using low-maintenance redwood lumber and lattice panels (in two-by-eight- and four-by-eight-foot sizes), a homeowner with basic carpentry skills and tools can build this structure in a couple of weekends. You can decide whether to build the gazebo as a cozy corner retreat or as a central backyard focal point; my choice was the latter. The redwood lattice provides dappled shade while letting in breezes.

To build, set the outer posts of the structure first, making sure they are plumb before setting the additional front deck-support posts in line with them. I set the posts three feet into the ground without using concrete.

Use zinc-plated carriage bolts for additional strength and rust resistance when attaching the 2×6 deck-support stringers to the support posts. Nail on the front 2×6 facing, which will support the front deck 2×4.

When I laid the 2×4 deck boards, I left a $3/8$-inch space between boards for drainage. Wait until the deck is attached before trimming the 2×4s to match the structural angles. Give the top of the structure a front-to-back slope of about seven inches to give illusion of spaciousness.

When it's time to attach the upper front 2×6 facing, be sure the front posts are the same distance apart at the deck and at the top. Nail on 2×4s to complete the top framing after rabbeting their inner faces to take the overhead lattice sections. Vertical lattice sections can be attached to the upright framing in one of two ways, depending on your tools. Either cut a groove in 2×2s the width of the lattice, as shown, or nail beveled cleats on each side of the lattice. One edge of each vertical 2×2 or cleat will need to be cut at an angle its full length to match the angle it will set against the 4×4 post.

The lattice sections can be easily cut

with either a handsaw or power saw, but handle the panels carefully to avoid dislodging the staples used in their construction. I designed the two front side sections at a shorter 45-inch height to give the structure a more open, airy feeling. The back panel is in two sections, with the top one hinged so you have the option of closing it for additional screening or dropping it for more ventilation. To wind up construction, you can add triangular decorative trim at the upper front corners.

When the structure is completed, apply a preservative like Woodlife. Afterward, you can apply a redwood stain if you wish to retain the red color. If no stain is applied, all redwood gradually changes to a weathered gray color.

Your own personal touches complete your leisure retreat. Twin cushioned redwood chairs on the deck invite backyard relaxing, and a matching chaise lounge may attract sunbathers to the semiprivate area in front of the structure. The intriguing design of the redwood lattice invites creative use of the remaining redwood scrap, such as forming a border trim along the front of an adjoining flower bed—*by Lois Poppe. Drawings by Gerhard Richter.*

Cover the ground under the structure with a heavy-grade plastic cover held down by gravel or rubble to prevent the growth of weeds.

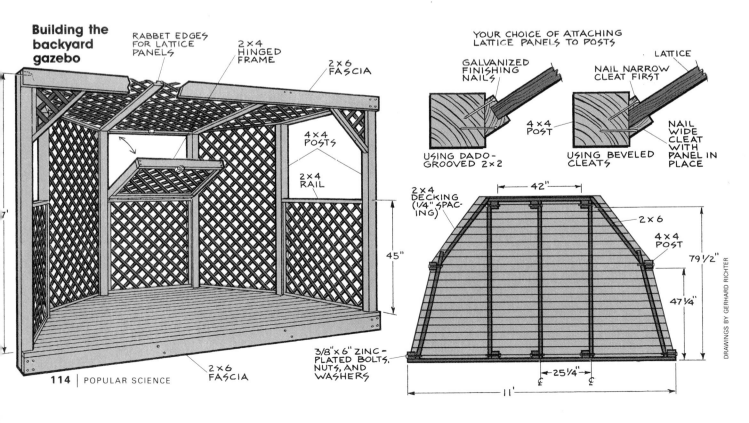

Building the backyard gazebo

RABBET EDGES FOR LATTICE PANELS

2×4 HINGED FRAME

2×6 FASCIA

4×4 POSTS

2×4 RAIL

7'

45"

2×6 FASCIA

3/8"×6" ZINC-PLATED BOLTS, NUTS, AND WASHERS

YOUR CHOICE OF ATTACHING LATTICE PANELS TO POSTS

GALVANIZED FINISHING NAILS

4×4 POST

USING DADO-GROOVED 2×2

LATTICE

NAIL NARROW CLEAT FIRST

NAIL WIDE CLEAT WITH PANEL IN PLACE

USING BEVELED CLEATS

2×4 DECKING (1/4" SPACING)

42"

2×6

4×4 POST

79½"

47¼"

25¼"

11'

DRAWINGS BY GERHARD RICHTER

your first deck

In "Decks," Dean and JoAnne demonstrate the technique for creating a 6-inch thick beam by nailing three "2-by's" together.

Building a deck is like adding a special outdoor living room. It's a great place to entertain, relax, or send the kids when you want them nearby but outside. And along with the fun it offers, a well-designed deck adds to the value of your home.

There are virtually limitless design possibilities for decks, but while you're working yours out, consider these points:

● Plan your deck so it'll provide some privacy. If it's going to extend to a property line, a privacy fence or screen would be in order. Before building, check local code and deed restrictions to learn about design and permit requirements.

● Although decks are open areas, they should have a feeling of enclosure. A simple perimeter railing is usually enough to accomplish this goal, but you have other options: Low benches, planters, and other built-in features can also enclose the space and serve both decorative and practical needs.

● Your deck should be large enough for your needs but in proportion to the rest of the house and property.

● Plan easy access to your deck from both your house and yard. Consider adding patio doors to open up the interior space to the deck. Besides providing access to the deck, you'll get the feeling the room is actually larger than it is.

● Locate your deck where it won't be subject to climatic extremes, and make provisions for shading and blocking stiff breezes. In many cases, the house or nearby trees will provide adequate protection.

Reprinted by permission of Homeowner Magazine.

● Use the right materials—buy only wood designed for outdoor use. Redwood, western red cedar, and cypress are naturally rot resistant and good looking; pressure-treated lumber also resists decay and is less expensive. (Note: When sawing or sanding pressure-treated wood, wear a respirator. And don't burn the scraps.)

PHOTO COURTESY WESTERN WOOD PRODUCTS ASSOCIATION

Multilevels, railings, benches and trellises add interest to this deck.

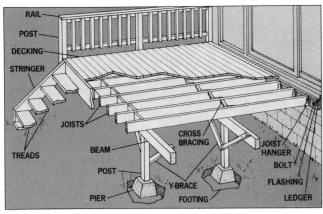

Parts of a typical deck.

Deck-building steps

Building a deck is a serious construction project, but it's eminently doable. The illustration below shows the parts of a typical deck. Use it as a reference to follow this basic construction sequence:

1. Plan your deck. Make a detailed drawing and translate into a materials list.
2. Buy the materials and arrange to have them delivered.
3. Fasten the ledger board.
4. Attach the end joists with temporary bracing.
5. Lay out the locations of footings.
6. Dig the holes and install concrete footing and piers.
7. Attach the posts to the piers.
8. Attach the beams to posts.
9. Install the joists.
10. Install the cross bracing.
11. Nail the decking to the joists.
12. Build the railings, steps, planters, and benches.

What follows is a closer look at the steps listed above.

Attaching the ledger

The ledger is a structural member that's bolted to the side of the house to support one end of the deck joists. Position the ledger so that when the decking is nailed over the structural frame, the finished surface will be 1 inch below the level of the interior floor. If your house has exterior siding, remove it from the area where the ledger will be attached. Tack the ledger in place and bore holes through it and into the interior floor frame. Permanently attach the ledger as shown in the illustration. (On masonry houses, you can attach the ledger with expansion bolts or lag screws in expansion shields; attaching to concrete block requires a fastener at the center of each block.)

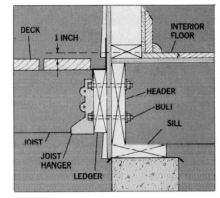

Fastening the ledger.

Insert aluminum or galvanized tin under the siding course above the ledger and bend it over the ledger's top edge as flashing. This helps the ledger shed rainwater.

Piers, posts and beams

The next task is laying out positions for the piers, the concrete foundations that the posts will rest on. First, attach the two end joists to the ledger; level and support them with temporary legs. To square up the end joists with respect to the ledger, use the "6-8-10 right triangle" method: Measure along the ledger from the outer face of the end joist and make a mark at 6 feet. Then measure along the top of the joist and make a mark at 8 feet. Starting at the mark on the ledger, run a tape measure to the mark on the joist to form the third side of a triangle. Adjust the position of the joist until the 8-foot mark aligns with the 10-foot mark on a tape. Nail a brace between the ledger and each end joist to hold them square.

Measure along the end joists to where you plan on placing the posts. Drive nails into the top of each joist at that point and run a string between

them. Measure along the string and at the preplanned intervals, drop a plumb line to indicate the centers of the holes for the footings. Use a posthole digger to make holes that meet building code specs for footing width and depth. Fill them with concrete to within 6 inches of ground level.

The piers rest on top of the footings to provide an above-ground bearing surface for posts. You can either poor your own concrete for piers or use precast ones. If you're pouring your own, make wooden forms and level them over the wet footing concrete. After pouring the piers, set nailing blocks into the tops while the concrete is still wet. The blocks make it easy to toenail posts in place. If you're using precast piers or masonry blocks, presoak them in water before setting them in position, about ten minutes after the footing is poured.

Toenail posts that are a little longer than you need to the piers. You can also mount the posts to piers with metal connectors, which offer more support than nails.

The posts support horizontal beams. The size for the beams depends on how many the deck design calls for and the span between the posts. Check your local code, but as a rule of thumb, an 8-foot span requires a 2×8 beam, a 10-foot span requires a 2×10 beam. With longer spans, you can use 4×8s, 4×10s and so forth. You can attach the beam to the top of the posts or to their sides so it's flush with the post tops.

Determine the height to which you must trim the posts by running a straight, level joist from the ledger to each one. Mark the post where the bottom edge of the joist crosses it. If you're attaching the beam to the post sides, cut the post at that mark. If the joists will rest on the top of the beam, mark the post at the bottom edge of the joist and, from that mark, measure down the width of the beam. Cut the post at that point.

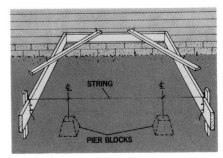

Laying out the footings and piers.

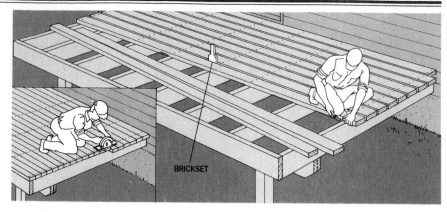

Installing the decking.

Installing joists

The joists will support the decking. The required joist size depends on the type of lumber, the spacing between them, and the length of the joist span between supports. The chart will help you decide on the size joists you'll need.

Mark off the joist spacing along the ledger—16- and 24-inch spacings are the most common. Also mark the spacings on the farthest beam from the ledger. Nail joist hangers to the ledger, centering them on the layout marks, then set the joists into place and secure them through the predrilled holes in the hangers. Nail wooden braces cut from joist scraps between each pair at about the midpoint for stability. Finish off the deck's structural frame by nailing a joist header to the joist ends.

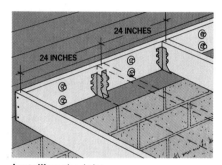

Installing the joists.

Joist spacing[1] (Decking span)

Species group[2]	Joist size (in.)	Joist spacing		
		16″	24″	32″
1	2 × 6	9′9″	7′11″	6′2″
	2 × 8	12′10″	10′6″	8′1″
	2 × 10	16′5″	13′4″	10′4″
2	2 × 6	8′7″	7′0″	5′8″
	2 × 8	11′4″	9′3″	7′6″
	2 × 10	14′6″	11′10″	9′6″
3	2 × 6	7′9″	6′2″	5′0″
	2 × 8	10′2″	8′1″	6′8″
	2 × 10	13′0″	10′4″	8′6″

1 Joists are on edge. Spans are center to center distances between beams or supports. Based on 40 p.s.f deck live loads plus 10 p.s.f. dead load. Grade is No. 2 or Better; No. 2 medium grain southern pine.
2 1—Douglas-fir-larch and southern pine; 2—Hemlock-fir and Douglas-fir south; 3—Western pines and cedars, redwood, and spruces.

Installing decking

The decking is the most visible part of the entire structure, so pick good lumber and install it carefully. Begin by laying the straightest board you can find alongside the house, making sure to leave a gap between the board and the house for rainwater to drain. Use nails or some other kind of spacer to set equal spaces between boards. Install decking boards with the curve of the end grain facing down—if the boards warp, they'll rise in the middle rather than form a cup that collects water. There's no need to align the edges of the decking boards—they should be a little longer than you need and should overhang a little past the points for the finished deck edges. Once all the decking is down, you can cut straight perfectly straight edges with a circular saw.

Drive two nails in 2 × 4 and 2 × 6 decking boards and three nails in 2 × 8s. Where decking boards must be fastened end to end, joints should fall over joists and should be staggered. For pressure-treated pine and fir, use ring-shank, galvanized nails, which have superior holding power and resist rust. Galvanized nails will stain redwood, cedar, and cypress; so with them, use aluminum, or stainless-steel nails.

Building the railing

The railing shown is only one of a variety of possible designs. Local codes may specify height, sturdiness, spacing of rails and balusters (uprights) and other elements, but you'll still have plenty of freedom with the overall design. In some cases, the posts for the railing could simply be an extension of the posts supporting the beams. Or, you might consider angling the railing out from the deck and building in benches around the deck sides.

A common method for building railings uses 4 × 4s for balusters, which are bolted to the end or side joists with a pair of carriage bolts. Drive one bolt through the lower hole, plumb the post, and tighten the bolt (use washers), then drill holes for the second bolt and fasten it.

Next, nail horizontal boards, in this case 2 × 4s, and then nail in the pickets. If you don't want pickets, use 2 × 6s for horizontal members. Finish off by nailing a 2 × 6 handrail to the tops of the posts.

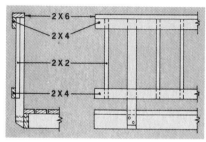

Building the railings.

Constructing stairs

Stairs consist of treads fastened to stringers that run from the ground up to the deck level. You can notch stringers to carry the treads, or you can nail cleats to the stringers to support them. Deck stairs usually have broader treads and shorter risers than household stairs. Stringers are normally made from 2 × 12s if notched, or 2 × 10s if they're supported by cleats.

If the stairway needs more than three steps, you should add a railing. Attach the posts to the stringers in the same way you attached the posts to the deck. And, like deck railings, make stair railings sturdy.

Once your deck is finished, just sit back and enjoy it. If you've followed our suggestions for lumber selection, the wood will weather to a pleasing silver-grey in just a year or so.

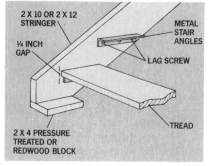

Building the stairs.

step-up deck for sloping yards

This well-designed deck solved two problems. Sharp slope of the lot created a drop from the back door; the only access to the yard was down a long, rickety stair, so the yard was never used. By projecting a large deck from the first-floor level, an "outdoor room" was created off the kitchen—ideal for alfresco dining and entertaining. Planters built into the 3-foot-high rail offer protected areas for growing herbs and flowers, safe from rabbits and deer.

Step-up deck

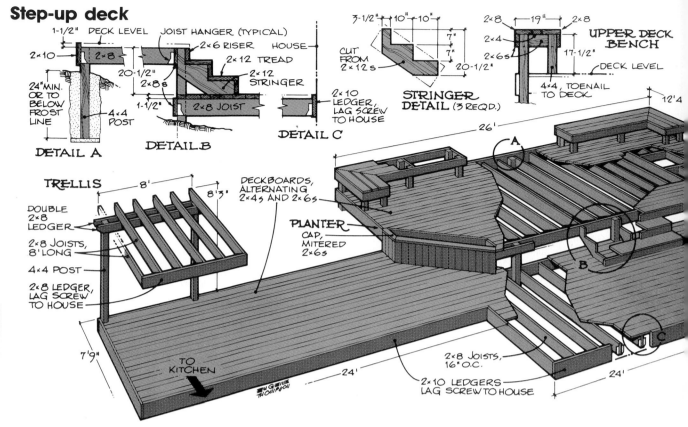

DRAWING BY EUGENE THOMPSON

The young homeowners were happy about their first house—until they walked around back. The builder had never properly regraded the backyard, and its pronounced slope ruled out laying a patio. The house itself was not at its best here, either: A series of setbacks fractured its rear elevation, and ironically, several back doors offered access to . . . nothing.

A major unifying structure was needed to tame the wild yard. So the couple took their problems to a local Georgia-Pacific Corp. dealer and formulated plans for a bi-level deck that flows around the jogs and beckons family and friends outdoors from nearly every room along the back of the house.

That's the purpose of the lower section, which was spliced directly to the house by means of 2×10 ledger boards lag-screwed into the foundation. Once you've stepped out onto this deck, you can either turn toward the left end, with its trellised barbecue area, or head to the right of the built-in planter and up three steps to an elevated section that features wide backless benches instead of a railing, and even wraps around a clump of existing trees. "For parties, especially," the homeowners report, "the platform is the most popular 'room' in the house.

And it's broad enough to take a table and chairs for more formal alfresco dining."

The amount of lumber you'll need depends, of course, on the area you want to cover, but the 663-square-foot deck shown here called for about 950 feet of 2×6s and 650 feet of 2×4s, mainly for decking (where the two widths are alternated). Construction also called for eight 10-foot 4×4s for posts, plus 2×8s, 2×10s, and 2×12s. The total cost for all materials, including 120 joist hangers and 100 pounds of No. 16 hot-dipped galvanized nails, came to less than $1,800. All the lumber was CCA pressure-treated southern pine. If you choose redwood or cedar instead, your lumber costs will be higher.

Angled planter marks the transition from lower deck to platform—it's built into the latter's framing. This is the view to the right as you step out onto the deck.

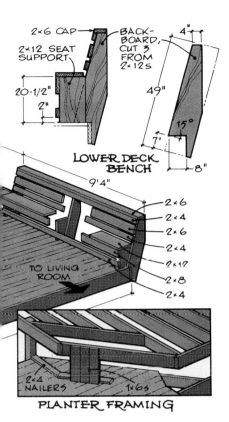

2×6 CAP
2×12 SEAT SUPPORT
20-1/2"
2"
BACK-BOARD, CUT 3 FROM 2×12s
4"
49"
15°
7"
8"

LOWER DECK BENCH

9'4"
2×6
2×4
2×6
2×4
2×12
2×8
2×4
TO LIVING ROOM
2×4 NAILERS
1×6s

PLANTER FRAMING

Left end of the deck has a trellis for hanging plants. It's all built of Georgia-Pacific pressure-treated lumber, with a sealer coat.

Preservative-treated lumber is sold with various levels of retention. For your posts (and any other wood that will be in contact with the ground), ask for a 0.40 level. For above-ground wood, 0.25 will suffice.

How you anchor the ledger to the house depends on how it relates to your foundation. Because it's the lower deck that abuts the house, you may have to attach your ledger boards to the masonry. (With higher decks you can often lag-screw ledgers directly into the house framing.) At any rate, you'll want to keep the finished deck surface below the thresholds of all existing or added access doors.

The 2×10 ledgers for the deck shown were attached by removing the house's bottom sheathing board to drill holes into the concrete blocks 2 feet apart; 6-inch lag bolts were driven into lag shields tapped into these holes.

To determine the outer corners, stake out your deck with string tacked to the ends of the ledgers, then dig holes at the post locations—about a foot in diameter and at least 2 feet deep. The homeowners on this project placed a concrete cap block in each hole, stood the post on top, and held the post plumb with staked braces while filling the hole flush with concrete. Be sure to let the concrete set 48 hours before loosening braces.

When all posts are in place, bridge them with 2×10 beams and band joists, outlining the entire lower-deck area. Check all installations with a carpenter's level before attaching them permanently. Nail joist hangers onto opposite inner faces (spaced 16 inches on center); drop 2×8 joists in place and nail them through the hangers. Now, nail the decking atop the joists, alternating 2×4s with 2×6s. All end-to-end butt joints must be centered on a joist, and these joints should be staggered so adjacent joints don't fall on the same joist.

In building the lower-deck bench, with its tall back, alternate 2×4s and 2×6s as shown in the drawing, using a 2×12 for the seat. Use angle-cut 2×12s, nailed to the band joist, to form the vertical back supports.

The 4×4 posts that support the outer corners of the upper deck extend 17½ inches above the deck's surface because they also support the built-in benches. Add 4×4 posts to the planter area and any framing around trees.

As with the lower deck, once all the outline beams and band joists are in place, install the inner joists and nail on the decking planks. Don't bother trying to cut the final planks in the rows to exact length before installing; instead, let them project raggedly beyond the band joist, and trim them flush with a portable circular saw after all decking is installed.

Assembly of the steps between the two decks is simple (see drawing)— but critical. Because the actual width of the 2×6 riser is 5½ inches and the actual thickness of the 2×12 tread is 1½ inches, the total height of each step will be 7 inches. The supporting stringers can be cut from 2×12s as shown; you'll need three, one at each end and one at the center.

When all construction is complete, you should brush on a water repellent. Or, if you wish to change the greenish tinge of treated wood, let it weather until this effect lessens, then brush on a pigmented repellent of the color you prefer—*by Al Lees.*

make yourself a panel saw

I recently had to do a roof-repair job that required cutting 4-by-8-foot sheets of plywood in half across the short dimension. I dreaded wrestling with the panels while trying to cut it to size with my table or radial arm saw, so I headed to the lumberyard to have it cut with a commercial panel saw. But once there, I realized that my money would be better spent buying materials to make a panel saw for my own workshop. I gathered my wood, went home, and started designing. The result: a convenient, portable panel saw that has since made jobs like cutting pieces for bookcases, tables, wall paneling—or roof decking—a breeze.

Building a panel saw that allows both crosscutting and ripping is sim-

ple. A portable circular saw secured to a carriage that slides on stiff twin tubes travels vertically for cross-cutting panels that sit securely in a sturdy frame. A pair of sliding-door closers acts to counterbalance the weight of carriage and saw, so little effort is required to move the tool through cuts.

Rotate the saw 90 degrees and lock the carriage at any point on the tubes; ripping is a matter of moving the panel against the blade. You can also add a removable ledge to support long boards at a comfortable height for sizing cuts.

The saw frame can be permanently attached to a long, bare wall—allowing for the frame width plus eight feet of panel—but I prefer to add the

hinged back braces so the unit can be used in either the shop or outside, on location.

The material you use doesn't have to be fancy, but it's essential that it be kiln dried. If you can select the boards at your yard, construction-grade lumber will do. Just be sure that it's free of any kind of distortion.

Nail the top beam to the two outside verticals, using a carpenter's square to ensure that corners are 90 degrees. Here and elsewhere, drilling pilot holes will guard against splitting and will make it easier to drive the nails. Do not attach the middle vertical now. This is added as a last step so it can be centered on the kerf line.

Add the bottom three beams, again using a square to ensure alignment.

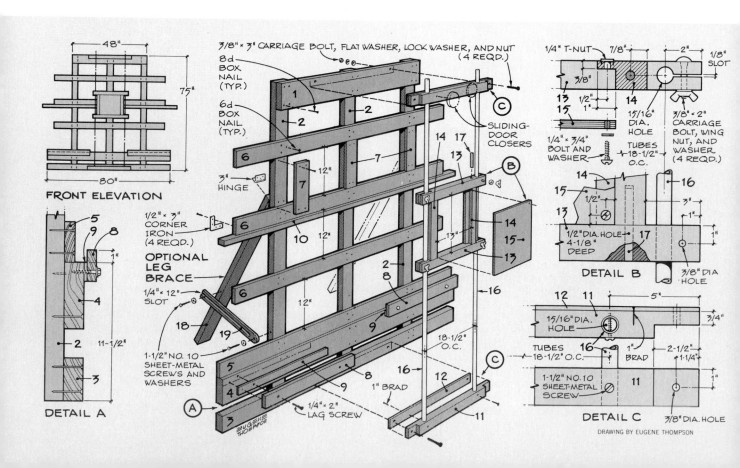

DRAWING BY EUGENE THOMPSON

The panel saw allows easier and more precise cutting than that accomplished by wrestling the panel onto a table saw.

The top edge of the 2×6 (Key 4) on which the panels will rest must be flat, straight, and smooth. If necessary, smooth it with a hand plane and sandpaper. The three bottom components can be longer than the ones I used for my project—a longer frame adds more support for panels being cut.

Add the three middle horizontal support pieces and the two outside fillers. The optional ledge is secured with corner irons; two placed at extreme points and two others spaced between them. If no screws are provided, use $3/4$-inch flathead wood screws to attach the corner irons. The ledge is used only when sawing lumber or small pieces of panel material.

The last step in constructing the frame is to add the retainers (Keys 8 and 9). Attach the shims ($1/4$-inch

hardboard or plywood) with brads and, while keeping the parts in place with clamps, drill pilot holes for the permanent lag screws.

Tracking assembly

The tracking assembly consists of matching top and bottom cleats and the steel tubes on which the carriage will slide. Start with a piece of lumber $4^{1}/_{8}$ inches wide. Drill the $^{15}/_{16}$-inch-diameter, $18^{1}/_{2}$-inch-on-center holes, and then form the end rabbets. Ripping the stock in two gives you duplicate cleats.

The tubes I used are $^{15}/_{16}$-inch outside diameter electrical tubing. You can rub it with fine emery paper or steel wool to minimize friction.

Use clamps to hold the cleats centered on the frame, and then slip in the tubes. When the assembly is

square to the frame and the tubes are parallel, drill holes and install the carriage bolts that secure the cleats. Do not secure the tubes at this time.

Make the top and bottom carriage members by following the technique described for the track-assembly cleats: Drill holes for the tubes and form the end slots before making duplicates. Before cutting the piece, check it on the tubes to be sure the holes have been drilled accurately. Next, shape the two verticals and the mounting plate on which the saw will be secured. Be certain that the plate is exactly 13 inches square.

Remove the tubes from the frame and slip on the top and bottom carriage components. Then use the mounting plate as a gauge when adding the remaining two pieces. Coat mating surfaces with glue and hold

Rotate the saw 90° and rip by pushing the panel into the saw. Place the material so its good side faces the frame. Clamps keep short pieces secure when cutting.

MATERIALS LIST

KEY	NO. OF PCS.	ACTUAL DIMENSIONS (in.)	MATERIAL
1	1	$1\frac{1}{2} \times 5\frac{1}{2} \times 48$	Lumber
2	3	$1\frac{1}{2} \times 3\frac{1}{2} \times 75$	"
3	1	$1\frac{1}{2} \times 3\frac{1}{2} \times 80$	"
4	1	$1\frac{1}{2} \times 5\frac{1}{2} \times 80$	"
5	1	$\frac{3}{4} \times 3\frac{1}{2} \times 80$	"
6	3	$\frac{3}{4} \times 3\frac{1}{2} \times 72$	"
7	3	$\frac{3}{4} \times 3\frac{1}{2} \times 12$	"
8	2	$\frac{3}{4} \times 2\frac{1}{2} \times 28$	"
9	2	$\frac{1}{4} \times 1\frac{1}{2} \times 28$	Hardboard
10	1	$1\frac{1}{4} \times 1\frac{1}{2} \times 88$	Lumber
11	2	$1\frac{1}{2} \times 2 \times 28\frac{1}{2}$	"
12	2	$\frac{1}{4} \times 2 \times 28\frac{1}{2}$	Hardboard
13	2	$1\frac{1}{2} \times 2 \times 22\frac{1}{2}$	Lumber
14	2	$1\frac{1}{2} \times 2\frac{3}{4} \times 13$	"
15	1	$\frac{3}{8} \times 13 \times 13$	Plywood
16	2	$\frac{15}{16}$ O.D. $\times 78$	Steel tube
17	4	$\frac{1}{2}$ D. $\times 4$	Dowel
HARDWARE			
	2		Sliding-door closers
	4	$\frac{1}{4} \times 2$	Lag screws
	4	$\frac{3}{8} \times 3$	Carriage bolts w/flat washers, lock washers, and nuts
	4	No. 10 × 1½	Sheet-metal screws
	4	$\frac{3}{8} \times 2$	Carriage bolts w/ washers and wing nuts
	4	$\frac{1}{4} \times \frac{3}{4}$	Bolts w/washers
	4	$\frac{1}{4}$	T-nuts
	4	$\frac{1}{2} \times 3$	Corner irons w/screws
			6d and 8d box nails
	1		Brads to secure shims
FOR OPTIONAL BACK BRACES			
18	2	$1\frac{1}{2} \times 3\frac{1}{2} \times 48$	Lumber
19	2	$\frac{3}{8} \times 2 \times 14$	Plywood
HARDWARE			
	4	No. 10 × 1½	RH sheet-metal screws w/washers
	2	3	Hinges

them in place with clamps. Then you can remove the tubes, but keep the clamps in place while you drill holes for and install the ½-inch reinforcement dowels.

Drill the holes for the four bolts that will secure the plate, and then install the T-nuts. Allow enough time for the glue to dry, then test the assembly by mounting it on the tubes. If you find that it does not slide easily, work on the tubes with fine emery cloth or lightly ream the holes in the carriage by using fine sandpaper wrapped around a ¾-inch dowel. When you are satisfied, drill for and install the sheetmetal screws that secure the tubes.

Adding the saw

Install the 2-inch carriage bolt and wing nuts, and tighten the nuts to hold the carriage at an arbitrary point so you can mount the saw. Retract the blade so it can't interfere, then use clamps to hold the saw while you drill a couple of holes through its base for small bolts that will secure it to the mounting plate. Be certain that the edges of the saw's base are parallel to the vertical members of the carriage. Turn on the saw and lower the blade to cut through the plate. The blade should project just enough to cut through ¾-inch material.

The sliding-door closers are attached with heavy sheet-metal screws to the top beam of the frame. Attach the hook-plates that come with the closers to the top member of the carriage. The closers are adjustable, so you can set them to provide just enough counterbalancing to ease moving the carriage. Don't make the pull so strong that you can't control the saw.

The last step is to run the saw down to establish the kerf line. Then add the middle vertical frame member and filler so they will be centered on the kerf line.

A note on ripping: The saw must be locked in the "on" mode while you move the work. If you don't have a saw that is equipped with a button that keeps the trigger depressed, use a length of soft wire to do the job. Another hint: Tie a couple of heavy bolts to the tool's cord so the cord won't tangle when moving the saw to the top neutral position.

You can, if you wish, add a couple of locking casters to the bottom of the frame so the unit can be moved about more easily. An occasional coating of hard paste wax to the tubes will keep them slick—*by R.J. De Cristoforo. Drawing by Eugene Thompson.*

3 versatile fences

Reprinted by permission of WORK-BENCH magazine.

A fence should do more than define your property line. It can help create privacy, act as a windbreak, keep animals out of your yard, or cover an eyesore. The three fences shown here fit the bill with style. Use the plans and construction tips that follow to recreate one of these fences in your yard, or as inspiration for your own design.

1. Lattice fence. A cedar slat fence made of rough-sawn 2 × 1s provides a measure of privacy, yet has a breezy look. Need more privacy? Plant a tree—or check out the fences in this article.

2. Redwood privacy fence. For the ultimate in privacy, build a solid screened fence from 1×6s nailed to a 2×4 frame. Our plans show fence and gate construction details.

3. Woven Lath Fence. A woven fence is easy to construct following our plans. Made from inexpensive lath, it's easy to maintain: A broken slat can be replaced by flexing a new one into place.

Lattice fence

This cleverly designed fence has a breezy look that still provides a measure of privacy. Built with rough cedar, the screen emphasizes horizontal lines by sandwiching 1×1 slats between 2×2 and 1×2 vertical pieces.

Lay out your fence location keeping the post spacing slightly more than 6 feet, to allow you to use standard 6-foot lengths of lumber. Remember that rough-sawn lumber measures close to its stated size.

Set the 4×4 posts in concrete then, after the concrete has hardened, install the lower rails. Nail 2×2s to the posts followed by the top rails. Install the intermediate 2×2s between the rails, spacing them 18 inches on center.

The 1×1 slats are nailed to the 2×2s and are spaced 1 inch apart. To create the sandwich, 1×2s are nailed to each 2×2 on the opposite side of the slats. A 2×6 top plate adds the finishing touch.

For more information:

Georgia-Pacific Corporation, Department RONR-11008-WN, PO Box 2808, Norcross, GA 30071. Decks and Outdoor Projects, a 36-page color booklet is $3.00; Western Wood Products Association, Department WN, 1500 Yeon Building, Portland, OR 97204. Write or call for free copy of Product Information Literature brochure.

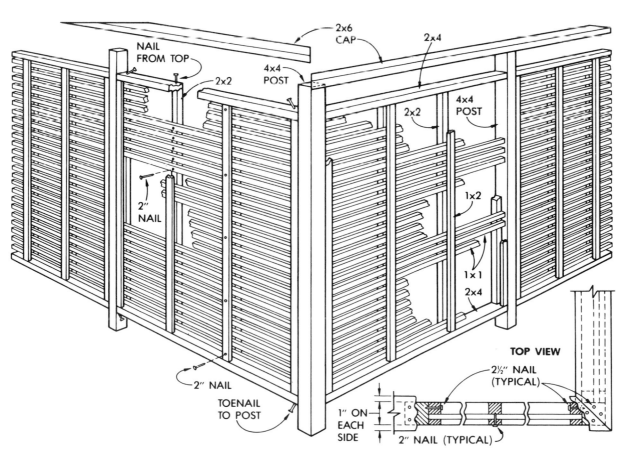

2x6 CAP

2x4

NAIL FROM TOP

2x2

4x4 POST

2x2

4x4 POST

1x2

1x1

2x4

2" NAIL

2" NAIL

TOENAIL TO POST

TOP VIEW

2½" NAIL (TYPICAL)

1" ON EACH SIDE

2" NAIL (TYPICAL)

Redwood privacy fence and gate

Visitors to this lovely California home enter through double redwood gates to the deck and entry area. The 6-foot fence provides privacy and is a pleasing backdrop for plants.

Construction Heart grade redwood was used for the posts and supporting structure of the fence. Clear All Heart—the top redwood grade—was used for the 1×6 screen.

Posts for the fence sections are 4×4s. Heavier 6×6s are used for the gate posts. Spacing of the posts should be about 6 to 8 feet. The gate posts are set first. Their spacing in this case is 8 feet, determined by the width of the gates. Set the posts in concrete and let it set up overnight. To construct the fence, toenail 2×4 rails to the posts, then attach the 2×6 cap to the top of the posts.

The fence boards are nailed vertically to the private side of the rails in stockade fence fashion with the top of the boards butted against the bottom of the cap.

The gates are heavy—one reason for the heavy gate posts. They are framed with mitered 2×4s. An X-bracing of 2×4s keeps the gate from sagging. They fit from corner to corner with a lap joint cut where they cross.

Square the frame and assemble the unit with construction adhesive and spiral nails. Nailing strips are fitted around the inside perimeter of the frame, then redwood siding is nailed to both sides of the frame.

Four heavy-duty brass butt hinges are used to hang each gate. The latch is black wrought (cast) iron.

For more information:

California Redwood Association, Department WN, 591 Redwood Highway, Suite 3100, Mill Valley, CA 94941. Send 60¢ for booklets on fence and deck construction.

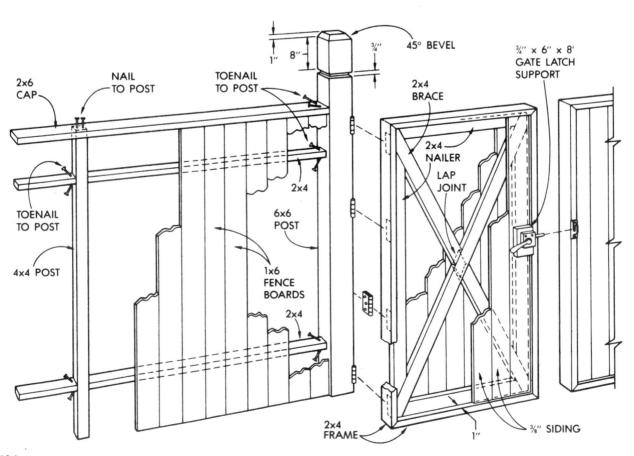

Woven Lath Fence

This fence is made of readily available materials, is inexpensive and easy to construct. It is also easy to maintain; broken slats can be replaced in seconds by simply flexing them into place. The appearance of the fence is the same on both sides and is just as attractive to your neighbors as it is to you.

Pressure-treated landscape timbers, which are less expensive than 4 × 4s, are used for the line posts. They have two flat and two curved surfaces and measure 3½ × 5 inches. For planning purposes, their width (flat sides) is the same as 4 × 4. They should be set so the flat surfaces face each other. The curved surfaces make landscape timbers unsuitable for corner posts, so use 4 × 4's at the corners.

The posts must be located exactly 8 feet apart or the lath will not fit and the design will not work. Maintain exact spacing by temporarily nailing 8-foot 2 × 4s between the posts.

Set the posts in concrete. After it has hardened, install the lower rails. Their height above the ground is not critical, but keep them level. Nail 6-foot 2 × 2s above the lower rail, centered on the sides of the posts, then

install the top rail. Locate and install the remaining 2 × 2s and 1 × 2s as shown in the drawing.

Before weaving the lath on the fence, the posts and rails were painted brown. The strips of lath were not painted, but allowed to weather naturally. Weave the lath beginning at the bottom rail and work upward. They do not need to be nailed.

The exposed ends of the lath are covered with prepainted (to match the posts) ½ × 1½ inch strips ripped from

a 2 × 4 which give the fence a more finished appearance. The lath can be easily removed in case broken strips need to be replaced.

I made a gate in a similar manner, but it is heavy and sturdy corner braces and heavy-duty hinges are used.

The cost of materials will vary across the country, but in my part of New York, the cost for 60 feet of fence including a 4-foot gate was about $200—*Robert L. Magee*

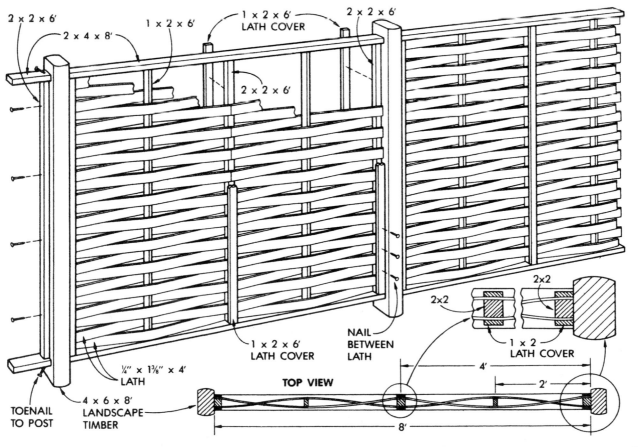

2 × 2 × 6'
2 × 4 × 8'
1 × 2 × 6'
1 × 2 × 6'
LATH COVER
2 × 2 × 6'
2 × 2 × 6'
2 × 2 × 6'
1 × 2 × 6'
LATH COVER
NAIL BETWEEN LATH
2×2
2×2
1 × 2
LATH COVER
¼" × 1⅜" × 4' LATH
TOENAIL TO POST
4 × 6 × 8' LANDSCAPE TIMBER
TOP VIEW
4'
2'
8'

planter fences and pergolas

Redwood was the lumber of choice for all three of these handsome projects. Its natural resistance to decay makes redwood ideal for outdoor exposure. And for massive timbers, such as those used here for posts, redwood will shrink less than other lumber, in dimensions greater than 2 inch nominal; this means timbers are less likely to split or check.

To shop intelligently for redwood, you should know about recent shifts in how it's sold. The redwood trees that are now grown and harvested as a commercial crop tend to develop more knotty lumber. This wood is labeled "garden grade" because of its appropriateness for outdoor structures such as fences. Garden grades include Construction Heart, Construction Common, and Merchantable.

For years, garden grades were only sold green (undried), so the lumber tended to be heavy with moisture—which eventually weathered out, causing some shrinkage and temporary darkening. Now, though, garden grades can be bought air-dried (seasoned); this makes them lighter in weight and more attractive. (You can still buy the cheaper green lumber, if you prefer to cut costs.)

In all three projects shown on these pages, the redwood was left natural. A water repellent containing mildewcide was brushed on surfaces. This application stabilizes the

1. Gateway pergola has an oriental grandeur that makes it an imposing entry on the street side of an enclosed yard—or into a fenced flower garden. The many projecting beams—of different milled dimensions—could support a variety of hanging plants. Though the prototype was built of Clear All-Heart-grade, garden-grade redwood could be substituted for at lower cost.

2. Planter pergola was designed by Eli Sutton and built by Hoddick, Berry & Malakoff at the end of a deck that stands high off a hillside—but it could be built along one side of a patio. The planter panels are redwood plywood, framed in one-by lumber. The support posts for the trellislike pergola are heartwood because they continue down to become part of the planter and are in contact with the soil.

3. Planter fence was built for *Popular Science* by Stevenson Projects. Each section has three tiers of planter boxes built in between the 4×6 posts. Face planks for both planter boxes and posts are beveled on all four edges. Redwood's resistance to rot lets you fill the pockets with soil (no liners required— but note holes to drain off rainwater). Fence could double as a retaining wall.

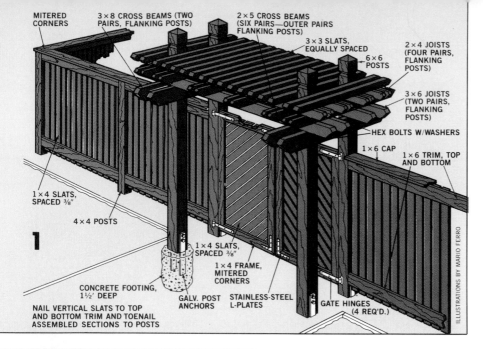

1

- MITERED CORNERS
- 3 × 8 CROSS BEAMS (TWO PAIRS, FLANKING POSTS)
- 2 × 5 CROSS BEAMS (SIX PAIRS—OUTER PAIRS FLANKING POSTS)
- 3 × 3 SLATS, EQUALLY SPACED
- 2 × 4 JOISTS (FOUR PAIRS, FLANKING POSTS)
- 6 × 6 POSTS
- 3 × 6 JOISTS (TWO PAIRS, FLANKING POSTS)
- HEX BOLTS W/WASHERS
- 1 × 6 CAP
- 1 × 6 TRIM, TOP AND BOTTOM
- 1 × 4 SLATS, SPACED 3/8"
- 4 × 4 POSTS
- CONCRETE FOOTING, 1½' DEEP
- NAIL VERTICAL SLATS TO TOP AND BOTTOM TRIM AND TOENAIL ASSEMBLED SECTIONS TO POSTS
- GALV. POST ANCHORS
- 1 × 4 SLATS, SPACED 3/8"
- 1 × 4 FRAME, MITERED CORNERS
- STAINLESS-STEEL L-PLATES
- GATE HINGES (4 REQ'D.)
- ILLUSTRATIONS BY MARIO FERRO

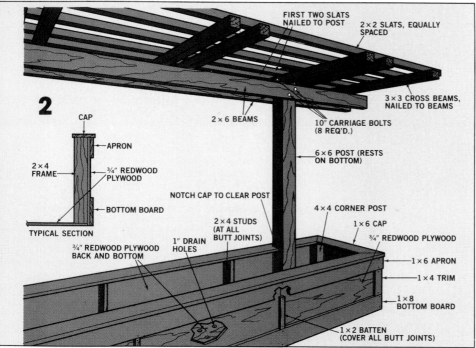

2

- FIRST TWO SLATS NAILED TO POST
- 2 × 2 SLATS, EQUALLY SPACED
- CAP
- APRON
- 2 × 4 FRAME
- ¾" REDWOOD PLYWOOD
- BOTTOM BOARD
- TYPICAL SECTION
- 2 × 6 BEAMS
- 3 × 3 CROSS BEAMS, NAILED TO BEAMS
- 10" CARRIAGE BOLTS (8 REQ'D.)
- 6 × 6 POST (RESTS ON BOTTOM)
- NOTCH CAP TO CLEAR POST
- 4 × 4 CORNER POST
- 1 × 6 CAP
- ¾" REDWOOD PLYWOOD
- 2 × 4 STUDS (AT ALL BUTT JOINTS)
- 1" DRAIN HOLES
- ¾" REDWOOD PLYWOOD BACK AND BOTTOM
- 1 × 6 APRON
- 1 × 4 TRIM
- 1 × 8 BOTTOM BOARD
- 1 × 2 BATTEN (COVER ALL BUTT JOINTS)

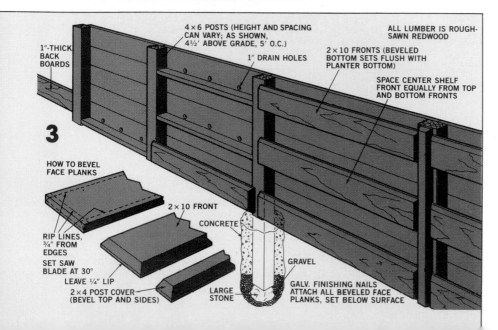

3

- 1"-THICK BACK BOARDS
- 4 × 6 POSTS (HEIGHT AND SPACING CAN VARY; AS SHOWN, 4½' ABOVE GRADE, 5' O.C.)
- 1" DRAIN HOLES
- ALL LUMBER IS ROUGH-SAWN REDWOOD
- 2 × 10 FRONTS (BEVELED BOTTOM SETS FLUSH WITH PLANTER BOTTOM)
- SPACE CENTER SHELF FRONT EQUALLY FROM TOP AND BOTTOM FRONTS
- HOW TO BEVEL FACE PLANKS
- 2 × 10 FRONT
- CONCRETE
- RIP LINES, ¾" FROM EDGES
- SET SAW BLADE AT 30°
- LEAVE ¼" LIP
- 2 × 4 POST COVER (BEVEL TOP AND SIDES)
- LARGE STONE
- GRAVEL
- GALV. FINISHING NAILS ATTACH ALL BEVELED FACE PLANKS, SET BELOW SURFACE

redwood color, delaying darkening of the lumber on its eventual way to driftwood gray. Water repellent reduces swelling/shrinking cycles. For assembly, use only noncorroding fasteners to avoid rust stains. Nails should be hot-dipped galvanized; carriage bolts and gate hardware should be stainless steel.

How you anchor the posts depends on where the structure is built. In the case of the gateway, galvanized post anchors were set in concrete; these footings were then covered by the gravel walkway. The anchors, with two bolts through each post, hold the ends just above the ground line. For the big planter, posts were tied into the box itself and into the deck railing. For a patio installation, you could extend these posts into the ground. How you set the planter-fence posts will depend on whether the planter is to be a free-standing structure or a retaining wall. If the latter, the posts must be set into concrete, below the frost line.

Since both planters are exposed to rainfall, drainage is important. Without it, any planter box will become a swamp. Should you elect to build planter boxes of other types of lumber, be sure you provide a liner of galvanized steel or heavy black plastic to keep the soil from contact with the wood—*by Al Lees.*

More on fence building

For a folder giving general tips and specific plans (how to determine your line of run; how to set posts and create the decorative tops shown above, etc.), send 50 cents to Western Wood Products Association, Department P-125, Yeon Building, 522 S.W. Fifth Avenue, Portland, OR 97204. For color brochures on redwood fences, send $1 to California Redwood Association, 591 Redwood Highway, Suite 3100, Mill Valley, CA 94941.

build a deck bench

Reprinted by permission of WORK-BENCH magazine.

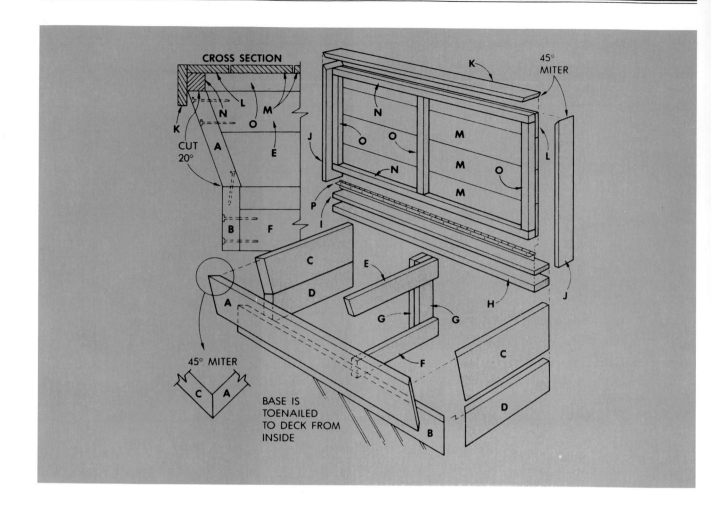

CROSS SECTION

CUT 20°

45° MITER

45° MITER

BASE IS TOENAILED TO DECK FROM INSIDE

45° MITER

ur bench is a convenient storage area for your hose and waterproof gardening equipment and is easier to build than it might appear at first. It abuts a house exterior wall and is cleverly designed to fit around the plastic gutter spout. Redwood lumber is used throughout.

Our drawing gives dimensions for a 16-inch high × 24¾-inch deep (front-to-back) bench. If you want it higher—say 18 inches—use 2 × 8s for the base instead of the 2 × 6s called for in the plans. Build it any length you need, but be sure to add seat supports every 24 inches.

The lumber used is nominal; so little rip-cutting is required. Determine your final dimensions before you buy materials.

Construction steps and tips

The base is made of 2 × 6 stock, and the angled front piece and vertical side pieces of 2 × 10 stock. The base pieces are mitered 45 degrees at the front corners and fastened together using non-corroding nails. Position the base where you want it and toe-

nail it to the deck with 6d (2-inch) galvanized nails. In our installation, we had to contend with a gutter downspout that ran through the deck. Rather than move the downspout, we built the bench around it.

The top and bottom edges of the 2 × 10 face are beveled 20 degrees. You can do this on a table saw, or with a tilting-base, hand-held circular saw.

Note the sides are vertical, not angled as with the face. Rip 2 × 10s to size for the sides and cut the front end of each side at a 20-degree angle. Next, miter the angled ends 45 degrees so they mate with the 2 × 10 face. All the 2 × 10s are toenailed to the 2 × 6s from the inside.

Install the lid/seat supports about every 24 inches. A 2 × 4 stretcher is placed next to the wall then nailed to the base and intermediate supports. We used a sabre saw to cut a notch at one end of the 2 × 4 so it would fit around the downspout.

The lid is framed with 2 × 2s and covered with 1-inch stock—a 1 × 4 and three 1 × 6s, or whatever suits your bench size. Another 1 × 4, notched to

fit around the downspout, is nailed on the top support to level it with the lid. Nail 1 × 4 trim, mitered at the corners, to the front and sides of the lid. Attach the lid to the hinge cleat with 1½-inch (open) brass continuous hinge.

The bench is not weatherproof; so do not use it for tools or other items that can be damaged by rain.

CUTTING LIST: DECK BENCH			
Key	No.	Part	Size (in inches)
A	1	Front	1½ × 9¼, length to suit (lts)
B	1	Front	1½ × 5½, lts
C	2	Side	1½ × 8¼ × 24
D	2	Side	1½ × 5½ × 21⅛
E	1	Lid support	1½ × 3½ × 22½
F	1	Base support	1½ × 3½ × 19⅝
G	2	Vertical support	1½ × 3½ × 13¾
H	1	Stretcher	1½ × 3½, lts
I	1	Hinge cleat	¾ × 3½, lts
J	2	Side trim	¾ × 3½ x 24¾
K	1	Front trim	¾ × 3½
L	1	Lid board	¾ × 3½, lts
M	3	Lid board	¾ × 5½, lts
N	2	Lid frame	1½ × 1½, lts
O	3	Lid frame	1½ × 1½ × 21
P	1	Brass piano hinge	1½ (open), lts

winged dinghy

Length, over all .... **12 ft.**
Beam .... **40 in.**
Beam, wing decks .... **53 in.**
Hull weight .... **125 lbs.**

ooking back over the popular series of boats the Stevenson crew has designed for *Popular Science* in recent years, we decided to come up with a boat that combined the most appealing features of our best build-your-own sailing dinghies.

A major design directive came from readers, who have often asked us for a small boat with true sloop rigging (mainsail and jib) instead of the lateens we've featured on past designs.

Then we were inspired by the new wing decks being fitted on the incredibly fast Italian lake boats. Crews of 11 hike out on the wing decks of these ultralight unballasted 45-foot rockets. So we developed our own scaled-down version with wings that two people can comfortably hike out on. The result: our easiest-to-buy-for, easiest-to-build boat project. This time we used stays that allow a lighter mast, so we could use chain-link fence parts for the rig.

That means you can make a single trip to a typical home center and come away with everything needed to build the boat from keel to mast top. We've even come up with jam cleats made from plastic pipe that really work.

And that trip to the home center will run you under $275.

Sails can be made in one afternoon with no sewing, using the tried-and-proven punched, laced, and taped method of our other sail plans. The mainsail is 72 square feet and the jib is 32 square feet, for a total of 104.

Our crew agrees this is the easiest sailing boat we've designed. With a strong jib and fully battened mainsail for better sail shape (note the four ribs in the silhouette), she really hauls. The mast rig slips apart into two sections so that no part of the boat measures over 12 feet. Her lightweight monohull has built-in lifting handles and tie-downs for easy car-topping, and the rudder raises when you pull forward on the tiller for easy beach launching.

If you *do* manage to flip her, she'll float on her positive flotation tanks. With sails that can't get waterlogged, this means she can be pulled on her side to drain the cockpit, then righted and sailed away with no dry-out wait.

Complete plans are $10 from Stevenson Projects, Box 584, Del Mar, CA 92014—*by Peter Stevenson. Drawings by Mario Ferro.*

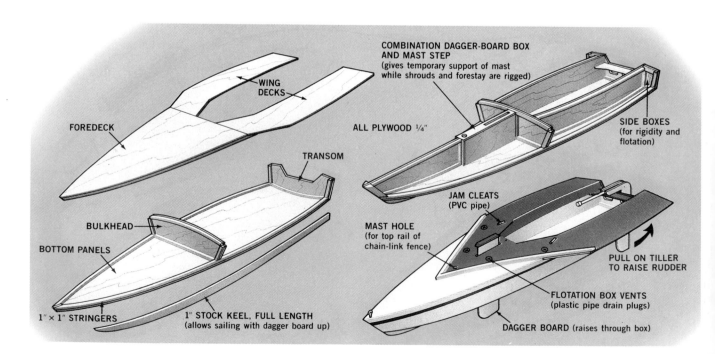

outdoor play center

Kiddiehaus **play center is easy** and economical to build and decorate. Knock-down design makes moving easy.

Here's something that will give your kids, grandkids, nieces, or nephews hours of fun and enjoyment. The 4-by-9-foot platform area provides plenty of play space for children aged three to ten. There's also lots of headroom and a tall door for bigger kids, yet the entire structure fits neatly even in modest-sized yards.

Stanley's *Kiddiehaus* comprises such attractive niceties as a deck, closable wood shutters, and working Dutch door. And because there are no openings on two sides, you can select a back-of-the-lot or corner location—unless, of course, you'd rather show off the play center's fine workmanship.

The Stanley
Kiddiehaus™

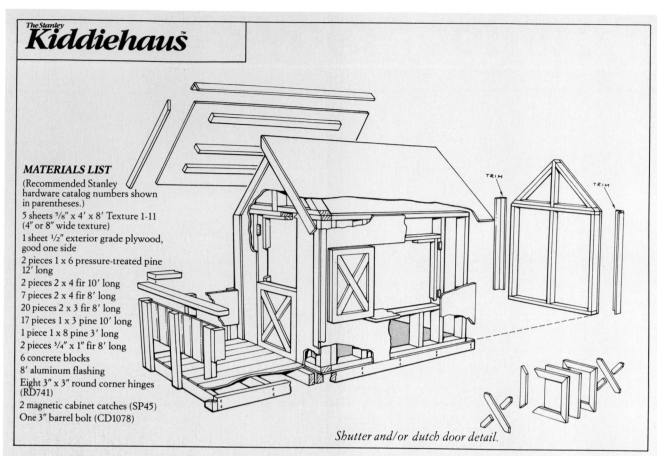

MATERIALS LIST

(Recommended Stanley hardware catalog numbers shown in parentheses.)

5 sheets ⅝" x 4' x 8' Texture 1-11 (4" or 8" wide texture)

1 sheet ½" exterior grade plywood, good one side

2 pieces 1 x 6 pressure-treated pine 12' long

2 pieces 2 x 4 fir 10' long

7 pieces 2 x 4 fir 8' long

20 pieces 2 x 3 fir 8' long

17 pieces 1 x 3 pine 10' long

1 piece 1 x 8 pine 3' long

2 pieces ¾" x 1" fir 8' long

6 concrete blocks

8' aluminum flashing

Eight 3" x 3" round corner hinges (RD741)

2 magnetic cabinet catches (SP45)

One 3" barrel bolt (CD1078)

Shutter and/or dutch door detail.

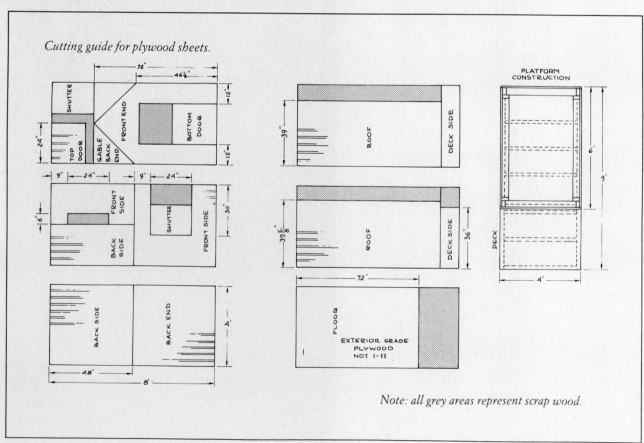

Cutting guide for plywood sheets.

Note: all grey areas represent scrap wood.

Shutters and door are held closed by magnetic catches that allow anyone inside to get out without help.

swing singly or jointly. Use magnetic catches to secure door and shutters. These will hold firmly in the closed position, yet allow anyone inside to get out without help.

Finishing touches

Be certain that all edges of texture 1-11 are protected from the elements by flashing or other construction details. Alternatively, you can seal edges with a protective finish to help prevent rot.

Roof, shutters, trim, and doors are all excellent candidates for color accents and other decorative touches. The high peaked roof, for instance, is a natural for American Gothic or gingerbread ornamentation as shown. Check out old homes in your neighborhood, photos from old books, and other idea sources. And remember *not* to add glass windows. It's safer and lots more fun if kids can crawl in and out at will, sit on the windowsill, or lean out on it as they follow the dictates of their imaginations—*by David Kataja. Photos and drawings courtesy Stanley Works.*

How to order more projects
Kiddiehaus is one of six projects featured in *Building Wooden Toys.* To order, send a check or money order for $1 to The Stanley Works, Advertising Services, Box 1800, New Britain, CT 06050.

Construction

Cuts for the *Kiddiehaus* are all at 45 and 90 degrees, so the work goes quickly and economically. The frame can be very light since the sheathing provides most of the strength.

Begin by building the platform on-site from 2 × 4s, raising it off the ground on at least six concrete blocks. Be sure to put a one-eighth-inch space between the deck boards for proper drainage. You can build the four side panels and two roof panels in your workshop or on-site, then simply nail them to the platform. Note in the drawings that the studs vary on centers, as opposed to the constant 16 inches typical in house construction.

Roof treatments include plain or painted texture 1-11, shingles, and a host of other possibilities. These photos show shingles. If that's your preference, you can probably save money by substituting two sheets of one-half-inch exterior plywood for two sheets of texture 1-11. Deck railing is built from 2 × 4s faced with 18-inch panels left over from the roof sheets. And if you plan on disassembling or relocating the *Kiddiehaus* later, simply replace the nails that join corners to corners and panels to platform with about twenty $5/16$-by-3-inch galvanized lag bolts.

Build the two door sections and shutters following the plan details. When you install them on-site, add a barrel bolt on the inside of the Dutch door so the door halves can

Finishing touches include barn-style door and shutter treatment, roof shingles, and gingerbread accent. Glass is purposely left out of window to make play safer and more fun.

backyard rocking horse

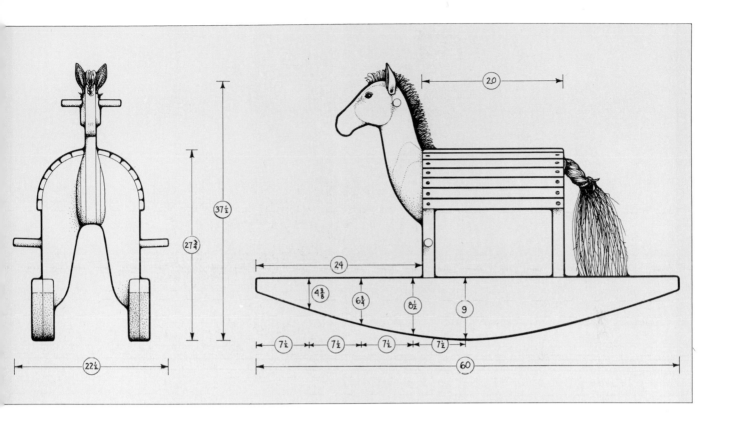

This sturdy solid-wood rocking horse is designed to stay wherever you wish to corral it, outside *or inside*. When properly finished, it will withstand the elements as well as most lawn furniture.

We built our rocking horse of kiln dried Douglas fir, but it could just as easily be made of any commonly available lumberyard wood in standard dimensions. Hardwoods are more durable but also require slightly more effort cutting and shaping. Softwoods such as pine are delightful and aromatic to work with, but are not quite as tough when exposed to a gang of hard riders. Our fir version weighs almost 50 pounds and, because of its size, weight, and stance, is quite stable. The horse will "gallop" along in a steady rhythm, and will even accommodate two small riders seated one behind the other.

Where to begin

You can build this horse as you would a piece of fine furniture, with delicately fitted joints and carefully matched grain; or you can build it in standard "playground" style with the accent on durability and sturdiness. Every horse needs a name, and we called ours "Strawberry" (note the strawberry "brand" painted on her hindquarters near her braided tail).

Begin by cutting out the rockers. They are 5 feet long and 9 inches from top to bottom at the widest middle point. The two pieces of 2-by-10-inch fir provide a 3-inch finished thickness for each rocker, since a 2-by-10 incher actually measures 1¹/₂ by 9¹/₄ inches. The rockers must be heavy and thick because they help balance the considerable weight of the horse and also smooth the rocking motion.

1

2

Each of the rockers could just as well be made of one single chunk of 4-by-10-inch wood instead of two pieces, but we choose to glue two smaller pieces together for greater resistance to splitting and warping. Another factor was price. Wood is cheaper in smaller dimensions, and the lumberyard let us select the best pieces from the stack. That gave us a much better choice of grain and appearance than we would have had with thicker dimension wood.

Lay out the rockers by drawing the pattern right on the wood. Make one perfect rocker and use it as a pattern for the other pieces. The curve of the bottom of the rocker must be accurate and continuous to provide a smooth ride at full gallop. We also attempted to match grain and color of all glued pieces as closely as possible by cutting them from the same plank.

Always spread glue on both surfaces before clamping regardless of what type of glue you use. (Fig. 1). Instead of clamping, you can also fasten the two pieces of rocker together with screws placed along each side in an attractive pattern. Countersunk holes can be filled with wood plugs, epoxy, or wood filler.

We rough-cut the rockers and other components to shape on a bandsaw, leaving about $1/16$ inch of wood outside the pattern line. Then we finished the curve with a compass plane set at the proper angle (Fig. 2). Mark the exact pattern clearly in pen on the wood and leave the line plus $1/16$-inch when rough-cutting. After glue-up, you can trim to the line with a jack plane and a square when doing final shaping, and finish with sandpaper on a block.

Legs

Front and back legs are cut, doweled, glued, and then joined together. The front and back legs are the same except that the underside cutout is slightly larger on the rear legs. Front legs are thus left larger to accommodate attachment of the head and neck piece. Both front and back legs are built of two pieces of 2-by-10-inch wood because of the width required, and are joined vertically on the centerline using $3/8$-inch diameter hardwood dowels and glue. Drill holes for dowels (Fig. 3), then glue and clamp halves of doweled legs together as shown in figure 4. Doweling gives additional structural support and makes gluing easier by providing perfect alignment when clamp-

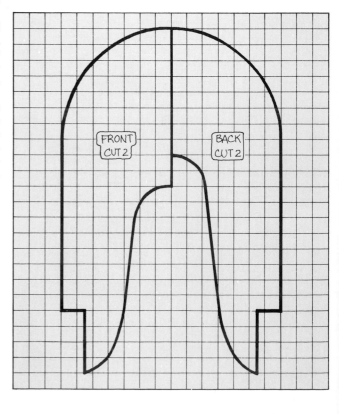

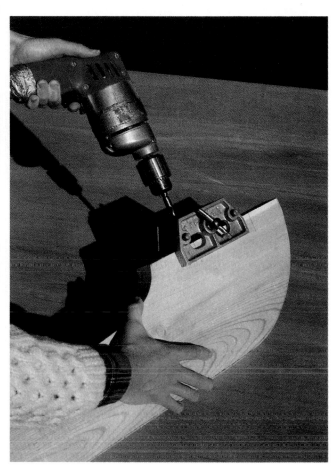

3

ing up the two separate pieces. Legs attach on either side to the rockers with a notch that is further reinforced with glue and a single No. 16 3-inch Phillips head wood screw.

Head and neck piece

The head and neck of the horse is the most challenging single piece in the structure and is subject to considerable personal interpretation. Much of the animal's personality lies in this part.

The center piece of the head and neck contains the basic profile (Fig. 5), and additional small blocks are glued on each side for added depth and realism (Figs. 6 and 7). Two blocks ³/₄ inch thick after shaping simulate the large jaw of the horse, and four blocks of the same thickness (two each side) fill out the shoulder and also provide a wider base for fastening to the front legs. These blocks should be clear straight grain to facilitate shaping and sanding.

Shaping the head and neck will spark your creativity and also let you use a number of enjoyable woodworking tools. For rough initial shaping, a sharp ³/₄- to 1-inch gouge with a light mallet is helpful, but must be used with restraint. Stand back and look at the piece often as you go, turning it from side to side (Fig. 8). Follow rough-shaping with a rasp or Surform tool, then finish shaping with coarse sandpaper. After final light sanding with No. 80 to 100 grit the head is ready to be attached to the body.

Join the head and neck piece to the front legs using four No. 16 3-inch Phillips wood screws and glue. Screws are placed from the backside of the leg into the shoulder. By removing about ¹/₄ inch of material from one side of the base with a plane, the head can be turned slightly to one side, giving the horse a touch more character. Be sure the entire base is flat to provide a proper glue base onto the front legs.

4

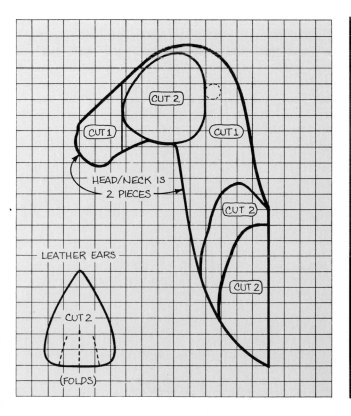

CUT 2

CUT 1   CUT 1

HEAD/NECK IS
2 PIECES

CUT 2

LEATHER EARS

CUT 2

CUT 2

(FOLDS)

5

6

7

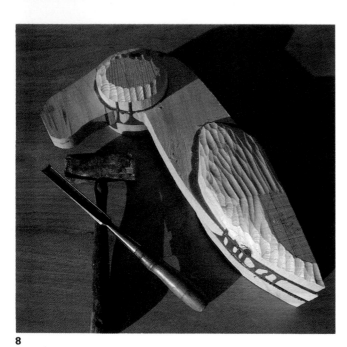

8

Staves

The staves are the 1½-inch-wide strips that attach the front and back legs together, forming the body of the horse and a seat for the rider. We chose clear vertical grain fir ¾ inch thick so the staves would match the rest of the horse. We secured the staves to the legs with No. 12 1½-inch Phillips head wood screws, then sealed the screw holes with contrasting teak plugs glued in place with epoxy (Fig. 9). The plugs are then pared flush with the wood surface using a sharp chisel before sanding. The staves—and all parts of the toy—should be splinter free, and all edges should be generously rounded. We used a carbide bit and router to cut a ⅛-inch round on the corners of each stave, and later when sanding we rounded all remaining corners slightly more for safety reasons (Fig. 10). For rough aggressive sanding we use a section of a coarse belt sander belt on an orbital sander. This quickly removes sharp edges and the sanding-belt material lasts much longer than sheet sandpaper.

Dowels

One-inch hardwood dowels are used for both hand-holds and foot pegs. The hand-hold dowel is inserted, one piece, into a 1-inch-diameter hole drilled through the neck (see front and side drawings). One way to avoid splintering the

wood as the drill exits the other side is to back up the wood with a scrap block. Or, when the point of the drill bit appears on the opposite side, stop and then carefully drill the hole through from that side. We used epoxy glue to fix the dowel in place; it will also support the dowel if the hole is not a perfect fit.

Foot-peg holes were drilled approximately 2 inches deep and also fixed in place with epoxy glue. We drilled these holes at a 10-degree upward angle to help keep small feet from slipping.

Ears, mane, and tail

We made the ears from a scrap piece of heavy leather cut to the pattern shown and tacked on with 1-inch-long bronze ring nails. Predrill a hole for the nail, then carefully nail the ears in place so they can be easily adjusted back and forth to give the horse a different look.

Mane and tail are made of manila rope sections ¾ inch in diameter. We used 6 feet of ¾-inch rope for both. Four-inch lengths were used for the mane and the balance for the tail. The mane holes were drilled ¾ inch deep with a ½-inch-diameter bit. Holes were drilled single-file in a straight line down the center piece of the head, the centers of the holes spaced ¾ inch apart. We used epoxy glue to secure a strand of unravelled manila into each drilled hole (Fig. 11), and followed the same basic procedure for the tail using three ⅞-inch-diameter holes. The tail holes were drilled in a triangular pattern and the full width of rope was inserted into each hole. Once the glue has dried, the rope can be brushed, combed, and even trimmed with scissors for authenticity. Each strand of rope should be unraveled and unwound by twisting against the lay of the manila, then brushed to remove loose short strands and give a uniform appearance.

Eyes and eyelashes

Most hobby or craft shops will have a selection of plastic eyes for the horse. We also applied large eyelashes, available in self adhesive strips. Eyes are attached using a ⅛-inch stem, for which a small hole is drilled into the horse at the proper location and angle. We painted the spaces around the eyes to take away some of the eye's roundness, then used a dab of clear silicone seal to cement the eyes in place and also provide a waterproof seal.

Finishing

There are a number of options for protecting your horse from splits, cracks, and darkening of the wood, particularly if it is to be left outside. If you choose a natural finish that shows off the beauty of the wood, you should provide some type of sunscreen to protect the finish as long as possible.

10

9

11

Two choices that have worked for us are sunscreen varnish and clear linear polyurethane (LP) paint. Varnish is much less expensive and easy to apply, while clear LP is comparatively expensive and relatively difficult to apply. Clear LP lasts much longer without retouching, however. It also provides a much tougher surface that may last four or five years while varnish normally requires retouching every year. Colored paint will protect the wood better and longer than any other type of finish, but the drawback is that you lose the natural beauty of the wood. Clear epoxy also provides the most durable undercoating for any of the above finishes. If used alone, however, it must be protected with a sunscreen additive. Whatever finish you use, be sure it is nontoxic. And be especially careful not to use paint containing lead—*by Paul and Marya Butler.*

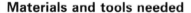

Materials and tools needed

2 × 10 Douglas Fir—35 lineal feet

1 × 6 vertical grain or clear select fir for shoulder and head blocks—4 lineal feet

Vertical grain fir for staves—15 pieces, $^3/_4$ by $1^1/_2$ by 20 inches

1-inch-diameter hardwood dowel for foot and hand pegs—2 lineal feet

6 feet of $^3/_4$-inch-diameter manila rope for mane and tail

Glue (epoxy or waterproof wood glue such as Weldwood)

Varnish, oil, or paint with disposable polyfoam brushes

Plastic eyes and eyelashes

8 No. 16 3-inch phillips head wood screws

10 $^3/_8$-inch hardwood dowels and a doweling jig

30 No. 12 $1^1/_2$-inch phillips head wood screws

30 hardwood plugs for stave-attachment holes

1 square foot of leather for ears

1-inch bronze ring nails for attaching ears to head

Sandpaper and/or sanding belts—coarse grit, No. 60 and 80 grits

Dab of silicone seal to attach eyes

Various-sized gouges, chisels, and hand tools

Surform tool with various blades

Disc sander and/or block plane, jack plane, compass plane, and spoke shave

Orbital sander

Hand-held jigsaw or bandsaw

house security: a guide to playing it safe

Although your home may be your castle, chances are it isn't surrounded by a moat. Consequently, lots of firms out there are hoping to convince you that electronic security (which these days can help with fire, medical emergencies, flooded basements, and even toxic gases) is cheaper and more effective than ever. They're right, but shopping can be confusing.

Actually, today's systems have much in common. All of them connect various kinds of sensors to a central controller, which triggers the alarm. The differences lie mainly in how these sensors are connected (wired vs. wireless), whether or not the system is professionally installed, how it reports an emergency (with sound alarms, autodialers, or central monitoring centers), and the sophistication of sensors and controller. As always, deciding which system to buy will involve a tug of war between keeping the price down and getting the latest gadgetry.

Reprinted by permission of HOME magazine.

Hard-wired systems

For years all home alarm systems were hard-wired; every sensor was connected to the central controller by wires concealed in walls, attics, and floors. The most expensive and elaborate alarm systems are still hard-wired, because they are the most reliable (transmitters don't have to communicate with the controller) and maintenance-free (no batteries to check). But owing to the sophistication and skilled labor involved in concealing wiring, they are also the most expensive—from $1,200 to $3,000 and up.

Wireless systems

In a wireless system, the sensors are teamed with mini-transmitters that talk to the central controller through radio frequency, infrared, or high-pitched signals. Although the first generation of wireless devices had a weakness for signals from jet planes and garage-door openers, more recent versions are much more dependable.

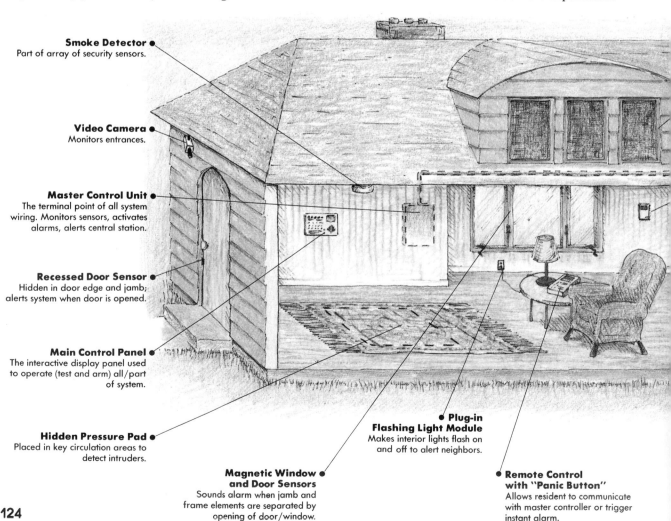

Smoke Detector
Part of array of security sensors.

Video Camera
Monitors entrances.

Master Control Unit
The terminal point of all system wiring. Monitors sensors, activates alarms, alerts central station.

Recessed Door Sensor
Hidden in door edge and jamb; alerts system when door is opened.

Main Control Panel
The interactive display panel used to operate (test and arm) all/part of system.

Hidden Pressure Pad
Placed in key circulation areas to detect intruders.

Magnetic Window and Door Sensors
Sounds alarm when jamb and frame elements are separated by opening of door/window.

Plug-in Flashing Light Module
Makes interior lights flash on and off to alert neighbors.

Remote Control with "Panic Button"
Allows resident to communicate with master controller or trigger instant alarm.

While some professional installers still look askance at wireless technology, most of them regularly put in the high-grade wireless systems to reduce installation costs or because the construction of some homes isn't suited to hard-wiring. These systems cost $1,000 to $2,000.

But there are also less expensive wireless systems geared for installation by the consumer, such as Schlage's KeepSafer and Black & Decker's Home Protector. Easily installed with a screwdriver, they offer basic break-in and fire protection that can be readily added to and can be taken with you when you move. Heath-Zenith and Radio Shack retail similar components. Manufacturers of these off-the-shelf systems offer starter kits for well under $500; they can be augmented with individually packaged components such as sirens, extra sensors, or an autodialer.

DIY wireless systems now include some interior sensors and even national monitoring stations. But they are less flexible than the most expensive systems and they don't give you the benefit of professional advice.

Bells and whistles

One of the major differences in systems is how they deal with the emergency once it is signaled by a sensor. The simplest systems feature an alarm in the central control unit. But most systems can be equipped with an exterior siren or bell, modules that flash interior lights, and/or an autodialer to phone for emergency help.

Worn down by false alarms, some police departments have begun to levy fines for repeated incidents. Subscribing to a central monitoring service for $15 to $30 a month

Window Screen Sensors
Maintain security with windows fully or partially open.

Infrasonic Detector
Presence of motion *and* heat trigger alarm.

Phone Link to Central Station
Master controller automatically dials, identifies home and type of emergency. Central station attendant calls appropriate authority.

Exterior Alarm
Siren or bell to alert neighbors.

Alarm Company Sticker
Maybe the single best deterrent for intruders.

Outdoor Lighting
Switched on and off by system at dusk and dawn.

Breakage Sensor
Signals controller for alarm when window is broken.

can help. Upon getting an automatically dialed emergency call from your system, their personnel respond by notifying the appropriate local emergency service—police, fire, or medical—often after checking for a false alarm. They will also phone a friend or neighbor. For maximum security, some services recommend a separate phone line, and a few respond with private patrols.

A wide variety of sensors is available. Some are perimeter devices (point-of-entry sensors such as magnet switches and breakage sensors), while others are more sophisticated interior monitors (such as infrasonic sensors—units that combine sometimes temperamental infrared and ultrasonic sensors, requiring them to agree before issuing an alarm).

State-of-the-art systems can include concealed microphones and video cameras that will patch in police while recording court-admissible evidence of a break-in. Also, security can be combined with lighting, heating, and so on in home automation systems.

Whether low- or high-end, make sure the system you're considering is easy to arm, disarm, and reprogram. Most hard-wired systems and some wireless models let you bypass ("shunt") openings and interior zones so that normal family activity doesn't disrupt protection: This capability is excellent *if* the master controller makes it a straightforward task. If not, you'll end up leaving the system disarmed—the leading cause of security system failure.

Professional installation

Professionally installed systems offer the most sophisticated sensors and alarms, and are the most effective in foiling professional burglaries. When you contract with a professional installer, you are buying both products and service. It can be hard to know where to turn. One safe approach is to rely on household names such as Honeywell, AT&T, and Wells Fargo, who either maintain their own centers or have affiliated dealer/installers. Another is to go with one of the huge security companies like Westec or ADT. Or check with neighbors whose homes sport signs with names of local dealers.

Although their components may feature names you're not familiar with (Ademco and Radionics are two high-grade suppliers), it's a dealer's reputation that should determine your choice. A poor installation will make even the best components unreliable. Favor well-established firms over companies with no track record; never deal with "tailgaters" who sell systems from pickup trucks.

Make sure to talk to several dealer/installers before making a decision. To get general price information on the phone, be prepared to describe your home's layout and type of construction, and to give a tally of its doors and windows. Prior to quoting a final price (detailed and in writing), most installers will want to visit your home. Don't sign a contract until all questions are answered and you've seen warranties and service agreements.

Doing it yourself

It pays to bring home a brochure of the DIY system you're considering, and to plan carefully before purchasing. Manufacturers like Schlage emphasize good dealer training and product literature. Requiring little more than a screwdriver and a long weekend afternoon, installation really isn't complicated for DIY systems.

Whether you buy an inexpensive do-it-yourself package or have a state-of-the-art system installed, you'll be buying peace of mind at the right time: *before* an emergency—*by Jeffrey Book. Illustrations by Christopher Clapp.*

how to install a driveway alarm

Buried sensor detects a vehicle. Two sensors are used for wide driveways.

New driveway alarms tell you when there's company—or a bold intruder. When a vehicle enters your driveway, these clever systems turn on outside lights, activate a burglar alarm, or even ring your doorbell.

The alarms are available from a variety of makers, and are all easy to install. Most, such as the Preferred Security Components' Car Tel model I tried, contain an underground probe (sensor); a length of cable (usually 100 feet); and a control panel, which is installed in the house. A basic system costs about $350.

To install the system, I began by digging a trench for the connecting wire, following the contours of the driveway to minimize lawn damage. The probe is buried 6 inches deep and parallel to the edge of the driveway.

A single probe covers a 10- to 12-foot-wide driveway. To protect a double-width driveway, the probe can be installed in the center, but I found a more practical solution is to use

two probes—one on either side of the driveway. They are connected in series at the control panel.

At the point where the cable enters the house, use a length of PVC pipe with an elbow below grade to prevent damage from your lawn mower and other garden tools. In the house, the probe cable connects directly to the control panel; the panel plugs in an AC outlet for power.

All systems have a sensitivity control. If the control is set too low, the system won't detect small vehicles; set too high, the system could be triggered by nearby traffic. Try different settings—over a period of a few days—for the best results.

Most panels contain a built-in buzzer to alert you of an arriving guest when a vehicle is detected. Some panels can be directly connected to the house circuits that control outdoor floodlights, doorbells, or burglar alarms; some require additional accessories to control external devices—*by Dave Petraglia.*

Car Tel includes a sensor, electronics panel, external alarm, and cable.

VEHICLE DETECTION MAKERS
B-W Manufacturers, Inc., 721 N. Webster Street, Kokomo IN 46901; **Delta Scientific,** 2031 N. Lincoln Street, Burbank CA 91504; **Engineering Equipment Company,** 1020 W. 31st Street, Downers Grove IL 60515; **Outdoor Security Systems,** 10845 S. W. Cascade Boulevard, Portland, OR 97223; **Preferred Security Components, Inc.,** 14 Main Street, Landisville, PA 17538; **Sarasota Automation, Inc.,** 1500 N. Washington Boulevard, Sarasota FL 33577; **Sparton Corp.,** 2400 E. Ganson, Jackson MI 49202; **Tapeswitch Corp. of America,** 100 Schmitt Boulevard, Farmingdale, NY 11735; **Winland Electronics, Inc.,** 418 S. Second Street, Mankato MN 56001; **Wolo Manufacturing Corp.,** 1 Saxwood Street, Deer Park, NY 11729.

converting to 3-slot outlets

Each year, according to the National Safety Council, more than 300 people are electrocuted at home. Amazingly, the small amount of power it takes to light a seven-watt Christmas-tree bulb can kill an adult. Think your home is safe? Not if it has older non-grounding electrical outlets. These have only two slots, instead of three, and with such outlets the risk of being severely shocked by a ground fault while using plug-in electrical tools and appliances is only an insulation's thickness away.

To protect yourself and your family against all-too-common ground-fault shock hazards of two-slot receptacles, your home electrical system may need updating. If you are familiar with electrical wiring, you can tackle this update yourself. Otherwise, hire a licensed electrician.

The National Electrical Code (NEC) lists three options for replacing a two-slot outlet: 1) replace with another two-slot outlet (no help with ground faults); 2) replace with a three-slot outlet that is truly grounded; 3) replace with a receptacle-type ground-fault circuit interrupter (GFCI). The method you may use depends on your house wiring.

If your house wiring provides some means of grounding a replacement outlet within the outlet box, a two-slot outlet *must* be replaced only with a three-slot grounding outlet (NEC Section 210-7[d]). Some of these sell for as little as 40 cents apiece. (Grounded receptacle GFCIs may be used, too.)

The required means of grounding consists of a bare or green-insulated wire in a nonmetallic cable wiring system or the continuous metal covering of an armored-cable or conduit system.

To find out whether grounding is available at the outlets in your house, cut the power to an outlet's circuit at the main service panel. The outlet should be electrically dead. Test it by plugging in a known-to-be-working light or appliance. Or plug in a neon tester (available at any electrical supplier). Be sure to test *both* outlets of a duplex receptacle. Once you're sure that the circuit is dead, remove the cover screw and wall plate. Next, to make sure that no electricity is present inside, apply the neon tester across the exposed lighter-colored terminals on one side of the outlet and the darker-colored terminals on the other side. If the lamp doesn't light, remove the two long No. 10-32 retaining screws that hold the receptacle to its outlet box. Without touching any bare wires (it pays to be cautious around electricity), stretch the receptacle out of the box on its wiring. Pull it far enough to enable you to peer inside the outlet box with a flashlight. You are looking for 1) a bare or green-insulated wire or wires or 2) a metal outlet box served by armored cable or metal conduit. If you find either, a means of grounding is available within the box.

As a double-check, bring a grounded jumper wire near the dead outlet—a car battery jumper cable attached to a continuous metal piping system will do fine. Using a multitester set on "R × 1 Ohms," clamp one end of the jumper to one tester lead while touching the other lead to the metal box. If the tester reads zero-ohms resistance, the box is grounded. If any resistance is indicated, however, the box is not grounded.

In all receptacle hookups use standard Code-approved outlet-box make-up procedures. (If your house has aluminum wiring, not copper, special wiring procedures apply.) In any case, every three-slot outlet's hex-head green grounding terminal *must* be connected to a ground. These receptacles may not be installed at any location without grounding.

The common nonmetallic-sheathed-cable house wiring with white-, black-, and red-insulated wires—but no bare or green-insulated wires—provides no means of grounding. If you find such cable entering the box, you may replace a two-slot outlet *only* with another two-slot outlet or with a receptacle GFCI.

Replacement with a receptacle GFCI solves the ground-fault shock-hazard problem. NEC Section 210-7(d)

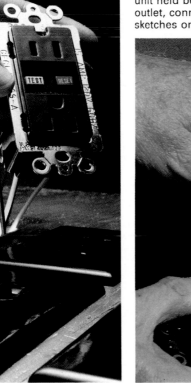

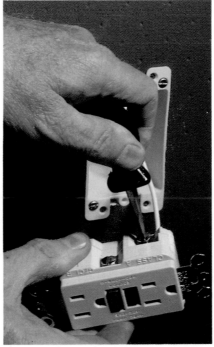

Receptacle GFCIs come with terminals (left) or with leads (the feed-through unit held below). To replace a two-slot outlet, connect as shown in either of the sketches on next page.

Feed-through connections
(To protect all outlets in circuit)

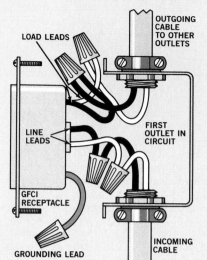

LOAD LEADS

OUTGOING CABLE TO OTHER OUTLETS

LINE LEADS

FIRST OUTLET IN CIRCUIT

GFCI RECEPTACLE

GROUNDING LEAD

INCOMING CABLE

Single-outlet connections
(To protect this outlet only)

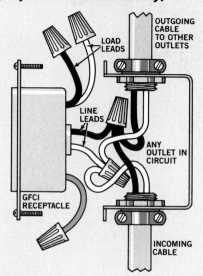

OUTGOING CABLE TO OTHER OUTLETS

LOAD LEADS

LINE LEADS

ANY OUTLET IN CIRCUIT

GFCI RECEPTACLE

INCOMING CABLE

Just what is a ground fault?

DRAWINGS BY MARIO FERRO

It's a line-to-ground short circuit. When ground-seeking electrons in the insulated hot side of a circuit find a pathway to ground, a ground fault occurs—usually through an insulation failure. For example, if the insulation on a live wire inside a power tool wears through and the bare wire contacts the metal tool body, the tool would take on a 120V potential to ground. Holding such a tool would be like having a hand clasped around a bare live wire. If you're standing on a concrete floor or damp earth, your body would complete the circuit to ground.

Having electrical tools and appliances properly grounded—plugged into a three-slot outlet—offers protection against ground faults. This is "equipment grounding," and the NEC requires it in new construction. Wayward electrons find it much easier to travel through a good conductor (grounding wires) than through a poor one (your body).

Plug-in grounding adapters with a pigtail lead offer no protection unless they themselves are well grounded. Attaching the pigtail lead to the center screw of a two-slot outlet doesn't ground the adapter unless grounding has been supplied to that outlet.

Exception recognizes that an ungrounded GFCI receptacle does offer a degree of shock protection, even though a tool or appliance plugged into it is not actually grounded. The GFCI receptacle thus protects where the old two-slot receptacle does not. Receptacle GFCIs in a number of brands are widely sold for about $11 to $20. Naturally, the receptacle GFCI you purchase should be listed by Underwriters Laboratories and bear the familiar "UL" designation ("CSA" in Canada).

A GFCI works by monitoring current flow in and out. As long as both are equal, though opposite, nothing happens. But when some current leaks to ground—even as little as 6 milliamperes—the in-out current becomes unbalanced. This triggers it to cut off the power within a few milliseconds. GFCIs protect only against line-to-ground shocks, not line-to-line or line-to-neutral shocks. Fortu-

nately, the latter are not nearly as common as ground faults.

Feed-through protection

Most receptacle GFCIs are designed to feed through their protection to other outlets. Two of the five leads or terminal blocks are labeled "line" and two are labeled "load," with the fifth one for grounding. (See first wiring pictorial.) Use of a GFCI in first-receptacle position will protect an entire branch circuit, except the wiring between the service panel and the first receptacle. Instructions with the GFCI tell how to locate the first outlet in a circuit and how to find the house line and load wires. With a GFCI wired for a feed through, you change this first outlet only. All outlets beyond it in the circuit must be left as two slot. Furthermore, a grounding conductor must not be connected between the receptacle GFCI and any outlet supplied from it.

A GFCI may be used in a non-feed-through installation by leaving its load terminals empty or placing wire nuts on the ends of its load leads, as in the second pictorial.

In connecting a receptacle GFCI, be sure to follow the instructions that come with it, though these do not generally cover its specialized use as a replacement for two-slot outlets. For home safety you not only want correct polarity at each GFCI, you want any two-slot outlets served by a feed-through GFCI wired with correct polarity. Check them to be sure. The narrow receptacle slots should be hot and the wide slots should be at ground potential (dead) when the circuit is turned on. Reversed polarity does not affect the operation of a GFCI, however.

Since the outlet box is not grounded, the Code does not require bonding of the receptacle GFCI's grounding lead to the box. This means that the grounding lead or terminal is left vacant. Being ungrounded has no effect on the GFCI's function, however. Care must be taken to be sure that it does not contact any uninsulated live parts inside the outlet box. If it's a lead, thread a wire nut on it; if a terminal, run the empty hex-head binding screw down tightly. And when mounting the receptacle to the box, be certain that any live wires are kept away.

To work properly, receptacle GFCIs need a "ground reference." In a properly wired house, this is provided by the service panel's neutral busbar, which is bonded—electrically connected—to the main panel enclosure and through this to the house grounding-electrode system. Most often, the grounding electrode is a buried water pipe.

If spare capacity is available, a circuit with grounding may be extended by adding additional wiring and outlets. An ungrounded circuit, whether it has GFCI or not, may not be extended. New outlets must be served by equipment-grounding conductors.

Remember to test all your GFCIs periodically as is directed in the instructions.

While your GFCI update does not provide grounding, it does give extremely sensitive, fast-acting ground-fault protection that can save someone's life. Still, having ground-fault protection is no reason for careless handling of electrical tools and appliances when you are wet or grounded. Using good electrical sense is still your best protection—*by Richard Day. Drawings by Mario Ferro.*

remote-control security lights

Today's remote-control transmitters let you light up your entryway as you arrive home at night.

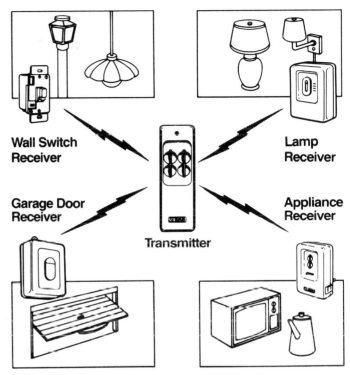

Zeus remote-control transmitter sends radio signals to Zeus receivers, which switch lights and appliances on and off.

C oming home to a dark house can be both uncomfortable and unsafe. Now it's also unnecessary. With the remote-control system featured here, you can turn on your home's indoor and outdoor lights from inside your car.

Zeus system lets you control both lights and garage-door opener with the same transmitter.

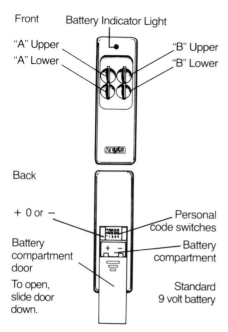

Front

Battery Indicator Light

"A" Upper
"A" Lower

"B" Upper
"B" Lower

Back

+ 0 or −

Battery
compartment
door

To open,
slide door
down.

Personal
code switches

Battery
compartment

Standard
9 volt battery

Zeus transmitter.

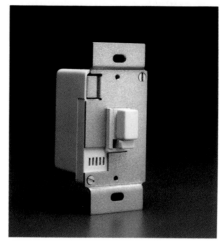

Zeus wall transmitter.

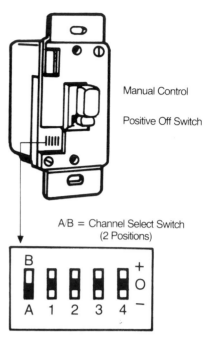

Manual Control

Positive Off Switch

A/B = Channel Select Switch
(2 Positions)

1-4 = Personal Code Switches
(3 Positions +, O, −)

High-technology improves a great idea

The idea of activating lights via remote control has been around for a few years. The problem was, no remote control was powerful enough to work at distances of more than 25 or 30 feet. That meant you had to be almost at your doorstep to operate the remote control. With the Zeus Extra-Distance Transmitter, you can turn on your home's lights and even the living room stereo or TV from up to 150 feet away. Zeus also features state-of-the-art security codes that prevent access from any other transmitter, boasts its manufacturer.

Zeus was invented and designed in the U.S. by Novitas, Inc. (1657 Euclid Street, Santa Monica, CA 90404). The company has made lighting controls for industry, universities, and hospitals since 1977. I asked the firm's president, James Himonas, about the evolution of the device for home use. "Zeus controls are a response to the growing concern of people for their personal safety," he explained. "We developed Zeus to take the worry out of coming home at night." Why did they call it *Zeus?* Himonas explained further: "As the supreme god of the ancient Greeks, Zeus was the protector of mortals. He was a symbol of power, rule, and law."

Before developing Zeus, Himonas conducted extensive consumer research in Boston, Chicago, and Los Angeles to determine what people wanted in the ideal remote control. He learned that the five features most wanted by the people surveyed were:
● Control of home lights from inside a car.
● A transmitter range of over 100 feet.
● Control of outside as well as inside lights.
● Capacity for two or more sets of lights.
● Personal codes to avoid interference with other remote controls.

Himonas then went to work designing those features and more into Zeus. The complete Zeus system consists of hand-held transmitters, wall-switch receivers, lamp and appliance receivers, and garage-door opener modules. The items are available individually, or in sets. Zeus controls outdoor and indoor lighting fixtures—both incandescent and fluorescent—as well as TV, audio equipment, even coffee pots and hair curlers. Added bonus: When the garage-door module is wired to an existing garage-door opener, you can toss away your bulky transmitter and control your garage-door opener *and* house lights with the Zeus transmitter.

Designed for easy installation

According to Brian Elwell, Novitas Chief Engineer, "Wall Switch Receivers for lighting fixtures are installed in the same way as common dimmer or toggle switches. Receivers for lamps and appliances simply plug into wall outlets. The Garage Door module is a simple low-voltage hookup to your existing garage door opener."

I decided to put Zeus to the test at my home. Situated in a hilly area, the house is approached by a steep, tree-lined access road that eventually leads to a dead end. Inviting by day. Foreboding after dark. I wanted the ability to control outdoor lights from inside my locked car. I

Parts of the Zeus wall switch.

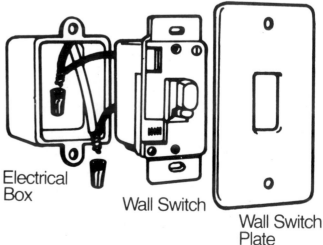

Electrical Box

Wall Switch

Wall Switch Plate

thought, if Zeus can handle my hill, it will surely function on a more typical suburban street.

I wanted to control my porch lights, a lamp in my living room, and my garage-door opener. And I wanted to be able to control each separately. The diagram on the Zeus package indicated I would need a wall-switch receiver for my porch lights, a lamp receiver, a garage-door module, and one transmitter to control all the functions. How long would this simple installation take? Following the package directions, it took me less than half an hour to set up my four-part Zeus system. Here's how I did it.

1. Preparing the transmitter

First, I put a standard 9-volt battery into the battery compartment of my transmitter unit. An important feature of Zeus is the personal Code Selector. It lets you select a secret code so that your receivers are operated only by you or your family's transmitters. Switches inside the battery equipment provide 162 different codes. The switches in the transmitter correspond to switches in each Receiver.

I selected my own code and moved the switches on my transmitter into place with a small, flat-tip screwdriver. My transmitter was now ready to perform.

2. Setting the wall switch receiver

When operated remotely, the Zeus wall switch is controlled by separate "On" and "Off" buttons on the Zeus Transmitter. The upper buttons are "On" and the lower ones are "Off." Separate buttons eliminate any doubt as to whether an out-of-sight fixture has been turned on or off.

The channel select switch on the wall switch receiver lets you designate which set (Channel) of transmitter buttons will operate a specific receiver. (See diagrams of the Wall Switch Receiver and the Transmitter.) I decided to use channel A (the buttons on the left of my transmitter) to control my porch light and reserved channel B for controlling my indoor light and garage door opener. With my small screwdriver I slid the channel select switch on the wall switch receiver down to the channel A position. Next I set the personal code switches on the *receiver* to match the code I had selected for my *transmitter*.

3. Installing the wall switch receiver

I installed the Zeus wall switch in the same way as an ordinary two-wire switch. Here's all you need to do:

a. Turn off power at the fuse or circuit breaker before wiring.
b. Remove the wall plate. Save the screws.
c. Disconnect existing wall switch. Again, save the screws.
d. Hold the Zeus Wall Switch so that the large section of the button controls is on top and the small section is at bottom.
e. Connect the Zeus wires to the wires that were connected to the switch using the wire nuts provided.
f. Push the wires and Zeus wall switch into the box.
g. Fasten the Zeus wall switch to the switch box using the screws from the removed switch.
h. Replace the wall plate by placing it over the button of the Zeus wall switch and replacing the screws.
i. Turn the power back on at the fuse or circuit box.

Once I had completed these simple steps my wall switch was operable from my Zeus transmitter. Less than 15 minutes had elapsed. On to the garage door opener!

4. Installing the garage door opener module

The set-up and installation of the garage door opener module was also very simple:

a. First, I set the channel selector so the garage door

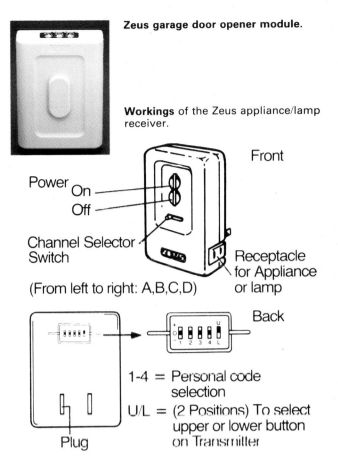

Zeus garage door opener module.

Workings of the Zeus appliance/lamp receiver.

Front
Power
On
Off
Channel Selector Switch
(From left to right: A,B,C,D)
Receptacle for Appliance or lamp

Back
Plug
1-4 = Personal code selection
U/L = (2 Positions) To select upper or lower button on Transmitter

opener module would operate on the B channel, lower button of my transmitter.

b. Then I set the code switches to match my personal code.

c. The next step was to mount the module to the ceiling beam near my existing garage-door opener. I located the two screw terminals on my garage-door opener that connect to the remote control switch that opens the door. After unplugging the garage door opener, I connected terminals 1 and 2 of the Zeus garage door opener module in parallel with the remote switch terminals on the garage door opener.

d. Next, I connected the Zeus transformer to terminals 1 and 3 of the garage door opener module.

e. All that was left was to plug in the transformer and the garage door opener. Now, both my garage door opener and porch lights were controlled by one Zeus transmitter. I had left the simplest project for last.

5. Setting up the lamp receiver

I had selected the B channel upper button on my transmitter to control the living room lamp. To activate the lamp receiver, all I had to do was set the channel selector switch on the front of the receiver to B, set the upper/lower switch on the back of the receiver to the upper position, and set my personal code. Next, I plugged the Receiver module into a wall outlet and inserted the lamp plug into the receptacle on the side of the Receiver.

By Zeus! I had my remote system in place. And in hardly any time at all. All the remotes operate reliably, and after everything was installed I discovered another feature I had overlooked: with Zeus I can operate my lights either by the manual buttons on the Receivers *or* remotely from the transmitter—*by Eunice Norton.*

putting in track lighting

Spang in the middle of many ceilings hangs a prosaic light fixture that typically wishy-washes the room with an overall glow, adding little character or contrast. If your home has one of these, maybe it's time for a makeover.

Contemporary lighting creates atmosphere and provides flexible illumination. With a good system, you can scallop a wall with light, highlight a piece of art and enjoy low-level ambient light—all at the same time.

Reprinted by permission of HOME Magazine.

Efficient low-voltage lamps on track create atmosphere, visual interest—and light.

Choosing a system

We removed the outdated pendant light in the study shown here and mounted a 4-foot Halo "Miniature Trac" fitted with three solid-state, low-voltage transformers and lampholders. We chose low-voltage lighting for energy efficiency, controlled beam spread, and the white color of the light, but incandescent lamps could be substituted for low-voltage.

A wide choice of fixtures is only one aspect of a track lighting system's flexibility. You can mount lampholders anywhere along a track's length, route track in nearly any direction, and control fixtures so they cast light only where you want it.

If an existing electrical box isn't ideally located, either check with an electrician about running a new circuit or buy special tract connectors to route the track from an existing box. This Halo model is powered by a connector that locks in anywhere along the track's length. You can also power a track with a live-end connector, or from an outlet with a cord and three-prong plug adapter.

Proper choice and placement of fixtures can be tricky. For a complicated lighting scheme, you may want to find professional help. Some interior designers specialize in lighting design and some quality lighting retailers offer skilled consultants.

Supplies for this system include one 4-foot track with toggle bolts and dead end connectors; floating canopy, mounting bracket, and connector; three solid-state, low-voltage transformers, gimbal-ring lampholder, and 25W PAR 36 lamps. You'll need only a few tools: tape measure, pencil, and drill with ½-inch bit, Phillips and flat-blade screwdrivers, and wire cutters or needle-nosed pliers. For greater control and more dramatic lighting effects, also consider getting a dimmer switch.

First things first

Be sure your new lights won't exceed the house circuit's electrical capacity (often 15 amps). This generally isn't a problem with a small low-voltage system, but incandescent lights may overload your circuit. Before installing, check your circuit for its amperage rating. Add up all appliances and lights drawing power from that circuit to figure the overall requirements. If this sounds confusing, get help from your lighting retailer or an electrician.

Don't overload the track: The one shown can handle a maximum of 20 amps per circuit if wired directly to an electrical box, or 10 amps if a cord with plug-in connector is used.

Before doing any work, be certain to shut off the power to the light—not just at the light switch, but at the fusebox or circuit breaker.

Helpful tips

After disconnecting the old lamp, make sure wires are suitable for connection; if necessary, clip ends and strip off ½ inch of insulation. Strip ends of new wires if they're not already stripped. Connect white wire to white and black to black. Ground the fixture's green wire to the house system's green wire, to an electrical ground wire or to the metal electrical box (according to codes). After you've tightened wire nuts onto the joined ends, gently push excess wire back into the outlet box to get it out of the way.

Before you screw the new mounting bracket to the electrical box, touch up the ceiling around the box with paint (if necessary). Be sure to orient the bracket so the track will run in the proper direction. It may be necessary to buy an adapter to modify your electrical box's hole spacing so that it matches the mounting bracket's holes.

This type of track can be cut to length with a hacksaw before mounting. Cut the track ⅛ inch shorter than the required dimension to allow for the dead-end fitting; follow the manufacturer's directions to add the fitting. Whether or not you have to cut the track to length, put dead-end fittings into the open ends of the track before you attach it to the ceiling.

The track can be mounted to drywall or plaster with toggle bolts, or screwed directly to solid wood.

Before you plug lampholders, transformers or the power supply into the track, note that it has a polarity line running along its length (see step 9). Each lampholder and transformer also has a polarity line for reference; be sure they align with the track's— *by Don Vandervort. Photos by John Reed Forsman.*

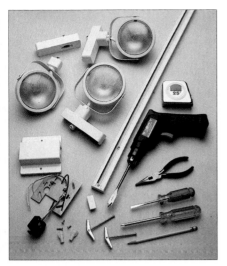

1. This is the collection of tools and materials needed for hanging a track light; see text for a complete list.

2. After shutting off power, remove fixture: First take off cover plate, then remove wire nuts and untwist wires.

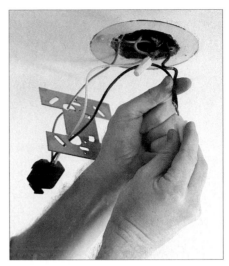

3. Run wires of power connector through holes in mounting bracket; connect wires using wire nuts.

4. Screw mounting bracket to junction box. If necessary, screw to an adapter that modifies hole placement.

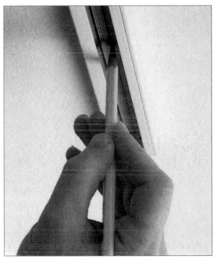

5. Measure and lightly mark track's placement on ceiling. Hold the track in place and mark hole locations.

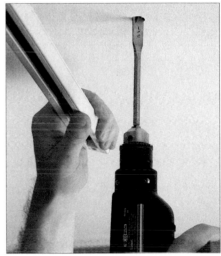

6. Drill ½-inch holes for toggle bolts in drywall or plaster. For a solid wood ceiling, drill pilot holes for screws.

7. Run bolts through track into spreading anchors, then insert toggle bolts into drilled holes and tighten (or use screws).

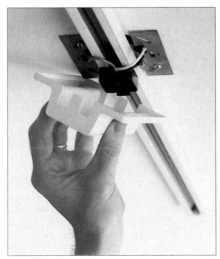

8. With power plug in place, tighten bracket's set screws on track and add canopy cover plate, tucking wires inside.

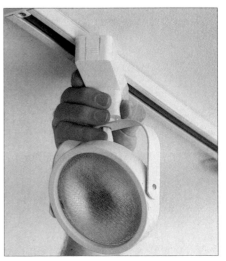

9. Lock light fixture and transformer into track. Be sure to properly orient polarity marks. Adjust direction of light.

adding masonry walkways

You can make a mortared brick walkway like this, or other designs in brick, stone or concrete if you master a few basic techniques.

Around most homes, walkways and footpaths serve both practical and aesthetic landscaping needs. Although there's a virtually endless variety of designs for walkway paving, there are essentially only two basic construction approaches: Paving materials such as bricks, flagstones, fieldstones, or precast pavers can be set in sand. Or, you can build walkways using concrete either as a primary surface or as the foundation for pavers set in mortar.

Many do-it-yourselfers choose the set-in-sand approach because it's lighter work and requires a bit less skill, but poured-concrete and concrete-based pavings are more permanent. And consider this: paving with or without concrete is pretty strenuous. If you're in good shape and can plan well, there's no reason why you can't give your home the benefit of all-masonry walkways.

Concrete facts

Concrete is a mixture of four materials: cement, sand, coarse aggregate (gravel or crushed stone), and water. Mixing these materials in the correct proportions is one of the keys to a successful job. The Portland Cement Association recommends a mixture of 1 part portland cement to 2¼ parts sand to 3 parts aggregate for walkway slabs. It's also important to order the correct size aggregate for a strong slab. For walkways, ¾- to 1-inch aggregate is about right.

Strictly speaking, you'd have to weigh each ingredient to achieve an accurate mix. For on-site mixing, it's easier to count out shovelfuls. As a rule, add 6 gallons of water for each 94-pound bag of cement used in the concrete. If you plan to mix it yourself, refer to the chart which lists the correct amounts of each ingredient you need for making various quantities of concrete.

For larger jobs, it's easier to buy ready-mixed concrete, which is delivered to the site. But whether you plan to order ready-mix or just the materials to mix the concrete yourself, first you've got to establish how many cubic yards of concrete you'll need for the job. You'll find you can buy it in amounts as small as ¼ yard.

To figure out how much you'll need, first make a measured drawing that shows the length and width of the walkway slab in feet. The other key dimension is the slab thickness, which must also be expressed in feet. To figure the total yards of concrete needed for your project, multiply the length times width times thickness of the slab, and divide the result by 27 ($[l' \times w' \times t']/27 = cubic\ yards$).

For example, if you wanted to order concrete for a walkway that is 30 feet long by 3 feet wide by 4 inches thick, you'd multiply 3 × 30 to get 90 square feet, then multiply 90 × ⅓ to get 30 cubic feet, and finally, divide 30 by 27 to find you need 1.1 yards of concrete for the job. In this case, you'd have to order 1¼ yards.

Reprinted by permission of Homeowner Magazine.

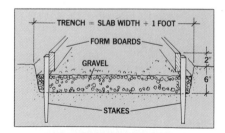

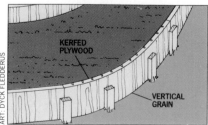

Details for straight and curved forms for concrete are shown above.

In "Patios and Walkways," Dean and JoAnne demonstrate paving techniques including setting bricks in a mortar bed.

Planning the path

After making a sketch of the walkway and figuring out how much concrete it'll take, take some time to plan the all-important drainage details and the work sequence for actual construction. In most communities, sidewalks designed for public access and walkways on or near property lines must pass muster with the local building department and zoning board, so consult with the proper authorities to learn what is required.

For a walkway to drain properly, the surface should slope 1/4 inch per foot—either from side to side or lengthwise. If the lengthwise slope is greater than 2 inches per foot, design steps into the walkway. And if the walk is close to a house foundation, be sure to pitch it away from the building.

Complete all site preparation before starting to pour the concrete. This means that all layouts, excavation and concrete forms must be done. And be sure to arrange beforehand to have enough help available when concrete ingredients or ready-mix is delivered. Many suppliers have a "sidewalk-delivery" policy, which means they'll drop off materials at the curb or in your driveway; it's up to you to have enough wheelbarrows and strong backs on hand to get materials from the curb to the location of the pour. Ready-mix outfits will slap you with overtime charges if the driver has to wait too long to unload your order. Depending on the size of the walkway, you'll probably need one or two helpers.

Site preparation and form work

Use stakes and string to make a rough layout for the walk. The area marked off should actually be about a foot wider than the walk will be. Dig out

SCREED

EDGER

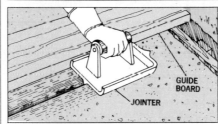

JOINTER

GUIDE BOARD

DARBY

STEEL TROWEL

SHEET PLASTIC

BURLAP

Pouring And Finishing Concrete

Although pouring concrete is heavy work, it's not really hard. But it's important to be organized to ensure you'll have enough time to work before the concrete begins to harden. The basic steps and tools for pouring concrete are shown in numbered illustrations at the left.

1. Pouring, spreading, and tamping. Start pouring concrete at one end while a helper spreads it. Tamp it into all corners. Space out pours along the form, working each batch just enough to fill the form completely.

2. Striking. Work a 2x4 across the top of the form with a rapid sawing motion to level the concrete.

3. Edging. Run a trowel between concrete and form, then follow with an edger for a smooth, slightly rounded edge.

4. Jointing. Use a jointing tool, guided by a straight board, to cut control joints into the surface every four to six feet.

5. Floating. Work the surface with a darby or wood float to smooth high spots and fill depressions. Overlap passes with the tool, then redo the edges and joints.

6. Finishing. After the sheen disappears from the concrete but before the surface becomes too stiff, finish the surface. For a smooth surface, use a wood float and follow with a steel trowel. For a nonskid surface, drag a stiff-bristle broom toward you across the surface, without overlapping passes. You can produce a variety of other surface finishes with special techniques: Seed the surface with small pebbles for an "exposed-aggregate" finish, or imitate the texture of marble, brick, stone or tile by tooling or stamping the soft concrete. You can even color the surface by dusting it with a coloring oxide.

7. Curing. Keep the concrete from drying out by keeping it covered. Place plastic sheeting or roofing felt over it for six days after it's poured. Leaving the forms in place for several days also helps the concrete to cure.

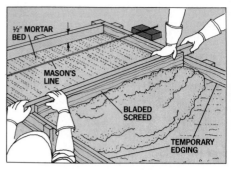
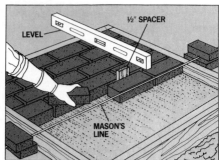
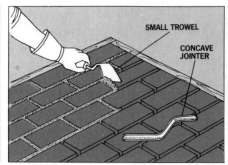

For mortared brick walkways: 1. Spread a ½-inch thick bed of mortar with a bladed screed over a concrete base. **2.** Bed and level bricks in the wet mortar using ½-inch spacers between them. **3.** Fill and finish joints.

enough earth inside the lines to accommodate 2 inches of gravel fill or a 4- to 6-inch bed of compacted sand (in locales where the ground doesn't freeze) that'll serve as a base, plus 4 inches of concrete. In most cases, you'll want the finished walk surface to be level with or slightly higher than the grade.

Use 2 × 4s to build the forms. Drive stakes into the ground every 4 feet, and nail the form boards to them. The top of each stake must be below the level of the form to allow for smoothing and finishing. Where the ends of two form boards meet along a continuous line, brace the joint with a 1-foot length of 2 × 4 centered over the joint, nailed on the outside of the form work.

If the ground naturally slopes so that the walkway will drain lengthwise, set the forms on both edges level with one another. If the end-to-end run is level, pitch the slab side-to-side about ¼ inch per foot by nailing one side of the form to the stakes slightly higher than the other.

MATERIALS NEEDED FOR MIXING CONCRETE				
Concrete Required	Cement* (lbs.)	Water (gals.)	Sand (lbs.)	Coarse Aggregate (lbs.)
1 cu. ft.	22	1¼	52	70
3 cu. ft.	65	3½	156	211
5 cu. ft.	109	6	260	352
¼ cu. yd.	147	8	350	475
½ cu. yd.	294	16	700	950
1 cu. yd.	588	32	1400	1900

*1 bag of cement weighs 94 lbs.
Courtesy Portland Cement Association

Straight forms are the easiest to build, but your layout may call for some curves. For gently curved forms, cut ½-inch plywood into 4-inch-wide strips, with the outer grain running up and down. Drive stakes into the ground to form points along the arc, and nail the plywood strips to them. For tighter curves, make form boards from ¾-inch-thick plywood with ⅜-inch-deep saw kerfs, spaced ½-inch-apart, cut across the strips.

In some designs, the form work is left in place for decorative edging and dividers between sections. Choose pressure-treated lumber, redwood or cedar for permanent forms. A specialty wood product called redwood benderboard is also available for making curved decorative forms.

Concrete walks need expansion joints spaced 10 to 12 feet apart to reduce stresses caused by frost and temperature changes. For these, use either asphalt-impregnated joint filler strips made expressly for the purpose or permanent wooden dividers. To support asphalt fillers during a pour, prop them against a temporary wooden divider supported by stakes nailed on the side that will be poured last. Once the first concrete section hardens, remove the wood divider. The standing concrete will support the expansion strip as the adjacent section is poured.

Coat the inside of all temporary forms with oil so it won't stick to the concrete, and treat all permanent forms with a wood preservative. Once all the prep work is finished, follow the steps presented in "Pouring and Finishing Concrete."

Brick-in-mortar walks

Pouring a concrete slab base is the first step in creating a mortared brick walkway. Mortar-set bricks can also be applied over sound existing concrete.

Once the concrete base is set, place a ½-inch-thick bed of wet mortar mixed to a whipped-cream consistency from Type M portland cement-lime mortar. Use the form work left over from pouring the base, or stake boards along the sides of existing slab, to act as a guide for your "bladed-screed," a tool made from straight pieces of scrap wood for leveling the mortar bed. Mix only as much mortar as you can use in an hour and screed only 10 square feet at a time.

Next, place the bricks in your chosen pattern, leaving ½-inch spaces between them. Bed each brick by gently tapping it, and use a level and mason's line to check the surface for flatness. Where it's necessary to cut bricks, use either a brick chisel or a circular saw with a masonry-cutting blade.

When all the bricks are set, pack more mortar into the joints. Use a concave jointer, dowel or other convex object to tool the joints. Scrub the paving several hours later with a burlap sack to remove any crumbs of dry mortar.

Stone walkways

While stone-in-mortar walkways also require a 4-inch thick concrete base, the procedure for setting stone in mortar differs from the procedure used for bricks. Instead of creating a large, level mortar bed, trowel only enough mortar onto the slab to make a bed for one or two stones at a time. Flagstones vary in thickness and their undersides are irregular, so you have to place enough mortar to fill all the voids.

Set each stone firmly in place by tapping it with a rubber mallet, and use a straightedge to level the surface from stone to stone. After the mortar has set for 24 hours, pack freshly made mortar between the stones. Smooth joints with a trowel and clean spills with sponge and water.

For concrete and mortar to cure properly it's important to keep the surface damp for about a week. The best way to keep water from evaporating too quickly is to keep surfaces covered with plastic. After that, they'll require little care except for occasional sweeping.

coloring concrete

They call it a stain. It comes in a plastic container, and you apply it with a brush. But any similarity between chemical concrete stains and the organic pigmented wood stains you're used to working with ends right there.

Chemical stains permanently color concrete, and the resulting colors vary in shade much as the colors of stones and other natural materials do—don't expect the deep color you can get with wood stains. Because the color is in the concrete and not just on its surface, it will not fade, chip, or peel the way concrete paints will. Chemical concrete stain can be used to color concrete slabs and even walls, but there are some guidelines: These stains can prove to be tricky.

When noted architect Wright designed a ski lodge at Sun Valley, Idaho, in the '30s (above), he textured the concrete walls by pouring against wood molds, then stained the concrete. Color has lasted 50 years.

Chemical stains are water solutions of metallic salts that penetrate and react with concrete to produce insoluable, abrasion-resistant (and thus long-lasting) color deposits in the concrete's pores. They contain a dilute acid that etches the concrete lightly and helps the staining ingredients penetrate deeper and react more uniformly.

Stains come in gallon bottles. Kemiko's stain is concentrated; you dilute it with an equal part of water for 200-square-foot-per-gallon coverage in two coats. The color of the stain in the plastic jug has little bearing on its ability to color concrete. For example, in the bottle, tan stain actually looks like a weak green thirst-quencher.

Little preparation is necessary. Concrete to be stained must be clean, dry, unpainted, and free of oil and grease. If it *is* clean and has fully cured to a uniform light color, just sweep it and start staining. Aged concrete can be a problem. Years of weathering and wear don't make for a good chemical reaction; the ideal age of concrete for staining is from a month to a year or two. Lightly sandblasting the surface helps the stain react more uniformly.

Be especially careful to protect yourself against the stain's acid content. Use rubber gloves and eye protection, and wear old shoes and old clothes. A rubber apron will help keep acid off your clothing. Indoors, provide ventilation so that you're not breathing the fumes.

A plastic dishpan makes a good mixing and application container. For staining small areas, apply the diluted stain with a small medium-soft acid-resistant brush. For larger areas use a 10-inch or larger broom-type brush.

Apply the stain liberally, but keep it from running or puddling; concentrated spots of stain will end up a darker color. Instead of painting-like strokes, rotate the brush in a circular or figure-eight motion, keeping it in contact with the surface. This will help prevent spatters and runs.

As the acid reacts, the stain must foam briefly. If there's no foaming, there's no staining reaction. During foaming, expand the stain out very slightly. But once the fizzing stops, don't brush the reacted stain into new areas; its staining ability has been used up. To avoid lap marks, additional applications should be brushed back into the wet areas to maintain a wet edge. At this point, the concrete color is not yet its final shade.

Allow eight hours for the first application to cure before giving the second. The surface must be kept moist during this time by sprinkling with water—the coloring reaction will stop if the surface dries out. Further applications of stain tend to even out the coloration, enriching it.

If a powdery salt residue shows on the surface after the stain dries, it should be removed by wet scrubbing with a stiff-bristled brush and water flushing.

To finish, sealers, clear or otherwise, will give the stained surface better wearing qualities. They also enhance the appearance, making the color look "wet." On inside areas and shuffleboard courts where you want a slick surface, colored Kemiko brand waxes may be applied.

A few other pointers

Chemical stains are primarily for slabs, but they can be used on concrete walls, portland-cement bricks, and blocks, provided they haven't been sealed first. Staining walls is difficult though, because the stain must stay on the vertical surface long enough for it to work fully.

An important point to remember is that any variations in the concrete surface composition will cause variations in color. For example, I stained three different concrete sections in front of my shop, dating from 1974 to only a month old. They ended up three shades of tan, all pleasing but all different.

In my experience black and brown are the most effective colors. The Malay tan and cola colors from Kemiko that I tried were also quite effective, though they look somewhat alike. Green-stained samples came out a very pale green. Kemiko's English red didn't do well for me at all—it merely made the barest blush.

Mixing stains might not be a great idea, according to Frank Ramirez, owner of Epmar Corporation, which markets the Kemiko line. "It doesn't work the way an artist mixes paints to get new colors," he says. "You might end up with mud." If you do experiment, test first.

Distribution of chemical stains for concrete is incomplete. I could find only one brand available to the do-it-yourself market: Kemiko's Stone Tone. Another manufacturer—L. M. Scofield Company—says it sells only to pros. So if dealers in your area don't have stains, contact Epmar Corporation (13210 Barton Circle, Santa Fe Springs, CA 90670). They will ship to you directly if no local dealer is available—*by Richard Day.*

custom-sized plastic shutters

Homeowners these days seldom rush to close their shutters at the first sign of a storm, yet they still spend hours painting and repairing wooden swing shutters because they like the look.

That's why molded plastic shutters were born—they fulfill the decorative functions but need no maintenance. And now they can be custom sized.

These durable shutters, made of high-impact polystyrene, are for looks only—they don't close; so they're easy to install. The plastic will last "forever," claims Mid-America Building Products Corporation (9420 Hubbell Avenue, Detroit, MI 48228), manufacturer of the Universal line of exterior shutters. The company also guarantees the finish against peeling or color change for seven years. The only maintenance suggested is an occasional hosing with water.

Although Universal shutters can be purchased already assembled, those who want a custom or odd-sized shutter can assemble one themselves in five minutes. The component parts include side rails, end pieces, and louvers. To assemble the shutter, cut the rails to the desired length and drill holes to hold fasteners that lock the end and sides together. Slide the louvers into tracks in the rails and lock the second end piece in place.

The cost for unassembled shutters runs about 45 cents per inch. Write the manufacturer for your nearest distributor—*by George Sears*.

Universal shutter is a decorative plastic shutter that can be constructed to fit any window. After measuring and cutting the side rails, drill corresponding holes in the rails and end pieces (above), and insert locking fasteners to join the sides and ends. Insert necessary number of louvers (above left) between the side rails. Attach the bottom end piece. The shutter is now ready to mount. Drill holes through the shutter into the siding (left), and screw it on. Because these shutters are for decoration only, no hinges are used. Universal shutters are available in eight colors and two styles. If you want to change the color later, paint the shutters with exterior latex.

rekindling a tired chimney

Before: Brick chimney lacks character. Repair and refinishing tools are shown.

Reprinted by permission of HOME Magazine.

Restored chimney adds rooftop charm, design interest to house. "Aged whitewash" finish—on irregular coating of thinned white paint—is applied with brush and rag.

Odds are, no matter how much you've done to renovate your home—from paint to petunias—when you step back to admire your work, one element stands out like a sore thumb: your brick chimney. If it's like many of its cousins, it is worn, smoke-stained and missing mortar. Before winter sets in, why not give the chimney a good, old-fashioned revival? Reverse its decline and offer it character. It will thank you by adding style to your home.

For our restoration, we repointed and refinished a relatively short rooftop chimney. You can apply the same techniques to any brick chimney or, for that matter, to a brick wall.

Repointing—replacing cracked, loose, or missing mortar—is a fairly easy job that can save you costly brick repairs later. We repointed our chimney in an afternoon and, including the purchase of a few mason's tools, completed the job for less than $40.

To give plain-Jane brick the character of the aged, whitewashed variety, we applied a brush-and-rub "skip" coat of thinned white latex paint. Though this doesn't require an artistic bent, you may want to practice the technique on the least visible side of the chimney, wiping the paint off with a wet rag until you achieve the effect you want.

Do the masonry work on a moderate day—preferably in the 50-to-75° Fahrenheit range. Too cold a day can freeze the new mortar; high temperatures, on the other hand, will dry it out too quickly.

The tools you'll need for the renovation are rubber gloves, work gloves, pail, scrub brush, whisk broom, protective glasses, cape chisel (for narrow joints) or a wider plugging chisel (for breaking out larger areas of mortar), hammer, trowel, tuck pointer, dropcloth, paintbrush, and rag. Depending upon the height and style of your particular chimney, you may also need a brick jointer and a ladder.

Required materials include muriatic acid, trisodium phosphate (T.S.P.), premixed mortar (or mortar ingredients) and latex paint.

To clean and prepare the brick for the new finish, scrub it with a solution of muriatic acid—4 parts water to 1 part acid, mixed in a pail. Use a stiff bristle brush and a pushing motion; don't pull it toward yourself or you may be splattered with acid. Remember that this chemical is hazardous, so be careful. Follow the label directions and be sure to wear rubber gloves and eye protection. Avoid skin contact with the acid and don't breathe the vapors.

The second preparation phase is to remove stains from the brick with a tri-sodium phosphate (T.S.P.) solution—4 tablespoons T.S.P. dissolved in a gallon of water. Follow up by scrubbing obstinate stains with a wire

1. Use a stiff brush to carefully scrub brick with acid solution. To avoid splattering, push brush—don't pull it toward yourself.

2. After cleaning the brick with T.S.P., wire-brush the surface. Wash down the roof and chimney and allow to dry.

3. Chisel out loose mortar, using a hammer and cape chisel (or plugging chisel). Brush away loose mortar and dust.

4. Using a tuck pointer, slide mortar off a trowel into the joints and work it in. Finish joints with a brick jointer or trowel.

5. Brush on paint in an irregular pattern, skipping some bricks and portions of bricks. Do small areas, then move on.

6. Blot wet paint with a damp rag, removing all brush marks and lines. Return to Step 5 and continue with rest of chimney.

The Art of The Chimney Sweep

A sweep is as lucky as lucky can be—if he has the right equipment.

Whenever you burn wood in a fireplace or wood stove, creosote—a tarlike substance—rises with the smoke, then cools, condenses and collects on the chimney's inner walls. The resulting long-term buildup can ignite into a dangerous flue fire that may spread to your house or nearby trees. Creosote accumulation also corrodes the flue and reduces energy efficiency.

Different woods emit varying amounts of creosote—hardwoods and properly cured woods less than softwoods or "green" wood. And airtight wood stoves and fireplace inserts produce creosote buildup much faster than open fireplaces. It's time to clean the chimney when about ¼ inch of creosote has collected on the walls.

Though the job is messy and requires a few special tools, you can probably do the chimney sweep's job and save hundreds of dollars over several seasons. If your chimney is particularly tall or your roof is quite steep, you may be better off leaving it to a pro.

To sweep it yourself, you'll need the tools shown in the photograph. You probably already own some of them—for example, a metal bucket, wire brush with scraper, flashlight, metal dustpan or ash shovel, goggles, dust mask, dropcloths, masking tape and work gloves. A shop vacuum (not the household kind) is handy but not required. You'll also need a chimney brush, sized and shaped for your flue. Choose metal bristles for a masonry flue, synthetic for

a metal flue. And you'll want extension rods or rope and a weight (a plastic bottle filled with water) for moving the brush inside the flue. Though it makes sense to buy the brush and extensions if you plan to do this more than once, you can rent them if you prefer.

Make sure the fire is completely out. Then mask off the fireplace opening, using a paper dropcloth and wide masking tape; be sure to seal it completely. In the case of a wood stove or freestanding fireplace, seal all openings.

From the roof, remove any chimney cap or spark arrestor (most are snapped or screwed in place). Either screw an extension rod into the end of the flue brush or screw an eye socket into the brush and tie a long rope to one end, a short rope and weight to the other. Lower the brush (or weighted brush) into the flue with the extension rod (or long rope), and scrub up and down a few times to remove soot and creosote. Do this until you no longer hear creosote dropping. Add extension rods (or extend more rope) to scrub the entire flue. When you're finished, remove the flue brush and extensions (or ropes and weight) and replace the chimney cap or spark arrestor.

Inside, lay a dropcloth on the floor around the fireplace or wood stove. Carefully remove the masking tape and paper from the mouth of the fireplace. Using the hand wire brush and scraper, clean the firebox and all areas you can reach. Then sweep out the accumulated ashes and creosote.

If you're cleaning a wood stove or fireplace connected to a stovepipe, you can disconnect the pipe at the stove and remove pipe sections for a thorough cleaning with a wire brush outdoors. (Before you do this, mark their order and alignment with a light pencil line to make reassembly easier.) Also remove any damper, downdraft equalizer or heat reclaimer.

If necessary, you can poke the flue brush's extension rod through a large paper bag, then tape the bag onto the exposed stack where it enters the room. Then when you scrub from below, the creosote won't come raining down.

When all of the parts have been cleaned, reassemble them. Complete the job with a thorough vacuuming inside and around the fireplace. **—D.V.**

brush. Again, wear gloves and eye protection. Hose off the brick and the roof when you are finished and let the brick dry.

To remove loose or cracking mortar, use a hammer and a plugging chisel for wide areas, a cape chisel for narrow mortar grooves. Wear protective glasses and work gloves. After chiseling out all loose and damaged mortar, brush away dust and bits of mortar with a whisk broom.

To replace the old mortar you can either buy premixed weather-resistant type N mortar—just add water—or you can mix up your own from 1 part Portland cement; 8 parts sand and 2 parts hydrated lime. Unless you are doing a huge job, the premixed mortar makes more sense. Add enough water to make a fairly stiff paste that you can push into the joints easily.

To protect the roof, spread a dropcloth around the chimney's base. Dampen the mortar joints with water; then scoop mortar onto a trowel's underside, and holding it mortar side up next to the joints, push wet mortar into the joints with a tuck pointer.

First fill the vertical joints and then the adjoining horizontal ones. Be sure to work the mortar all the way into the cracks and crevices in the old mortar, filling the joints completely. Scrape excess off brick surfaces before it has a chance to harden. Do about 1 square yard and then go on to the next step.

If existing mortar joints are concave, draw a brick jointer along the new mortar to duplicate that profile. For flat joints, strike off the mortar with the trowel, flush with the brick. To match V-grooved joints, use the trowel tip.

When you've finished all wet mortar joints, return to the previous step and begin another square-yard area.

After you've repointed the entire chimney and the mortar is set, use the trowel or a flat stick to scrape off any protruding pieces of mortar. Then scrub down the chimney with a wet brush and hose off the chimney and roof. The mortar will cure in about four days; spray it with water daily during this period.

To apply the "aged whitewash" finish, mix equal amounts of white exterior latex paint and water. Working in about a 2-foot-square section, brush on the paint in an irregular pattern, skipping some bricks and portions of bricks. Blot and blend paint with a damp rag, removing all brush marks—*by Don Vandervort. Photos by John Reed Forsman.*

4 easy patches

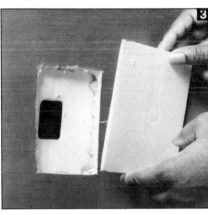

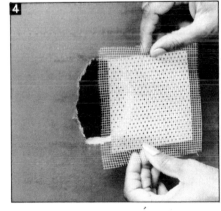

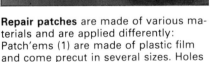

Repair patches are made of various materials and are applied differently: Patch'ems (1) are made of plastic film and come precut in several sizes. Holes must be sized to fit Pro Patch (2), and cardboard-type Holpatch (3) is cut to fit hole. Aluminum-mesh Repair Patch (4) is ready-cut in a variety of sizes.

No, I hadn't played several rounds of golf in my living room, but there were holes in the walls just the same. They were caused by typical household mishaps: a doorknob repeatedly banging into a wall; nails and toggle bolts used to hold up heavy shelves and pictures had ripped out unsightly cavities in the gypsum board. Eventually, I accumulated wallboard hole-patch kits from four suppliers: One patch can be applied to a wall just by pressing against its adhesive backing. The others are a little more elaborate—and permanent—involving finishing compound and sanding.

● Patch'ems made by Atlanta Sundries, look as though they are Band-Aid adhesive bandages and can be applied in seconds.

● A square of wallboard with a paper border, Pro Patch from P&H Products, blends in well with the wall, so it's hard to tell there was a hole.

● Cascade Development's Holpatch embodies the wall-patching technique used by most homeowners: a piece of cardboard with string attached goes behind the hole to hold the spackling compound in place. Holpatch improves on that approach, using another piece of cardboard to fill in the hole.

● Pace-Setter Repair Patch, a thin sheet of rustproof aluminum covered with nylon mesh, combines aesthetic value with strength, says Jack Goddard of Goldblatt Tool Company. It is completed by lightly applying finishing compound and sanding.

The four hole-patch kits are applied in various ways. Larry Owens, president of Atlanta Sundries, calls the thin Patch'ems "the McDonald's of hole patches." They work in two steps: Peel off the adhesive backing and place the patch on the hole, then paint over it. Repainting is simple because "it already has primer," says Owens, who is also the inventor. A pack of 22 assorted-size patches is $8.

"Pro Patch is best used by homeowners who don't want to do the job again," says Dave Olman, vice president of sales and marketing for P&H Products. Though the results are professional-looking, Pro Patch is more tedious and messy to apply, I found. First you size the hole to match the patch. Then you apply a thin coat of Quickset adhesive around the hole's edge and a generous coat on the patch's paper border, insert the patch, let the Quickset harden, and sand. Lastly, apply a coat of finishing compound, let it dry, and remove any ridges with a wet cloth. A kit with Quickset, finishing compound, a putty knife, and two patches is $7.

To use the two-piece Holpatch kit ($4), you push the adhesive-faced in-wall backing part through the hole. Peel off the protective strip and pull the patch against the back of the drywall through the center hole. Once the backing is in place, cut the cord that connects the second, finishing, part. Then cut that second piece of board to fill the hole; spackle, let dry, and sand.

Repair Patch is easy to use: Strip away its adhesive backing, make sure the metal area covers the damaged spot, and press firmly. Spackle lightly and let it dry, then sand to a smooth finish. "You can nail up to a 30-pound picture over it," claims Goldblatt's Goddard. Repair Patch is available in various sizes, two to a pack. A 12-pack box costs $48—*by Sherrill Clarke. Photos by Greg Sharko.*

DRYWALL-PATCH MANUFACTURERS' ADDRESSES
Atlanta Sundries, 6480 Chupp Road C-8, Lithonia GA 30058; **Cascade Development,** 500 E. Carson Plaza Drive, Carson CA 90746; **Goldblatt Tool Company,** 511 Osage, Box 2334, Kansas City KS 66110; **P&H Products, Inc.,** 6840 Second Street NW, Albuquerque NM 87107

PHOTOS BY GREG SHARKO

lead-free plumbing repairs

Get the lead out!" cries the Environmental Protection Agency. Since most copper water piping in U.S. homes is soldered with a 50-percent-lead alloy, most of us drink water containing traces of lead. The EPA estimates that 40 million of us are exposed to higher levels of lead in our water than the 20 parts per billion the EPA considers a safe maximum contaminant level. To minimize this exposure, other means of making water-line joints must now be used: Old-time solders have been outlawed for this purpose.

If you were determined to banish all lead risk from your drinking water, you'd have to break existing lead-soldered joints and replace them, using one of the systems below. However, unless you've had your water tested and know the lead content is high, your main reason to learn about the alternative systems is for any *extensions* of supply lines you make.

Do all new sweat soldering with lead-free solder. The old tin-lead solders (40/60, 50/50, or 60/40—the tin number always comes first) are still fine for jobs where lead's toxicity isn't a problem. But for water lines, you can choose a lead-free solder; 95/5 contains 95 percent tin and 5 percent antimony, and it's made by Oatey Company, Alpha Metals, Inc., Kester Solder Company, and others. It's harder to use than 50/50 because it has a higher melting point—464°F rather than 421. This increases the chance of burning the flux out of the joint. Flux is needed to prevent oxidation of the copper or brass surfaces and to lower the surface tension of the molten solder so it will flow.

Tighter flow range

Also, tin-antimony solder has a shorter plastic range than tin-lead. This is the temperature range over which the solder starts to melt but does not yet become liquid—the range when solder is most workable. Where tin-lead offers a 60° range, tin-antimony offers only 14°.

"When overheated, the solder becomes runny and won't flow into a joint as easily," says John McMillan of Oatey. So Oatey markets a lead-free flux designed to ease the problem; ask for Oatey #95 Tinning Flux. "Even if the flux should be burned out," says McMillan, "solder will flow into the joint because the flux contains pow-

1. New solder is trickier to use than tin-lead type it replaces. You need the right flux on fully cleaned joints—plus care not to overheat the joint.

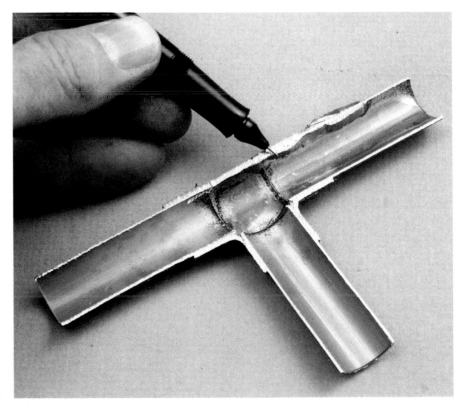

2. Cutaway of sweat-soldered tee shows how excess solder can flow past joint, along inside of tubing (at pen point), increasing exposure of lead to water. Photos 3–5: alternatives to soldering.

dered lead-free solder that tins the copper surfaces."

Tin-antimony solder costs about twice as much as 50/50. An 8-ounce container of the special flux sells for about $6—perhaps a lifetime supply for a do-it-yourselfer.

Another lead-free solder uses silver-bearing alloys to replace the lead. Not truly silver solder (which has more silver and a high melting point), silver-bearing solder is about 90 to 95 percent tin with the balance a combination of silver, antimony, zinc, or copper. The good news is that it offers a plastic range of 35 to 50 degrees. This makes silver-bearing solder work more like familiar tin-lead solder. The chief difference is that it takes longer because the joint must be hotter than when using a tin-lead solder.

Oatey's Safe-Flo silver-bearing solder has 96 percent tin and 4 percent silver and melts at 430 degrees F; Alpha Metals' Lead-Free Silver Solder has 98 percent tin, 2 percent silver, and melts at 450°F.

There are others. As with tin-lead and tin-antimony, all can be sweated with an ordinary propane torch. The correct soldering flux is required, often being packaged with the solder. Silverbearing solder costs 30 to 50 percent more than tin-antimony solder. Both kinds of lead-free solder produce joints that exceed the rated pressure on copper tubing.

Rather than sweating joints with lead-free solder, you can assemble copper-tubing joints using epoxy resin. No flame is required. A personal-use report on the brand shown in our photo appears on this page.

Plastic fittings

Instead of using standard sweat-type fittings you can replace them with an easier-working kind of fitting. The simplest replacements to install are mechanically coupled plastic fittings. There are several brands, all made for use with polybutylene, or PB, tubing, and some will work with copper tubing as well. Just be sure you get fittings made of chlorinated polyvinyl chloride, or CPVC.

CPVC fittings are large enough that the old sweat-soldered fittings can often be sawed out, clear of any solder deposits. Make the tube ends square and free of burrs, lubricating them with a little petroleum jelly. Push the tubes full-depth into the fitting. It's a good idea to mark the tubes at proper depth for full insertion to

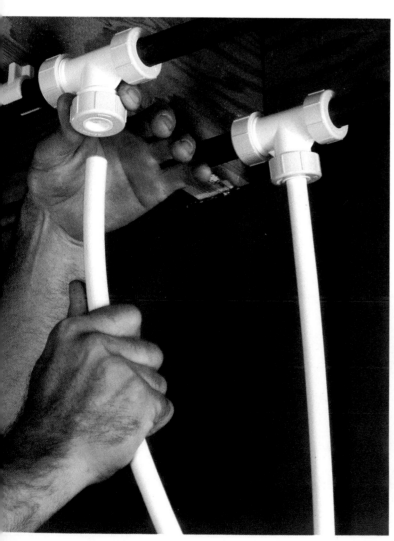

3. CPVC tees let you add supply branches to a copper plumbing system; Genova's Uncopper fittings use rubber O-rings for water sealing, while metal grab-ring holds fittings on tubing.

4. Compression fittings don't use solder.

5. If you want to use standard elbows and tees with copper tubing, you can join them with two-part epoxy adhesive.

indicate when the tube has entered all the way into the fitting. Tightening the fitting's collar completes the joint. CPVC fittings are available in both $1/2$- and $3/4$-inch copper-tubing sizes in couplings, 90-degree elbows, and tees. The water-supply system need not be drained for this kind of fitting replacement.

With more effort, sweat fittings can be replaced with brass fittings in compression or flared. These may be had as couplings, 90-degree elbows, and tees. Compression fittings are easier to handle than flared, which require the use of a flaring tool.

If you extend your home water-supply plumbing, you'll want to do it without lead soldering. The easiest and cheapest way is to use plastic hot-and-cold tubings and fittings. Choose flexible PB, rigid CPVC, or a combi-

nation of the two. Mechanically coupled PB tubing is the easiest method; solvent-welded CPVC makes the best-looking job; a combination lets you use either a flexible or a rigid tube. Not limiting you to PB only, mechanically coupled CPVC fittings will work on all four kinds of water-supply tubing: flexible copper, rigid copper, CPVC, and PB—*by Richard Day. Photos by Greg Sharko.*

rounding wall corners

Reprinted by permission of HOME Magazine.

A rounded corner softens the look of and adds a plastered effect to drywall.

The look of hand-plastered adobe has special appeal yet is often hard to achieve in a house of drywall interior surfaces. A technique we found employed in the McGilvray-Schow house goes a long way towards creating that look.

The tools and supplies you'll need are pictured opposite. You can find 8- or 10-foot lengths of rounded metal corner bead at most good builders' supply stores; we recommend the undrilled, taped type. You'll also need two types of joint compound: regular, for adhering the tape to drywall and a topping compound, for the final coat. Carefully follow the packages' directions for mixing and drying times.

Measure and cut the corner bead to length, taking care not to damage the actual round corner. If you have kick plates, floor moldings or carpet, be especially careful to make the bottom cut clean and even.

Hammer in the drywall nails every 10 inches on either side of the corner bead so that the head of the nail is over the edge of the metal bead flange; do not nail through the metal. Offset opposing nails slightly.

To adhere the tape to drywall, fold back the tape with a long, vertical crease; apply the joint compound in a smooth, thorough coat, then press the tape onto the compound with the 6-inch taping knife. Clean off any excess bulges or trailing edges.

When the tape is secured (depending on the temperature, it could take a few hours), apply the first coat of joint compound. Using the 8-inch knife, apply the compound with the edge of the knife striking the edge of the rounded corner bead (be sure not to damage the round corner). You are trying to build up the corner with compound without making it too heavy. You can apply the compound with smooth up or down strokes; just keep the strokes even.

After the first coat dries (four to six hours, depending on temperature), apply a second coat, again building up edge of the corner with compound.

When the second coat dries, sand the flat surfaces lightly with the sanding block. Be sure to use a very fine sandpaper (120 to 220 grade) or a fiberglass cloth (also fine grade). Do not sand the corner; you can use the sponge, which will form to the rounded surface without damaging the corner.

The third and last coat is a topping coat, which is applied thinly over the two other coats. When dry, sand and sponge lightly; the surfaces are now ready to paint—*by Charlie Posoneil.*

1. Tools: cutters, corner bead, taping knives, compound bucket, sanding pole, sponge, hammer, nails and respirator.

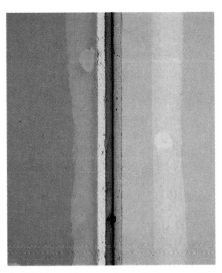

2. When nailing up drywall, leave a ½-inch gap between edges of drywall so the edges won't touch corner bead.

3. Hammer drywall nails through tape so the nail heads pin the metal bead to drywall; do not hammer through metal.

4. Crease tape vertically in order to apply joint compound behind tape; the crease will disappear when covered.

5. With a 6-inch taping knife, carefully apply joint compound behind the corner tape, smoothing over the entire surface.

6. Applying even pressure, squeegee the knife over the tape to adhere it to compound; remove excess.

7. Extend edge of the 8-inch knife slightly over corner; apply compound to build up corner; wait six hours; repeat.

8. After second coat dries, sand surfaces with a rigid block and fine sandpaper or fiberglass cloth.

9. Because compound is water-soluble, you can clean up corner with a soft sponge before applying topping.

float a hardwood floor

Reprinted by permission of HOME Magazine.

Underneath the wall-to-wall carpeting in most older homes lies a hardwood floor begging to be set free. If you live in a newer home, however, you may discover only plywood or a concrete slab beneath the carpet pad. Hardwood can be installed over these surfaces, but laying, sanding and finishing strip flooring has never been a job recommended for the weekend warrior.

No longer. In the last few years, Swedish mills have begun exporting a prefinished product, used widely in Europe, that is referred to as a "floating floor." Installed without nails over a high-density foam underlayment, it literally floats in place, accommodating seasonal expansion and contraction of the wood and the peculiarities of the surface on which it is laid.

The flooring itself is laminated—a triple-decker sandwich consisting of a hardwood surface layer $1/8$ inch thick, a core of cross-banded pine strips, and a plywoodlike backing layer. The beech flooring used here comes from Harris-Tarkett.

If the room is of average size, installing the flooring is a weekend job. You'll need a hammer, a crosscut saw of any kind, a pry bar, a razor knife and white glue in a squeeze bottle.

The flooring comes in shrink-wrapped bundles of 8-foot planks, each about $6\frac{1}{2}$ inches wide. The planks have tongue-and-groove edges and ends to make for a tight, almost seamless finish. Resist opening the bundles prior to installation, or laying them will be more difficult and shrinkage cracks will appear later on.

The $1/8$-inch high-density foam underlayment comes with the flooring. The foam smooths out minor irregularities in the subfloor and helps deaden noise, particularly in the room below.

Installing the flooring is a straightforward job, but there are a few professional tricks for topnotch results:

● Check to see that the room is square. If it's badly skewed, you'll have to rip the first and last boards along their length for proper fit. But in this or any other step, be careful not to chip or compress the planks' thin veneer.

● A $1/2$-inch expansion gap at all walls is vital. Lay the first boards against $1/2$-inch spacers set every 18 inches or so. Place the plank's groove toward the wall, because you'll be squeezing the glue into the grooves of succeeding boards and tapping them home.

● As you proceed, stagger the end joints at least 24 inches from those in the previous course. Cut only the first and last pieces in any course so that the boards are joined on all edges by a tongue and groove.

● Because there's no room to hammer the last course home, you'll have to use a pry bar, a wood scrap and the $1/2$-inch gap to force this last board into place.

● Once you've set the last finish nail on the baseboard or molding, the floor is ready for use. But many contractors strongly recommend a coat or two of finish over the completed floor—*by James Keough. Photos by Jeff Weissman.*

Swedish beech "floating floor" took just a day to install in this porch-turned-study, but it gives the room the natural warmth and focal point it lacked.

1. Starting in a corner of the room, pull up wall-to-wall carpeting and foam padding. Remove tack strips with care.

2. Using a scrap of flooring and foam underlayment as a guide, cut the door casing so flooring will slide beneath it.

3. Cut the foam underlayment with a razor knife to fit the room; use duct tape to keep seams together and lying flat.

4. Lay first course of planks against spacers to create a ½-inch expansion gap wherever the flooring abuts a wall.

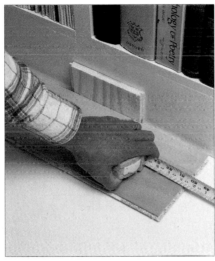

5. Measure remainder of the first course; remember to account for the ½-inch expansion gap at each end wall.

6. Use handsaw or backsaw (shown here) to cut board to length. Use the cut-off piece to begin the next course.

7. Squeeze narrow bead of white glue into the groove of the second course. Wipe up any spills with a damp cloth.

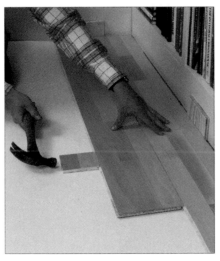

8. Drive second course tightly against the first with a hammer, using a scrap of flooring to protect the tongue.

9. Repeat with succeeding courses. Finish off by nailing in quarter-round or base-board molding; set the nails.

tile a tabletop

Reprinted by permission of HOME Magazine.

Vibrant tile top is a handy addition to a wooden appliance cart: The tile is durable and easy to maintain and won't be damaged by over-hot pans.

Take a new look at tile for wooden table or appliance cart tops: you can use it on a serving tray or hot-plate trivet; it's sturdy enough to stand up to some pretty hard use; it's very low maintenance; and perhaps best of all, it's easy to apply.

You'll need tile (we used a Mexican ceramic), mastic (an organic adhesive), cement-based grout, a notched trowel and a squeegee. Because there are so many choices, it can be overwhelming to select the tile, grout and mastic; it's helpful to consult a tile dealer about the project.

Measure your tabletop and decide how many and what size tiles you'll need—usually no larger than 4 inches by 4 inches. If they need to be cut to fit perfectly, ask if your dealer offers that service—or you may be able to rent or borrow a tile cutter from the dealer to do it yourself. Buy a few extra tiles in case any break or chip.

There are many special trim profiles available; so ask the salesman for advice. We used quarter-round pieces in a contrasting color for the cart edges.

Make sure you buy a mastic that can be used on wood. It doesn't have to be intended especially for wet areas (like bathtubs or backsplashes), but it shouldn't dissolve if it gets splashed with water occasionally.

When you begin to tile you'll start with the trim pieces, so apply the mastic to the edges first. Study the directions, then spread the mastic—between 1/4 and 1/2 inch thick—with the smooth side of the trowel. Next hold the trowel at a 45-degree angle to the surface and comb the mastic with the notched edge; press firmly so the adhesive forms ridges. Spread only the amount of adhesive you can cover before it sets (read the directions to determine the open time; it's usually about 30 minutes). Apply the trim pieces, then the flat tiles, spacing them by eye. (You can buy tile spacers to ensure perfectly even intervals, but for a small table surface it's not really necessary.) Allow the mastic to dry for at least 24 hours, then wipe the excess off the tile surface with a wet sponge before grouting; if it's hard to wipe off, try chipping it off with a putty knife.

For this project you'll use cement-based grout mixed with water; you can choose a matching or complementary color. Apply the grout with a squeegee, making sure all the joints are filled. Let the grout dry, then wipe the tiles with a clean, barely damp sponge. When the grout is completely hardened, polish the tile with a soft cloth—*by Terri Hartman. Photos by Stuart Watson.*

1. You'll need tile, mastic, grout, a rubber faced squeegee and a notched trowel. Make sure the wooden surface is clean.

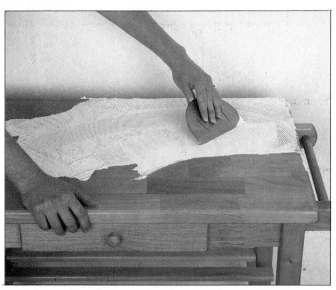

2. First apply with the smooth edge of the trowel, then comb the mastic with the notched edge.

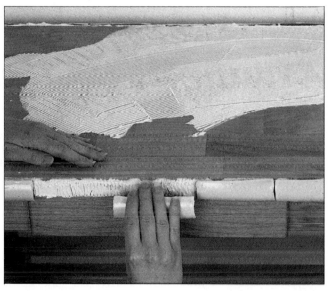

3. Apply trim pieces to the edge of the table before laying the flat tiles. Twist the tiles into the mastic.

4. Lay flat tiles. For a large table, you might want to use plastic spacers between the tiles for even joint lines.

5. Squeeze grout into the joints with a squeegee; use the rubber face to scrape the excess off the tiles.

6. Once grout has dried, wipe the surface with a barely damp sponge until the joints are smooth and level with the tiles.

troubleshooting electronic fuel injection

One source gives 1957 as the first model year fuel injection was offered by American car makers. The setup was a revolutionary new option on certain Chevrolet, Pontiac, and Rambler engines, though it may actually have been pioneered as early as 1910.

In any case, it's taken too long for this highly efficient fuel-intake system to take center stage away from the carburetor. Now that it has, though, do-it-yourself mechanics are being told that today's electronic fuel injection (EFI) is too complicated for them to tackle. That's baloney.

Once you get the hang of it, troubleshooting your car's EFI system is *less* complicated than working on a carbureted system. There's not much a professional technician can do for you that you can't do for yourself.

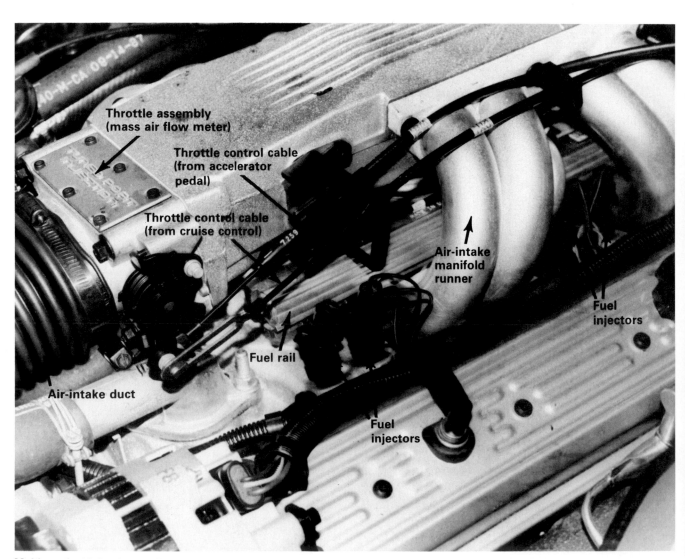

Multiport fuel injection on Corvette has eight fuel injectors—four of which are visible here. The gas they receive through the fuel delivery line (called a rail) is sprayed into the combustion chamber at the intake valve of each cylinder. There, it mixes with air entering through an air-intake duct, throttle assembly, and air-intake manifold runner.

Types of systems

There are two types of fuel injection systems: throttle body injection (TBI) and multiport injection (MPI). A TBI system uses one or two fuel-injection nozzles or *injectors*. Mounted atop the intake manifold as a carburetor would be, the throttle body itself even resembles a carburetor at first glance, especially with the air cleaner over it. Remove the air-cleaner top, however, and the differences become apparent (Fig. 1).

Look inside and you see one or two fuel injectors. They spray gasoline down the throat of the throttle body, past a throttle valve into the intake manifold. Unlike the multitude of parts inside a carburetor, the inside of a throttle body contains only the fuel injectors and a throttle valve. Don't let terms confuse you, by the way. Central Fuel Injection (Ford) and Single Point Fuel Injection (Chrysler), for instance, are both throttle body systems.

Multiport Fuel injection is, in essence, no different from TBI. MPI is also called port injection, and tuned-port injection. Whichever designation is used, an MPI system is characterized by one fuel injector per cylinder. Thus, a four-cylinder engine with MPI has four fuel injectors, a six-cylinder has six, and an eight-cylinder has eight. Each fuel injector is inserted into the engine's intake manifold where it can spray gasoline at the intake valve or valves for that cylinder.

Another term that may be used in connection with an MPI system is "sequential fuel injection." The word *sequential* refers to the way in which the injectors are designed to open—one by one in concert with the spark-plug firing order, instead of two at a time or all at once as with other MPI systems.

Timing the fuel-injector pulse

To work efficiently, the fuel injectors in your car's TBI or MPI system must be kept open just long enough to spray the optimum amount of fuel into the cylinder at any given time. How long they're open varies depending, say, on whether you're cruising comfortably down a straightaway or pulling a trailer up a steep grade. Electronic sensors monitor changing coolant temperature, manifold pressure and temperature, oxygen content of the exhaust, the angle of the throttle valve, and vehicle speed. The data is then transmitted by those sensors to an electronic control module (ECM), sometimes called a computer or microprocessor. The ECM then controls injector pulsing—or, how long the injectors stay open to meet constantly changing driving conditions.

You don't have to check out your EFI's electronics to see if its parts are working properly. The fuel injection system and the electronic control system, although they work together, are two separate systems. If the tests described here reveal that the parts of the fuel injection system are okay, however, the electronic system is probably at fault.

When one or more parts of a TBI or MPI system malfunction, the results can read like an encyclopedia of auto ailments. They include hard and no starts, stalling, loss of power, detonation (pinging/spark knock) and dieseling, hesitation, sag, stumble, rough idle, poor fuel mileage, excessive exhaust emissions, and a rotten-egg odor from the exhaust.

Depending on the symptom, you can sometimes make an educated guess as to a possible EFI malady. For instance, if the engine idles roughly, suspect the idle air control device. But, before you replace any fuel injection component, be sure the reason for trouble lies in the fuel injection system and with the part you suspect.

Fig. 1. Throttle body injection resembles a carburetor—at first. But with the air-cleaner cover off, you'll see one or two electrical connectors serving one or two fuel injectors.

The parts of a fuel injection system are divided into those that help deliver gas to the engine, and those that help deliver air. While gas and air mix in the throttle body of a TBI system, in an MPI setup, they take different routes before they blend together to form a combustible fuel mixture.

Moving from inside the fuel tank forward as gasoline travels, the parts responsible for delivering gas are much the same in both TBI and MPI systems. They are: a fuel sock on the gas pickup; electric fuel pump; in-line fuel filter; fuel-delivery line; fuel pressure regulator; fuel-return line; and fuel injector(s).

Air force

The parts responsible for getting air to the engine with TBI differ somewhat from an engine with MPI. However, both systems use an air intake duct and air-cleaner assembly.

With a TBI system, air follows the same path it follows in a carbureted system—through the air intake duct and air filter, and down the throat of the throttle body where it mixes with gas before passing through the throttle valve into the intake manifold. The throttle valve is opened when the driver presses on the accelerator pedal. When the throttle valve is closed—at idle or when decelerating—an idle-speed control device keeps the throttle valve cracked, letting in just enough fuel to keep the engine from flooding and stalling.

An MPI air system also uses an idle-speed control device that opens an air bypass, letting air flow into the engine under similar conditions. With your foot on the accelerator

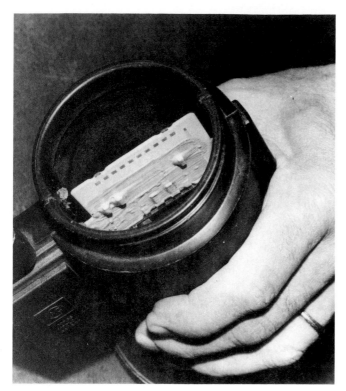

Fig. 2. Mass air flow meter of many MPI systems contains a sensor as well as the throttle valve. The sensor transmits data about the air to the electronic control module (computer). Based on this data, the electronic control module adjusts the pulse rate of the fuel injectors. If all else fails to reveal the reason for an engine driveability problem or if the engine light on the dash flashes, have this sensor tested.

pedal and the throttle valve *open*, the flow of air into an engine with MPI proceeds through the air intake duct, air filter, and throttle body. Don't confuse this throttle body with one on a TBI system. While this one also has a throttle valve, it handles no gas.

On some MPI systems (many of GM's, for example), the throttle body contain a sensing device that monitors the characteristics of the air entering the engine. This type of throttle body is often referred to as a *mass air flow meter* (Fig. 2). Throttle bodies of other MPI systems (Chrysler's, for instance) house only the throttle valve.

Air passes through the mass air flow meter or throttle body into the intake manifold (sometimes called the air plenum) above each intake valve, where it mixes with gas. The mixture then enters the cylinder as the intake valves open.

Where to begin

Two tests reveal if the reason for an engine problem lies with the gas-delivery components of your TBI or MPI system. One establishes whether there's an interruption of electricity to the fuel injector(s). If the fuel injectors don't get current, they don't open, and the engine doesn't get gas. The other—a fuel pressure test—helps you zero in on other faulty gas delivery components.

The purpose of the electrical test is to establish two facts: (1) that electricity is reaching each fuel injector; (2) that electricity is switching on and off to pulse (open and close) each injector. To make the test, you need a tool called an EFI-LITE.

Before buying an EFI-LITE (Fig. 3), detach the wire connector from one of the injectors. Note whether the injector terminals are pins or blades and make a sketch of them to show the auto parts dealer. You don't want to end up with the wrong kind of EFI-LITE.

If the dealer can't help you, send the sketch and information concerning the make and model of the vehicle to Borroughs Tool & Equipment Corporation (2429 North Burdick Street, Kalamazoo, MI 49007) or Kent-Moore Tool Group (29784 Little Mack, Roseville, MI 48066). The EFI-LITE costs between $5 and $10.

To use the EFI-LITE, disconnect the wire from one of the fuel injectors and plug the tool into the connector. Crank the engine, which may start if it has more then one injector *so be careful where you put your hands.* The EFI-LITE should give off a pulsating glow. If it gives off no light or gives a steady glow, there is an electrical failure. On the other hand, if the EFI-LITE flashes, current is getting to the injector and the injector is being pulsed. Follow this procedure from one injector to the next, assuming you have an MPI system (Fig. 4).

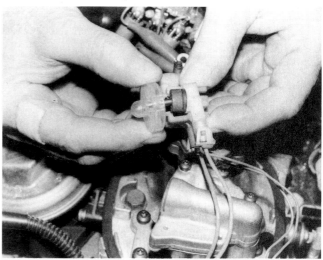

Fig. 3. EFI-LITE diagnostic tool must be the right one for your car. This one is being plugged into the wire connector serving a GM throttle body fuel injector.

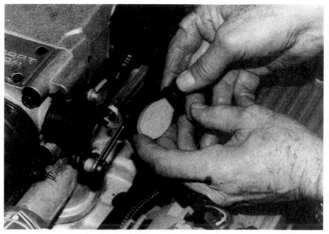

Fig. 4. This EFI-LITE is being used to test for current at the fuel injectors of an *MPI* system.

The gas delivery system

If each injector is getting current, troubleshoot the components that handle the gas. With a TBI system, take off the air cleaner and look to see whether the tip of the fuel injector is visible. If not, perform a fuel-system pressure test.

If the tip of the injector is visible, simply keep your eyes on the tip as a helper behind the wheel turns on the ignition switch without cranking the engine. Do you see an evenly formed spray of gas squirting from the injector? If so, the gas delivery parts of your system are in good shape (Fig. 5).

Important: When checking for the delivery of gas or replacing a malfunctioning gas delivery component, take the following precautions:
- Don't smoke.
- Keep a dry chemical (class B) fire extinguisher where you can grab it quickly if necessary.
- Wipe up any gas spills promptly.

Releasing fuel system pressure

Before doing a fuel-system pressure test, you'll have to release fuel-system pressure on systems where you must disconnect the fuel line to connect the pressure gauge. If your system has a diagnostic valve to which the gauge is connected, however, you can skip that step.

Most MPI systems have a diagnostic valve on the fuel delivery line or *fuel rail*, to which the fuel pressure gauge is connected (Figs. 6 and 7). The valve, which has a cap over it, resembles a tire valve.

If your MPI system doesn't have a diagnostic valve, release pressure and disconnect the fuel-delivery line where it attaches to the fuel rail; then connect the gauge.

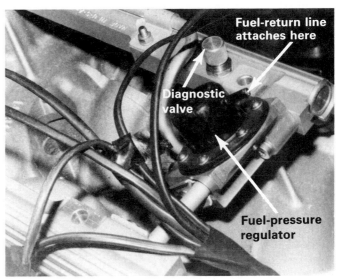

Fig. 6. **Before going a fuel-pressure test,** check if there's a diagnostic valve. If so, attach the fuel pressure gauge to it. There is no need to bleed pressure.

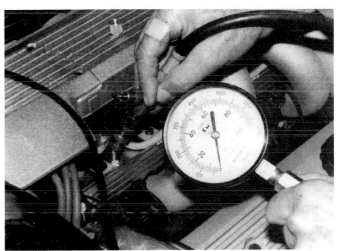

Fig. 7. **Connect the fuel pressure gauge** by removing the cap over the diagnostic value. Be sure to securely tighten the gauge's fitting to the valve.

Ford stands out as the one manufacturer that puts a diagnostic valve on its TBI system. The valve is on top of the throttle body. If there is no diagnostic valve on the throttle body of your TBI system, you have to release pressure and then disconnect the fuel-delivery line at the throttle body so you can connect the gauge (Figs. 8 and 9).

Each make of vehicle requires a different pressure-release procedure. With GM systems, remove the fuel pump fuse from the fuse panel, start the engine, and let it run until it stalls. Then crank the starter another five seconds and reinstall the fuel pump fuse.

With Chrysler systems, examine the area around the fuel tank to find the fuel-pump wire connector. Pull the connector apart. Then, start the engine, let it run until it stalls, and crank the starter another five seconds.

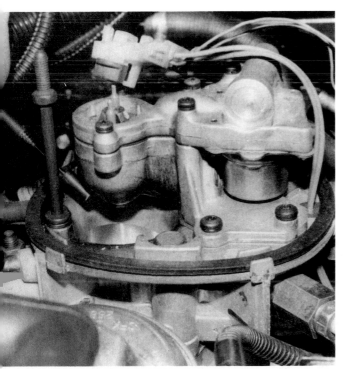

Fig. 5. **Gas spraying from tip of injector** (inside) tells you that the gas-delivery parts of your TBI system are working. Be sure electrical connector is reattached to the top of the fuel injector after using the EFI-LITE.

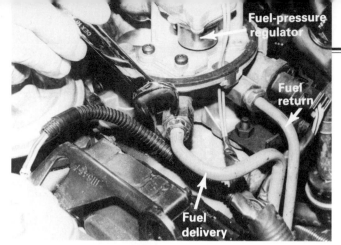

Fig. 8. **Remove the fuel-delivery line** to connect fuel-pressure gauge to a TBI system. *Remember:* The fuel delivery line has a larger diameter then does the fuel-return line.

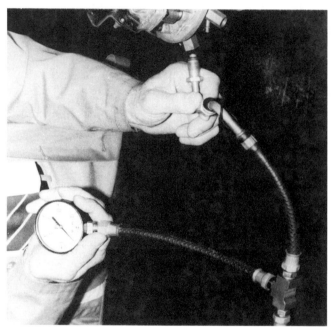

Fig. 9. **Fuel-pressure gauge is connected** to the fuel-delivery line on one end, and to the fuel-inlet port of the throttle body on the other.

Look in the luggage compartments of FoMoCo cars for the fuel pump shut-off (inertia) switch. To deactivate the fuel pump and release fuel pressure, unbolt this switch and turn it upside down. Reattach the switch. Then, start the engine, let it run until it stalls, and crank the engine another five seconds. To reset the switch and reactivate the fuel pump, press the button again. If your switch has two buttons, press both.

Making the fuel-system
Pressure Test

Find out the fuel-pressure specification for your system. It could be as low as 9 or more than 50 psi. The spec is in the shop manual. If you don't have the manual, call the dealer's service department.

Important: The pressure gauge has to record a reading that's at least 10 psi above the specification.

If you have to disconnect the fuel-delivery line at the throttle body to connect the gauge, don't confuse it with the fuel-return line. The fuel-delivery line has a larger diameter. Use two wrenches to loosen the line—one to turn

the fitting and one to hold the coupling nut. Double-wrenching will keep the line from twisting. Connect the gauge between the throttle body and the end of the disconnected fuel-delivery line.

Now as you watch the gauge, have a helper turn on the ignition switch without cranking the engine. Note the reading—you'll get one of four:

1. Normal pressure reading. If a check of air delivery components reveals no malfunction, look to another part of the engine for the cause of the performance problem. A good place to start is with vacuum hoses and components that require vacuum to operate, such as the EGR and PCV valves.

2. Zero pressure reading. The trouble you're having with your engine is that it won't start. More than likely, the electric fuel pump has died or the sock (filter) at the fuel pickup, located inside the tank, is clogged (Fig. 10). You can get an idea if the fuel pump is working by listening at the fuel tank as someone in the car turns on the ignition switch. If you don't hear a whir, the pump's not working. Before dropping the fuel tank and removing the fuel pump/sock assembly, though, determine if there is a fuel-pump relay in the car. It and the wire feeding current to the pump may have gone bad. Also check the fuel-pump fuse.

3. Lower-than-normal pressure reading. This is a fuel-starvation problem, and the two parts usually responsible are the in-line fuel filter and fuel-pressure regulator. But it is also possible that the fuel sock is partially clogged.

Find out by releasing fuel-system pressure and disconnecting the fuel-pressure gauge. Then disconnect the fuel-inlet line at the fuel-tank side of the in-line fuel filter and make another test. Now if pressure isn't to specification, the trouble is inside the fuel tank with the sock. But if normal pressure is recorded, release fuel system pressure, disconnect the gauge, reconnect the fuel line to the in-line fuel filter, then make the test again—this time on the output (engine) side of the fuel filter.

A normal reading now tells you the trouble is either with the fuel-pressure regulator or the fuel-delivery line, which may be kinked. Inspect the line, and if that's okay replace the fuel-pressure regulator. A lower-than-normal reading tabs the in-line fuel filter as the culprit. Replace.

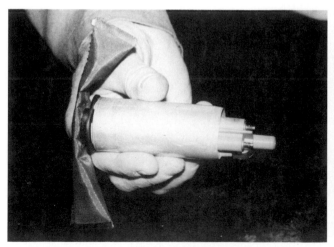

Fig. 10. **Electric fuel-pump with in-tank fuel sock.** When an engine equipped with EFI doesn't start and a fuel pressure gauge shows a reading of zero, suspect electric fuel pump.

4. Higher-than-normal pressure reading. A higher-than-normal fuel pressure reading will cause engine flooding. This doesn't happen often, but when it does there's little doubt as to the reason. Examine the fuel-return line attached to the fuel pressure regulator. It's through this line that gas bleeds back into the fuel tank to allow pressure in the system to be maintained at the normal level. Higher-than-normal pressure means there's a kink in that line somewhere. The blockage is preventing gas from flowing back to the fuel tank, thereby creating high pressure in the system. This, in turn, is causing the engine to flood.

Important: If you must release fuel-system pressure to attach the pressure gauge, remember that after doing the test you must again bleed pressure *before* disconnecting the gauge. You must also release pressure to replace a faulty part.

Air-delivery checks

There are a few performance problems that should make you suspicious of a malfunction with a part of your EFI system that handles the delivery of air. These are hard starting, rough idling, stalling while idling, and a fast idle that doesn't wind down. Fast idling is common when you first start an engine equipped with fuel injection, but that speed is supposed to drop after about 15 seconds.

The one malfunction that disrupts the intake of air most often is a tear in the air-intake duct. A close inspection between the folds of the duct will reveal this (Fig. 11). Also make sure the air duct is connected tightly (Fig. 12).

Don't forget that as with a carburetor, your EFI system has an air cleaning element. If this filter clogs with dirt, air flow is curtailed. The resulting overly rich fuel mixture will continually flood the engine. And that means prolonged cranking to get started, then rough idling and possibly stalling.

The other parts that handle the delivery of air—the idle-speed control device and mass air flow meter—usually cause the engine warning light on the dash to glow and a trouble code to be stored in the computer when they malfunction. When either fails, air flow is usually reduced, which forces the engine to try and run on too much gas.

Note: If the engine warning light comes on, you'll need instructions on how to get the computer into it self-testing mode. You'll also need the trouble code interpretation chart. This material is in the shop manual.

Checking the fuel injectors

Accurately testing the fuel injectors requires expensive equipment, such as the fuel injector balance test kit recommended by GM (Fig. 13). It costs over $150.

Luckily, the greatest cause of fuel injector damage in the early days of EFI systems—contaminating agents in gasoline—has all but been resolved. If you use a nationally advertised gasoline, it probably contains agents to keep fuel injectors clean. But there is no guarantee. Therefore, if you've gotten this far without uncovering the cause of your engine problem, have injectors cleaned by a professional shop if the injectors pass the test I'm about to describe. If they don't pass, have them tested professionally.

Note: This test cannot be done if the ignition coil is an integral part of the distributor as it is in GM models.

Attach the end of a jumper wire to the negative terminal of the ignition coil. Then place the tip of a long-shanked screwdriver on one of the injectors and hold your ear to the handle. Have someone in the car turn on the ignition switch. Now, alternately touch the other end of the jumper wire to a metal component, and then draw it away.

Fig. 11. Inspect the air-intake duct closely for a crack through which air is leaking. Excess air will hurt performance.

Fig. 12. Tighten air-intake duct clamps as needed with a screwdriver.

Fig. 13. Fuel-injector test equipment is easy to use, but expensive. The good news is injectors don't malfunction often.

If you hear clicking from the injector, it suggests that the injector is working. Therefore, the only reason why the injector may be hampering engine performance is that a little dirt is clogging the spray end. Obviously, all injectors used in your EFI system should be tested.

Cleaning the injectors isn't difficult. But the Kent-Moore injector-cleaning tool you'll need to do the job is expensive (about $150), especially considering how infrequently you'll use it. If dirty injectors are the problem, you'll probably come out ahead by bringing the car to your dealer— *by George Sears.*

25 illustrated car care tips

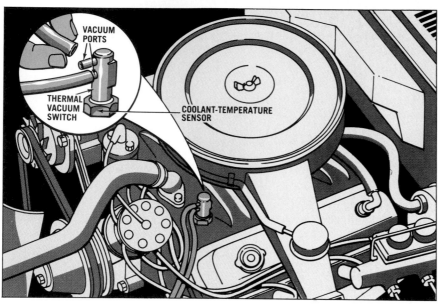

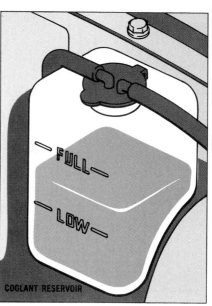

cooked distributor thermo-vacuum switch

Does your engine idle too fast and ping? Is it equipped with a distributor thermo-vacuum switch, or DTVS? Has the engine overheated recently? It's possible that the overheating damaged the switch. The DTVS allows the ignition to go to full advance when an engine overheats. (This has a cooling effect on combustion-chamber temperatures.) But if the overheating is sufficiently severe, the DTVS can be jammed in the full-advance position, causing the previously mentioned engine problems. Refer to the vehicle's repair manual for the specific diagnostic procedure for your DTVS.

ruptured reservoir

Remember to keep the fluid level up in the coolant system's plastic coolant-recovery reservoir. But when you refill, use only a 50/50 mixture of anti-freeze and water. A winter refill with just water could result in a ruptured reservoir—if outside temperatures drop sufficiently low.

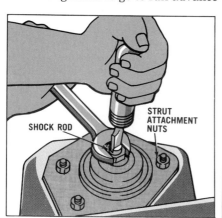

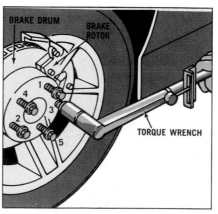

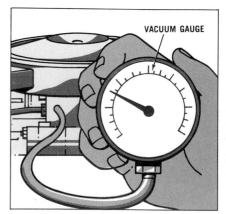

strut stuff

When a MacPherson-strut-equipped car hits a curb or nails a deep pothole, a bent strut is likely. To check for strut straightness, loosen the strut nut in the center of the shock tower. Then rotate the strut rod 360 degrees. If the top of the tire moves in and out, the rod is damaged, and the strut cartridge must be replaced.

wheel-nut warning

When tightening lug nuts, do not use an impact gun or long-handle wrench. Use a torque wrench in a crisscross pattern. Overtightening or uneven tightening can warp the brake rotors and drums. This will cause the brake pedal to pulse gently against your foot. The cure is new brake rotors and drums, or possibly resurfacing.

gauging performance

A vacuum gauge is inexpensive and easy to install. Besides the obvious benefit of tattling on vacuum leaks, the handy instrument can warn you of a clogged or collapsed catalytic converter. A gradual needle drop may indicate a progressively worsening exhaust restriction that could put your car on the road's shoulder.

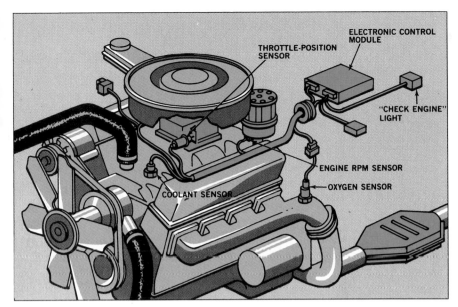

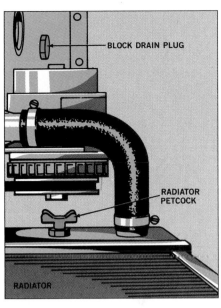

confused computer control module

Intermittent flashing of the on-board computer warning light can be caused by improper routing of the computer's wiring harness. A computer wire located too close to a high-voltage or high-current cable can pick up erroneous signals. These false signals can even cause stalling and stumbling. If a computer wire runs parallel to coil wires, spark-plug wires, starter cables, or battery cables, position it at least 5 inches from these interference emitters. Computer wiring that must cross such high-current cables should do so at a right angle to reduce the possibility of interference.

flush facts

When flushing a cooling system, check the engine block for a coolant drain plug (A V-type engine might have a drain plug for each bank.) Make sure the block plugs and radiator petcock are open to ensure complete drainage. Note: Apply sealant to the plug before reinstallation.

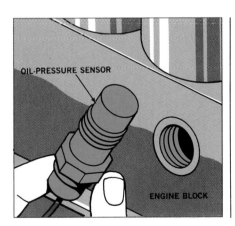

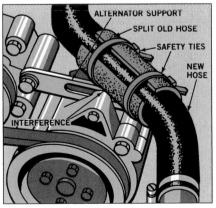

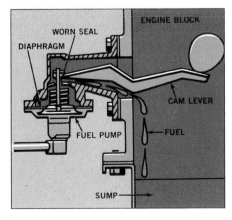

sensor savvy

Some types of engine and transmission sensors use a single wire. When installing such an oil-pressure or coolant-temperature sensor, do not use flourocarbon-resin tape to seal the sensor's threads. The tape will insulate the sensor from the grounded transmission housing or engine block, and the sensor's gauge won't operate.

hose sleeve

You can extend the life of a new radiator or heater hose by examining the old hose for interference wear due to rubbing. If the interference can't be eliminated, protect the new hose with a section cut from the old hose. Split the section of old hose and slip it over the new hose. Then secure the hose sleeve with safety ties.

leaky fuel pump

If you've checked the crankcase oil level in your car and the mark has moved *up* on the dipstick, chances are the additional fluid is gasoline, not oil. Some crankcase-mounted fuel pumps can dump gasoline into the sump when the diaphragm inside the pump deteriorates. Change the defective pump, the oil, and the oil filter.

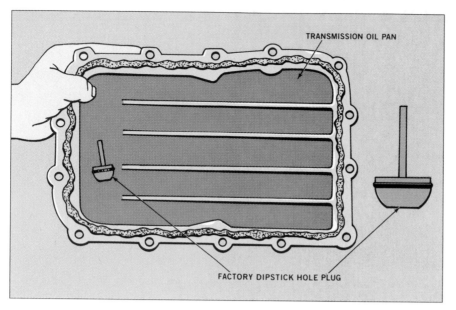

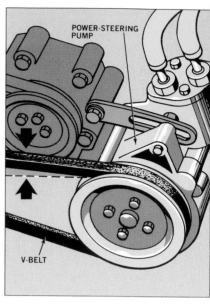

mystery plug

If you're a careful car owner, you may eventually find yourself changing automatic transmission fluid (ATF). During an ATF change, some conscientious mechanics have been puzzled—and possibly upset—by a small important-looking component lying loose in the bottom of the transmis- sion pan. But if you find one of these man-made mushrooms with an O- ring, don't be concerned. It's simply a safety plug used to keep foreign mat- ter out of the transmission during manufacture. During the installation of the dipstick tube, the plug is simply pushed down into the transmission body.

steering stutter

If your vehicle's power stutters (alter- nately losing and gaining power) as you negotiate a turn, check for a loose or worn V-belt. The erratic perfor- mance of the steering is caused by the intermittent loss and resumption of hydraulic assistance from the sys- tem's belt-driven pump.

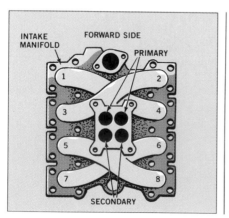

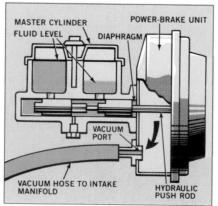

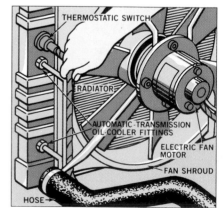

carburetor clues

Most V8 intake manifolds are de- signed so that opposite bores in the carburetor feed alternate cylinders in the firing order. For example, when the firing order is 1-8-4-3-6-5-7-2, the left bore feeds cylinders 1-7-4-6; the right bore feeds 8-3-5-2. This infor- mation can be handy when you're troubleshooting carburetor gremlins.

disappearing brake fluid

Is brake fluid vanishing from your car's master-cylinder reservoir but you have no leaks in the car or traces on the driveway? Are gray-white clouds of smoke spewing out of the tailpipe during hard stops or sharp turns? A master-cylinder seal has probably given up and is allowing fluid to be sucked into the engine.

fan fare

If an engine is obviously overheating and the electric radiator fan is not spinning, check the connection at the radiator's thermostatic fan switch. If the fan operates when you jiggle the connector, the connector or switch ter- minals are loose or corroded. After the engine has cooled down sufficiently, make the simple repair.

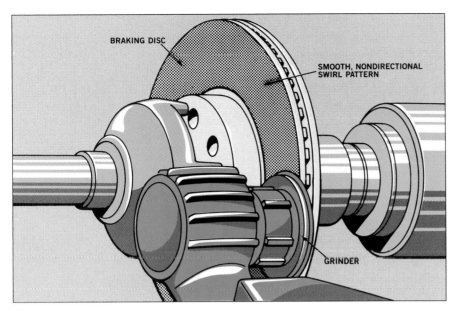

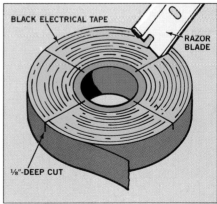

finishing touch for your brakes

Do you hear a clicking or tapping noise coming from the front disc brakes when you brake to a stop? Have your brake rotors been recently resurfaced? If so, the problem may be that a final brake-refinishing procedure was omitted. When a service technician resurfaces a rotor on a brake lathe, the cutting-tool bits leave a spiral finish on the rotor similar to that of a phonograph record. If this directional, grooved finish isn't polished off with a special rotary grinder, the brake pads will follow the track when the brakes are applied and will strike loudly against the caliper assembly.

lead lookout

If you suspect your car has been mistakenly fueled with leaded gasoline, there's a preliminary visual check. After a cruise, examine the opening inside the tailpipe. If the residue inside is gray, it's a strong indication your engine is burning leaded fuel. Unleaded leaves a tan coating.

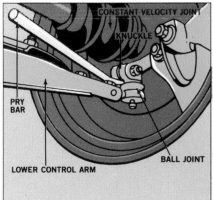

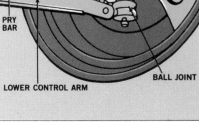

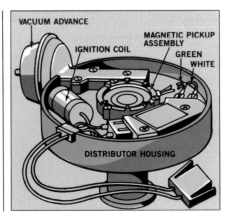

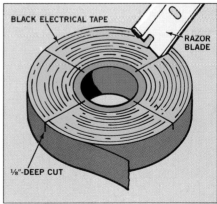

ball-joint check

To check for lower ball-joint wear on a front-drive vehicle with MacPherson struts, do the following. Jack and support the vehicle by its frame, with weight off the wheels. Position a pry bar between the lower control arm and knuckle. Push down on the bar, then release the tension. If there's movement, check the service limit.

sparkless ignition

If a General Motors High Energy Ignition refuses to spark the plugs, the first items to check are the white and green wires of the magnetic pickup assembly. Are they intact, and are their electrical connections clean and tight? The pickup coil is in the distributor housing under the ignition coil, distributor cap, and rotor.

tape tip

Plastic electrician's tape is great for patching worn auto electrical systems. But tearing a piece the proper length from a loose roll of tape can be a hassle. To eliminate sticky situations, try cutting four equally spaced $1/8$-inch-deep grooves in the roll's face with a single-edge razor blade. Pieces will tear off evenly and easily.

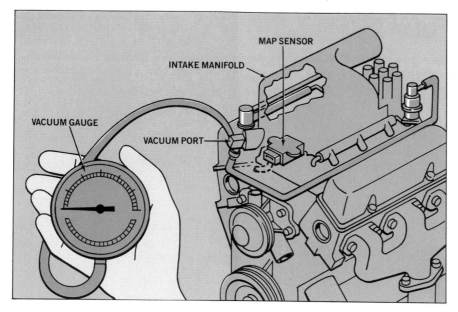

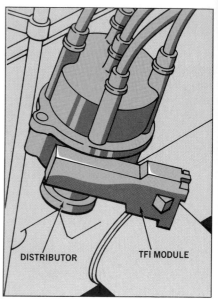

of manifold importance: MAP

One of the important new electronic-fuel-injection, or EFI, components is the manifold absolute-pressure (MAP) sensor. It samples intake-manifold vacuum for the on-board computer. If your EFI-equipped vehicle is using extra fuel and is down on power, the MAP sensor may not be reading true manifold vacuum. To check vacuum, remove the sensor's line and install a vacuum gauge. At start-up the engine should immediately jump the gauge needle to about 18 inches. If the needle is sluggish or shows low vacuum, the manifold line is plugged or an engine problem is affecting vacuum.

handle not

On late-model Ford distributors, don't use the thick-film ignition (TFI) module as a handle when adjusting the timing or removing the distributor. The module's plastic housing can easily separate from its metal base, causing a no-start or tough-to-trace intermittent stalling problems.

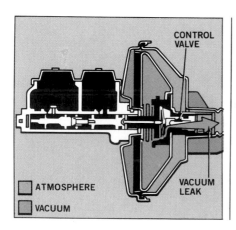

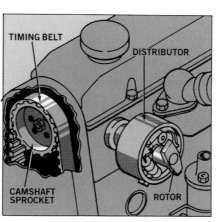

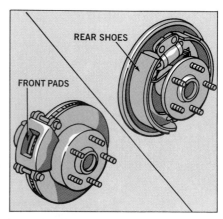

idle concerns

Does your car idle roughly at stoplights? Have you noticed that it only happens when the brake pedal is depressed? If so, you've probably got a vacuum leak at the floating control valve in your master cylinder. This can be tough to spot because engine checks aren't usually performed with an operator's foot on the brake.

timing-belt tip

Many four-cylinder engines use a timing belt between the camshaft and crankshaft gears. And unfortunately, broken belts are often misdiagnosed as bad ignition modules. To check the belt, remove the distributor cap and see whether the rotor spins when the engine is turned over. (The distributor is driven off the camshaft's end.)

shoe shuffle

When replacing worn front-brake pads, be sure to replace the rear shoes also—even if they don't appear worn out. Much of their gripping power has been diminished by time and heat. If you leave the old shoes in place, their lack of stopping muscle will accelerate front-pad wear and lengthen stopping distances—*by Steve Mercaldo.*

keeping nuts tight

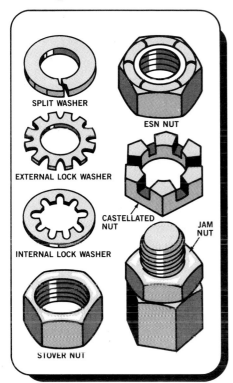

SPLIT WASHER

ESN NUT

EXTERNAL LOCK WASHER

CASTELLATED NUT

JAM NUT

INTERNAL LOCK WASHER

STOVER NUT

Few people would argue that a loose or lost nut can be a nuisance. But wiser and sadder are mechanics who have experienced a loosened fastener that caused expensive damage to moving parts—or even grave personal injury.

The best way to be wiser without being sadder is to make sure nuts are tightly and correctly fastened. But before discussing stay-tight methods, a word about tightening: Always tighten automotive fasteners with a torque wrench. And, if possible, refer to the index in a service manual for the correct tightening torque.

One of the easiest methods to ensure continued tightness is to apply either silicone rubber or a chemical locknut directly on the bolt threads. Sold under a variety of brand names, room-temperature vulcanizing (RTV) rubber in a tube—or any bathtub sealer or caulking compound—will provide a tenacious grip on bolt or stud threads. The other thread-coating method is the application of a squeeze-bottle compound that creates a chemical bond between the nut and bolt or stud. Labels on brands like

Loctite generally recommend the use of a cleaner-catalyst before applying the bonding agent. These chemical locknut products usually come in various grades of strength or removal resistance, with the strongest usually requiring fastener destruction for removal from the bolt or stud.

Another method of tightening nuts involves a variety of mechanical devices. These include locking washers, jam nuts, and self-locking nuts. Lock washers come in dozens of designs. One of the most common types is the split washer—a heavy washer with a single diagonal cut. A second type of lock washer comes in two types: internal and external. The internal type has serrations along the inside diameter of the washer. The external type has spoke-like serrations along the outside edge.

A jam nut, or locknut, is simply a second nut screwed down tightly against the face of the first nut. Jam nuts are most frequently used against tall nuts called high nuts. High nuts are designed for use with high-strength SAE grade-eight bolts—which are inclined to strip the threads out of shorter ordinary nuts when fully tightened to their higher pound-foot specifications.

There are three common types of self-locking nuts: castellated, elastic stop nut (ESN), and stover. Castellated nuts are used where loose, exact adjustment is necessary. In use, a hole is drilled through the bolt or stud. The nut is adjusted, then a cotter pin is slipped through the castle-like openings in the nut's face and the holes in the shaft. An ESN nut uses the resistance between a nylon bushing inside the top of the nut and metal threads to lock the nut in place. The stover nut has an egg-shaped collar on its top face that resists turning by the friction required to force it to conform to the round bolt.

In an emergency, locking devices can be improvised. Here are three favorites:

One old-timer's method of bonding a nut and stud together is to use a few drops of battery acid judiciously applied before tightening. Naturally, use extreme caution and wear protective eye wear and gloves when

handling these highly caustic chemicals—and be forewarned that the nut will probably have to be removed with a cold chisel or cutting torch.

Cutting a small notch into the stud threads with a cold chisel is another effective way to secure a nut. Again, because of the destructive nature of this stay-tight fastening method, it can only be recommended for on-the-road emergency situations.

The final emergency fastening method uses a field-improvised locknut. To improvise: Use a hacksaw to saw halfway through the nut. (A fine-toothed saw blade will reduce burrs. If possible, run a tap through the nut after cutting.) Then close the kerf with several sharp hammer blows. Install the nut on the stud. The nut's slightly distorted shape will be forced back to its original dimension, and the spring action will hold the fastener tightly in place—*by Doug Richmond.*

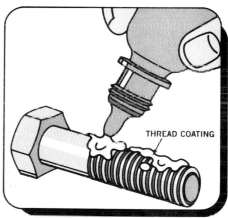

THREAD COATING

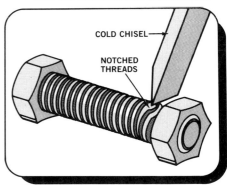

COLD CHISEL

NOTCHED THREADS

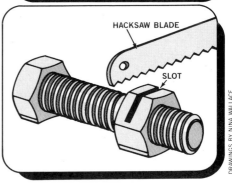

HACKSAW BLADE

SLOT

DRAWINGS BY NINA WALLACE

10 picks of the pros

Do you have pet tools that are a bit out of the ordinary? That's what we asked five of our tool-savvy contributors. They did indeed. All of them prepared lengthy lists, from which we winnowed ten choices.

Our participants are Richard Day, a Southern Californian who specializes in plumbing and concrete work; R. J. De Cristoforo, a Northern Californian whose tool-techniques articles, books, and videos are famous in the field; A. J. Hand, who has extensively enlarged his house in Connecticut; Thomas Jones, a Pennsylvania furniture maker and tool expert; and Iowan Phil McCafferty, a workshop professional whose masterwork may be the "Ultimate Workbench" featured in the 1988 Yearbook.

A. J. Hand

Ryobi half-inch plunge router simplifies starting a cut in the middle of the stock—lets you use guide bushings for pattern routing.

Half-inch plunge router

Although I've had this tool for only a little over a year, it has already become a solid cog in the workings of my shop. Mounted upside down under my tablesaw extension, it can turn out joinery, cabinet doors, and fancy millwork that were once possible only with an expensive and bulky shaper.

Removed from the table, it is like any other router, but its plunge capabilities make it more convenient and versatile. How? Two quick examples: 1) It simplifies starting a cut in the middle of your stock because you can place the base firmly on your work first, then plunge the bit downward to start cutting. This is much easier and safer than lowering the whole tool under power. 2) Plunge capability makes it possible to use guide bushings and templates for pattern routing, or for cutting mortises. (I constructed a simple jig for this.)

There are quite a few good half-inch plunge routers around, but the Ryobi has the most convenient controls—and the best price—I've found.

Thickness planer

The thickness planer is one of those tools you probably consider a luxury. But once you own one, you'll never want to do without it. I discovered this about five years ago when I got my first planer from Shopsmith.

A planer is so quick and easy to use that I find myself running nearly every board I buy through it. Just a whisker-thin pass will remove the washboard surface left by commercial planers, plus dirt, stains, grade marks, and other minor blemishes. That pass also assures me that all my stock is uniform (lumber commonly varies in thickness by as much as $1/16$ inch), so my joinery is neater and stronger.

The planer lets me buy rough-cut hardwoods at about the same prices I used to pay for pine, so I now do more work in cherry, maple, oak, and walnut. If I need some stock made thinner than the usual $3/4$ inch, I can produce it in minutes. I can also resaw stock, plane it smooth, and produce beautiful matched panels.

I still have my Shopsmith planer and would recommend it to anyone. But after trying the little Ryobi 10-incher, I think it's a logical choice for most home shops. It is light and compact, does an excellent job, and sells for about half what you'd pay for a bigger machine. Its 10-by-5-inch maximum capacity is a couple of inches less than you'll get from more expensive machines, but it's adequate for most home-shop needs.

Phil McCafferty

Foot-inch-fraction calculator

For years I used one of those shortcut methods they teach you in school for adding and subtracting fractions. Then I started converting fractions to decimals and using a calculator. That was pretty easy because I memorized the decimal equivalents. But it was slow.

Now I have a calculator that lets me tap in the feet, inches, and fractions just as I measure them. It's called the Measure Master-Plus fraction calculator, and frankly, I'd be lost without it.

It instantly adds, subtracts, multiplies, and divides feet, inches, and fractions of an inch down to 64ths, in any mix. And it functions as a regular calculator with memory, so I don't need a separate machine for standard math. For good measure, it also converts any displayed measurement from foot-inch fractions to decimal feet, inches, yards, or meters—even square and cubic measurements. It instantly calculates area and volume from any of those formats, and solves right-triangle calculations. This 3½-ounce wonder rides in my pocket much of the time.

Measure-Master Plus fraction calculator takes the error—and guesswork—out of figuring area, volume, and other woodworking calculations.

Safe-t-planer

I confess to owning not one but two Wagner Safe-T-Planers. One fits on the arbor of my radial-arm saw; the other has a shank that chucks into my drill press. These are precisely machined aluminum-bodied tools about 3 inches in diameter; they have three nearly hidden hook-shaped high-speed steel cutters that will almost effortlessly plane away wood.

I also confess to being lazy. And for a short run (planing, rabbeting, tenoning, panel raising, or making molding), in many cases I find it easier and faster to pop one of the Wagners onto the saw or drill press than to set up a planer, dado head, shaper, or some other tool.

If you don't have those latter tools, the Safe-T-Planer makes even more sense. By using one with the head flat I can surface-plane. Cutting with the edge gives me square-cornered rabbets and tenons. By tilting the head I can make moldings, raised panel, bevels, tapers, and decorative cuts. By planing a tad here and there, a Safe-T-Planer is unmatched for truing up cupped or twisted boards.

The tool is particularly good for working on short or thin pieces that might be difficult or unsafe to cut on a conventional power tool. Because of the way the Safe-T-Planer is designed, it is almost impossible, when it's used properly, for this accessory to grab workpieces or kick back.

Electronic Radial

R.J. De Cristoforo

Powered hand plane

I use a powered hand plane for many routine, and some not-so-routine, woodworking chores. Example: The time I had to reduce the width of a number of 12-foot-long 2 × 4s. Ever try to plane the edges of 12-foot-long stock on a jointer?

Then there was the time I had to fit a half-dozen doors. The powered hand plane is great for trimming any large workpiece.

It is on my list of favorite tools not because it removes a lot of material in a single pass, but because it can be used with the delicacy required when only a smidgen is to be removed from the edges or ends of lumber, or from projects that are already assembled.

Working on hard or soft wood, panel material, or particleboard, only the expert craftsman with a conventional hard plane can rival the results I get with my Sears Craftsman $3/4$-hp, $3 5/8$-inch powered plane. and he has to work a lot harder.

Cordless screwdriver

It isn't difficult to appreciate the advantage of driving and removing screws with power. All it takes is to have done those chores thousands of times with your fist gripped around a manual screwdriver. And with a *cordless* power screwdriver I have the speed and convenience of power on a roof or ladder, or in a crawl space, without yards of extension cord.

Some cordless drivers have an adjustable clutch, so that heavy or light screws can be driven to precise depths without fear of damaging work surfaces. That's a useful feature. But even the inexpensive drivers without fancy features can be excellent tools.

The little Skil Twist, for example, looks and acts much like a conventional screwdriver—but with the speed and ease power buys. When I first saw it, I sneered: How could an itty-bitty battery-powered tool drive screws? (I remembered a battery-powered drill of a few years back that couldn't drive a quarter-inch bit into cream cheese.)

I was wrong about the Twist, and now there's no going back.

Richard Day

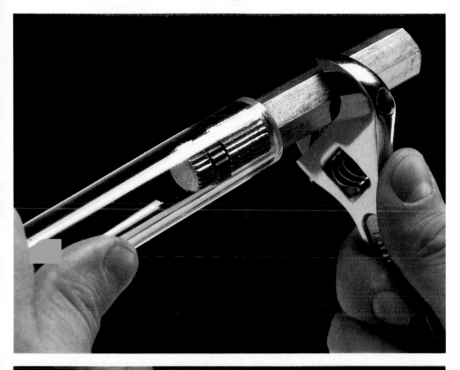

Inside pipe wrench

What do I do when a pipe breaks off inside a fitting, leaving a stub that's too short to grab with a pipe wrench? I reach for my inside pipe wrench.

What's an inside pipe wrench? Its only moving part is a toothed eccentric cam that nests in a slot in one end. To use the wrench, you insert that end into the broken-off pipe. As you turn the inside pipe wrench (use an adjustable open-end wrench), its little cam swings out and jams against the inside of the pipe. (For the photograph, the pipe is acrylic so you can see inside it.) Without much fuss you can thus remove a broken-off pipe.

You need one inside pipe wrench for each pipe size. Mine's a half-incher—probably the most generally useful size. I've had it for about 20 years. I don't use it often, but when I need it, nothing else will do.

Magnesium float

If you're casting a concrete patio, sidewalk, or driveway, you'll find a magnesium float makes working with air-entrained concrete easier and quicker.

The Portland Cement Association calls for using air entrained concrete for all outdoor projects in climates where freezing and thawing occur, and strongly recommends it for other climes as well. This concrete contains an agent that makes billions of microscopic bubbles. When the mix hardens, these bubbles provide space into which freezing water can expand.

But the bubbles also increase surface drag, so working air-entrained concrete with a wood float tends to tear the surface, leaving a finish that is too rough for good cleaning. So you have to follow with a steel troweling.

A magnesium float, however, glides over the surface, producing a neat, non-skid finish that is ideal for outside surfaces—as is. You can skip the tedious troweling step.

SOURCES OF THE PROS' PICKS
Cordless screwdriver: Skil Corporation, 4801 W. Peterson Avenue, Chicago IL 60646; **Fraction calculator**: Calculated Industries, 22720 Savi Ranch Parkway, Yorba Linda CA 92686; **Half-inch plunge router**: Ryobi America Corporation, 1158 Tower Lane, Bensenville IL 60106; **Inside pipe wrench**: Chicago Specialty, 750 Northgate Parkway, Wheeling IL 60090; **Magnesium float**: Goldblatt Tool Company, Box 2334, Kansas City KS 66110; **Powered hand plane**: Sears, Roebuck and Company, Sears Tower, Chicago IL 60684; **Safe-T-Planer (Wagner)**: Gilmore Pattern Works, Box 50034, Tulsa OK 74150; **Scroll saw**: Delta Intl. Machinery Corp., 246 Alpha Drive, Pittsburgh PA 15238; **Tenoner accessory**: Delta Intl. (address above); **Thickness planer**: Ryobi America (address above).

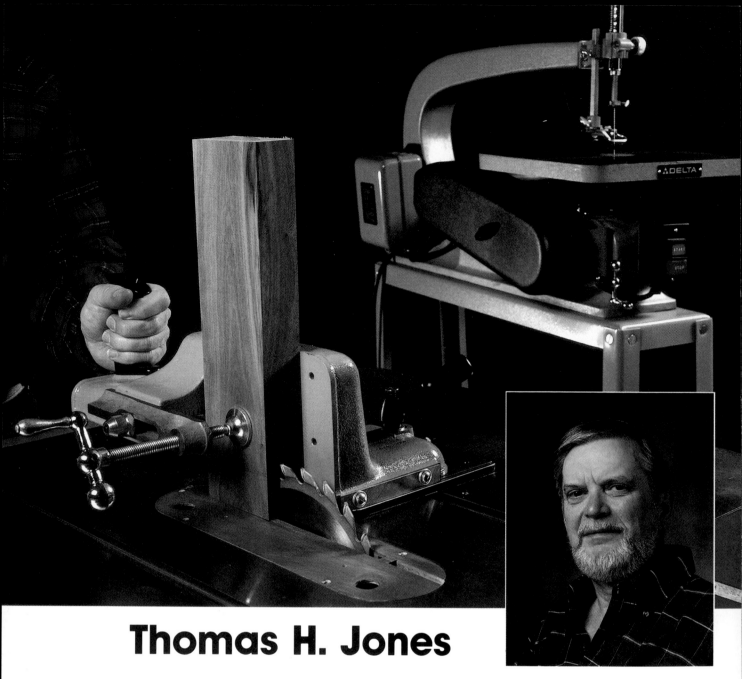

Thomas H. Jones

Scroll saw

If I had to be limited to one—and only one—power saw in my shop, it would have to be a scroll saw. Of course, I would hope to have a router too, and a bench-mounted belt or disk sander. With that combination, I can and have built furniture (including a Hepplewhite rolltop desk). And years ago, with only a scroll saw, I cut the two-bys and plywood for a house addition.

The going would have been a lot faster with a table or circular saw, but the scroll saw is tops when it comes to versatility. Its blades can follow curved and squiggly lines through tighter curves than a band saw's. It can do all the intricate sawing you would like to do with a saber saw but can't.

With the proper blade and at the correct speed you can saw through any cuttable material: mild steel, brass, aluminum, plastic, veneer, ivory, even seashells. A scroll saw will accurately cut out small sheet-metal parts without leaving tin-snip edges.

When it gets down to a particular scroll saw, I like the Delta 40-406. It has a 24-inch capacity, variable speed, and two-way table tilt. For fast work, it can be run as a saber saw; detach the overarm, and the workpiece capacity is limited only by what you can handle in your shop.

Tenoner accessory

A tenoner accessory for a table saw, on the other hand, is not at all versatile. It does only one thing: It holds a stick firmly while you saw the cheeks of a tenon or cut an open mortise in the end.

These can be touch-and-go operations on a table saw without a tenoner. Safety is a problem because you have to operate the saw without the blade guard. And the hazard is made worse by the awkwardness of holding the wood vertically to run it through the blade.

You can build your own tenoner of wood (I have made several), but a good, solid tenoner guided by the saw's miter-gauge slot lets you push wood through the blade for accurate, repeatable cutting, with the work held solidly and your hands well away from the blade.

The massive 27-pound weight of Delta's 34-172 tenoner makes it rock-solid on the saw table. It is my favorite. With two blades and spacer collars, I can do both cheeks of a tenon with one pass.

3 for your shop

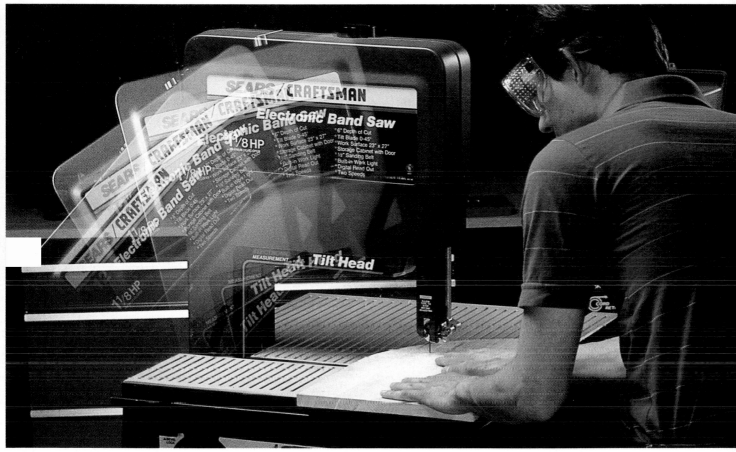

Tilting head of the new Sears band saw is controlled by a rack-and-pinion drive. You turn a knob to pivot the head.

c ouble-jointed 10-incher

PHOTO BY GREG SHARKO

When I last reported on power miter saws, I found only two that could cut compound miters. Both were light-duty models with 8¼-inch blades.

Now Sears offers a serious 10-inch miter saw that can make compound cuts. A drum-shaped pivot joint between the table and arm allows the blade to be swung from vertical to 45 degrees, so you can cut accurate bevels.

A compound-miter saw is extremely useful for making shadow boxes, tapered stands or boxes, and when cutting crown moldings. I found that the power of this one, the smoothness of cut—and even the accuracy—are excellent. That pivot joint does not compromise the rigidity of the saw. Nice feature: A clever mechanism lifts the clear-plastic blade guard as the arm is lowered.

The Sears Craftsman model 23461 compound-miter saw weighs 64 pounds and sells for about $220.

tilting band saw

The newest band saw from Sears, Roebuck and Company has an electronic readout, a 12-inch throat, a 6-inch depth of cut, a storage-cabinet base, and a 23-by-27-inch table. That list of features could make it irresistible to any workshopper.

But the best feature of this new saw is the way it handles bevel cuts: The head tilts—up to 45 degrees—while the table stays put. With other band saws I've done some messy bevels because I could not hold the workpiece on a small tilted table. With this one's large table, which remains flat, I found it amazingly easy to control bevel cuts, even on fairly heavy stock.

A rack-and-pinion drive tilts the head as you turn a knob. The saw's electronic readout (accurate to $1/2$ degree, I found) displays the angle. The electronic readout also displays the blade's tension and speed. You adjust tension by setting the readout to the width of the blade you are using. With tension properly locked in, you avoid a too-taut blade—which can break—and a too-loose blade—which tends to twist out of the line of cut.

Blade speed may be the least important readout because the saw has two fixed speeds, 3,000 and 1,500 feet per minute. Nevertheless it is useful because it reports a *drop* in speed—your warning that the blade is dull or you are feeding too fast, or both.

Disadvantages? I found it a little hard to get at the belt to change speeds. But overall this innovative saw is a quiet, as well as smooth-running, performer.

The Craftsman electronic band saw (model 24741) has a $5/8$-hp motor, uses 80-inch blades from $1/8$ to $1/2$ inch wide, has a built-in work light and sawdust ejector, and sells for about $440. The same tilt-head feature is available for $290 on a nonelectronic single-speed saw (model 24721).

wire-feed welder

Welding wire is pulled off spool by a drive roller powered by a variable-speed motor (not drawn). Trigger near nozzle feeds out wire.

DRAWING BY MARIO FERRO

I am not a first-class welder, but a novel arc welder, also from Sears, has made me a whole lot better.

Instead of welding rods—metal electrode sticks coated with flux—this machine uses flux-core wire that is fed off a spool inside the welder.

Wire-feed welders have been around for several years. But the other homeshop models I've seen use solid wire along with "shielding" gas (pressurized argon or carbon dioxide), which serves the same purpose as flux: It hinders the formation of oxides so that the metals will bond. With the Sears unit, you avoid the expense and care required when using shielding gas.

I found I could neatly weld sheet metal from 18-gauge up to $3/16$-inch steel plate in one pass. Welding $1/4$-inch metal required beveling and multiple passes. I made respectable vertical welds—which I could never do with a stick welder. The instructions say the arc welder will make overhead welds, the toughest kind. I'm working on that.

The welder weighs only 66 pounds. It runs on 120 volts and draws 18 amps; output is 18 volts and 75 amps. Sears sells the model 20100 welder (with helmet) for about $350—*by Phil McCafferty. Photos by Greg Sharko. Drawing by Mario Ferro.*

tapeless measures

Eight feet three inches," the precise female voice announces from a little plastic box about the size of a chalkboard eraser. In case I didn't catch it, she repeats it, and then tells me that the room temperature is 72° F. A few more measurements and I've completely sized my living room. Time spent: a few seconds.

ETEC's Ultra Measure is one of nine ultrasonic measuring devices I tested—and the only one that talks. The others show dimensions digitally on liquid-crystal displays. These portable battery-operated devices size up a room in seconds for calculating paint, carpeting, wall-paper, paneling, and flooring requirements. Some of them automatically give new readings as you move, so they are handy for visualizing changes: "An eighteen-foot addition would come out to here," you can quickly learn while walking backward from your existing wall. When it comes to stairwells, high ceilings, and the like, these electronic gadgets will measure where using a tape would be unsafe, time consuming, or nearly impossible.

But electronic tape measures will not replace the standard steel type. They are not precise enough for some purposes, and steel

Electronic tape measures vary in price and features. Some of the instruments are strictly linear measures. Others allow you to enter two measurements and calculate area. Some will directly calculate volume and even store the answer for future totaling. Others have a regular calculator built in. Units with this added calculator tend to cost more, as do those that read out to less than an inch and those that have longer ranges.

The average electronic tape measure has a range of about 2 to 35 feet, rounds to the

nearest inch, and is supposed to be about 99.5 percent accurate. I calculate that to be plus or minus $1^5/_6$ inches at 30 feet. As noted in the table, some round to $^1/_4$ inch. Sonin Inc. makes two long-distance models: One measures up to 150 feet and the other to 250 feet. These models have longer ranges because they are supplied with a separate electronic target. The measuring instrument sends infrared light to the target, actuating its ultrasonic transmitter. These incoming sound waves are received by the measuring instrument and then computed and displayed within seconds.

Before testing the electronic tape measures I was skeptical about their performance. I took care to test all the units under the same conditions: Time of day, room temperature, and air stillness were all controlled. I clamped the units onto a table to ensure that they were pointed perpendicularly to the wall in both planes and tested them at distances of precisely 5, 10, 15, 20, and 30 feet. I repeated the readings five times each to make sure they were consistent.

The measuring unit for the Sonin 150- (above) and 250-foot models sends an infrared signal to an electronic target (next page), actuating its ultrasonic transmitter. The measuring unit receives the sound waves and calculates distance.

tapes can sometimes be more versatile.

The electronic measures work like some autofocus cameras: They transmit an ultrasonic signal, which bounces off the target object and reflects back. An integral electronic stopwatch measures the time it takes for the signal to return, converts that to distance, and almost instantaneously displays the distance.

Although we list 11 models here and checked out nine of these smart instruments, new brands and models with more features can be expected.

To my surprise, under those conditions not one of the units was off by more than one inch at any of the distances, and typically those designed to read out to a fraction of an inch gave readings accurate to less than an inch. All were accurate within the makers' promises.

I then proceeded to test the longer-range devices: the Sonin 150 and 250. Before I could test these units I had to use a standard steel tape to mea-

sure out the test distances: 100, 150, 200, and 250 feet. To get truly accurate readings I had to take care that the tape was not too slack or too taut before each measurement. In addition, I had to calculate a temperature adjustment for the tape. Just handling such a length was unwieldy.

In contrast to all that preparation with the steel tape, each measurement with the electronic devices only took a second or two. And the accuracy was impressive: For example, at 100 feet the measurement was 1/2 inch off; at 150 feet it was perfect; and at 250 feet, 1 1/2 inches off. In eight trials there were no variations more than three inches and most were under two inches. All were well within the promised 99.85 percent accuracy, which works out to 1 5/6 inches at 100 feet and 4 1/2 inches at 250 feet.

Indeed, for measuring longer distances the electronic devices could be more accurate than standard tape measures because they do not have the inherent inaccuracies of tape ex-

pansion and contraction—or tape stretch and slack.

But under less-controlled conditions, I discovered that you can get some bizarre readings with the electronic tape measures. Here are some tips for getting accurate readings:

When out of range or

confused, the devices display an error code. The voice on the Ultra Measure tells you to "try again." When there is a small object in front of a larger one, you may get two different and/or incorrect readings as the device tries to make a decision between them.

Soft surfaces such as drapes and some acoustical-tile ceilings may soak

Display on Exact Technologies' Mach 5 (front) is typical, giving feet, inches, and decimal inches; most convert to metric on demand. Clockwise from front: ETEC's talking Ultra Measure also tells you room temperature; EMS model includes a programmable calculator that handles trigonometry; the Estimator 39-035 from Stanley measures continuously as you move; while the Digitape from Houseworks gets a low-cost award.

up the sound and reflect too little for the device to register. Turbulence can disturb the sound pattern and affect accuracy. Thus you should avoid taking measurements in turbulent air zones around heating and air-conditioning outlets.

Weather also can contribute to inaccurate readings. Barometric pressure and humidity affect the speed of sound transmission, and temperature extremes can affect accuracy. This could hamper outdoor measurements on cold days. Check the particular model for instructions about allowing the instrument time to adjust to new temperatures. Adjustment times range from 2 to 15 minutes.

You can get an incorrect reading if you are at much of an angle to the target surface, so make sure the device is as level as possible. Likewise, you will get a bad reading if the beam is pointed into a corner. The instruments include their own depth in the measurement and have flat backs or bases. Thus you can hold them against a wall or other perpendicular surface so that the sound waves will hit the target surface squarely.

Clearing a path

A final consideration is that the conical sound beam leaves the instrument at up to a 15-degree angle and the cone widens as it travels across a room. Make sure the beam follows as uncluttered a path as possible. If there are objects in the center of a room, two readings can be taken and added—each from the center of the room to the opposite wall. If there is a large object, say a cabinet, near a wall, and you need to know the wall-to-wall dimension, shoot to or from the cabinet, measure the depth of the cabinet with a conventional tape, and add it to the dimension you got electronically. For this type job, electronic and steel tape measures are good companions.

For occasional use, any of the simpler units should work well; for measurements beyond their range, simply measure each way from the center of a room and add them together. But for more serious use involving longer distances, you might choose the Sonin 150-foot or 250-foot model. The electronic target units have a 1/4-inch 20-thread bushing on the bottom for tripod mounting. So measuring can be a one-person operation.

In the end, these tape measures are truly convenient. Realtors and contractors use them to quickly check room sizes, calculate wiring and plumbing runs, and determine volumes for heating and air conditioning. You'd probably find one handy when buying home furnishings, or when building or remodeling.

The truth is, I have the uncomfortable feeling that these smug little boxes may be more accurate than I am with a tape. Certainly they are a lot faster—*by Phil McCafferty. Photos by Greg Sharko. Drawings by Eliot Bergman.*

Comparing the tapeless measures

Company	Brand, model	Sugg. retail price	Range (ft.)	Oper. temp. (range °F)	Size (in.)	Wt. (oz.)	Battery	Display	Rounds to nearest	Stated accuracy (%)	Features
EMS 295 Lake Shore Dr. Pleasantville NY 10570	EMS FT 4100	$280	4–100	50–86	6.5 × 6.0 × 1.5	8	9V	LCD	1/10 ft.	99.5	Carrying case; built-in Texas Instruments TI66 programmable calculator; feet-meters switchable
ETEC 3208 Commander Dr. Carrollton TX 75006	ETEC Measure Mate Model-E	88	2–35	40–105	4.4 × 2.6 × 1.3	6	9V alk.	LCD	1/10 ft.	99.5 +	Pouch; reports temperature and continuous distance; metric model available; auto shut off
	ETEC Ultra Measure	129			5.3 × 2.6 × 1.5	8		Voice	in. or 1/10 ft.		Pouch; reports temperature and continuous distance; calculates area in feet or yards; feet-yards-meters switchable; auto. shut off
Exact Technologies Corp. Box 973 211-B Old Laurens Rd. Simpsonville SC 29681	Exact Mach 5 DMC-100	200	1–50	14–104	6.00 × 3.00 × 1.75	7.5	9V alk.	LCD	1/4 in. up to 10 ft.; 1 in. beyond 10 ft.	99.5 +	Belt pouch; feet-yards-meters switchable; calculates areas directly; calculates volumes; built-in calculator has memory; reports temperature; auto. shut off
International Consumer Brands 126 Monroe Turnpike Trumbull CT 06611	Houseworks Digitape TLM-70N	40	2–33	32–100	5.00 × 2.62 × 1.62	3.5	Built-in 3V lith.	LCD	1/10 ft.	99 +	Auto. shut off
Measurement Specialties 1133 Route 23 Wayne NJ 07470	Measurement Specialties Measurmatic*	50	2–30	32–100	4.00 × 3.00 × 1.25	5	Built-in 3V lith.	LCD	1/10 ft.	99 +	Beeps when measurement is established; auto. shut off
Sonin Inc. 672 White Plains Rd. Scarsdale NY 10583	Sonin 60	100	1.3–60 +	32–100	5 × 3 × 1	6	9V	LCD	1/4 in.	99.85 (in still air)	Belt clip; feet-meters; calibration adjustments; automatic temperature compensation; reports continuous distance; directly computes area and volumes; adds, subtracts; door covers sensors when not in use; auto. shut off
	Sonin 150	135	3–150 +		5 × 3 × 1 (each unit)	6 (each unit)					
	Sonin 250	150	3–250 +		5 × 3 × 1 (each unit)	6 (each unit)					
Stanley Tools 600 Myrtle St. New Britain CT 06050	Stanley Estimator 39-035	80	2–35	40–105	4.4 × 2.6 × 1.3	6	9V alk.	LCD	1 in.	99.5 at 30 ft.	Reports temperature and continuous distance; auto. shut off
	Stanley Estimator 39-030*	40	2–30		2.75 × 4.75 × 1.00	6	2 built-in 3V lith.	LCD	1/10 ft.		Clip-on carrying case; beeps when measurement is established; left- and right-hand switches; auto. shut off

* Not available for testing or photos

monster routers

I've been working with wood for more than 30 years, and during that time I've accumulated four routers, all of them quarter-inchers. Oh, now and then I'd look at those big routers with half-inch chucks, but until recently I could never justify actually buying one. Then, just a few months ago, I finally broke down and did it. Now I have some advice for you: Do the same.

I'll be the first to admit that a half-inch router is not as light or maneuverable as a quarter-incher, and it will cost you a few dollars more; but once you get past the bulk and the bucks, the half-incher has all the advantages.

- Power. Half-inch routers have lots of it, usually around 2 horsepower as a minimum. That means they have the guts to swing big bits and make heavy cuts without bogging down. Sure, you can often do the same work with a smaller router by making two or more passes at lighter settings, but that takes extra time; and it multiplies your chances for error. Never forget that there are some types of cuts—dovetails, for example—that *must* be made in a single pass of the router.

- Durability. With that extra power comes the kind of heavy-duty construction that adds up to longer life. I've worn out more than one light-duty router, but I doubt I'll ever be able to kill my half-incher.

- Mass. Poor cuts are no mystery: After dull bits, vibration is their main cause. The slightest amount of flex or wobble will result in washboard cuts.

And that's not the worst: With stringy woods like oak and ash, vibrations usually translates into chipping, splintering, and ruined work.

The heavy motor and beefy shaft of a half-inch router run virtually flex- and vibration-free. And half-inch bits are roughly four times stronger than quarter-inch cutters.

Make two identical cuts, one with a quarter-inch router and one with a half-incher, and chances are you will feel and see the difference in smoothness immediately.

- Bits. Power, durability, and smoothness are important, but the major reason for buying a half-inch router is to gain access to the amazing library of bits made only with half-inch shanks.

It's these bits, most of which have appeared on the market during the past couple of years, that finally persuaded me to go to a half-inch router. As the illustrations reveal, a good selection can turn you and your router into a full-fledged millwork shop. At the flip of a switch you can crank out frame and panel doors, window sash, dozens of custom moldings, and raised panels in several different styles. You can mill tongue-and-groove lumber, finger-join stock end to end, or make durable lock-miter joints.

Just a few years ago, you needed an expensive shaper that cost from $450 to $2,000 to do this kind of work. Now all you need is a router and some kind of router table (see sidebar). The result is what Freud's Barry Dunsmore calls "the poor man's shaper."

—*A. J. Hand*

Half-inch-shank router bits let a router do new jobs. Panel-raising bits like these from Freud (top left) come in a plethora of profiles. Freud's Multiform bit (top right) is surrounded by some of the moldings it can produce. Cabinet-door sets from ZAC (above left) and Freud (above right) let you make elegant raised-panel doors. Freud's set has a bit to shape the door edge, a set to mold frame parts so they interlock and accept the panel, and a bit to make the raised-panel cuts; it works only with ¾-in. stock. ZAC's set has fewer bits and works with any stock but requires more router passes.

The poor man's shaper

To get the most out of a half-inch router, you should mount it in some kind of router table. Generally, the big bits just can't be used freehand.

There are several routes to a router table. I hang my router under the wooden extension wing of my table saw (see photo). This lets me use my saw's rip fence with the router. Most shaping operations call for the bit to be partially buried in the fence, so I clamp a sacrificial hardwood fence with an acrylic bit guard to the rip fence and let it take the beating. When it's worn beyond use, I make another.

This system has advantages: It doesn't tie up precious shop space as a separate router table would; and it lets me make use of the easy adjustability of my rip fence. Disadvan-

tages? My shaper setups sometimes conflict with table-saw operations.

If you'd like to build your own router table, Freud's slick booklet by longtime POPULAR SCIENCE Consulting Editor R. J. De Cristoforo will help. It includes complete router-table plans (and comes with Freud's cabinet-door bit set).

You can also buy a router table. Porter-Cable's model 696 comes with an adjustable split fence, and it's prewired to its own switch so you don't have to rely on the router's (often inaccessible in under-table use). Though it's designed for Porter-Cable routers, you can drill the table to accept routers from other makers. List price is $150, but I've seen it for $105.—*A. J. H.*

Half-inch bits: a wealth of possibilities

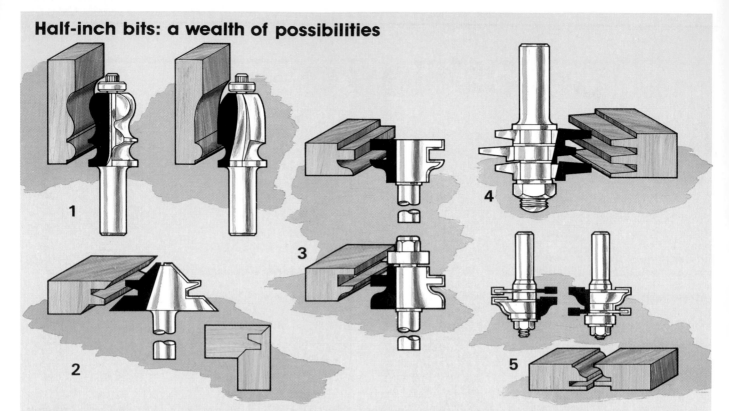

DRAWINGS BY MARIO FERRO

Half-inch router bits come in some unusual profiles. Examples above hint at what's possible.
1) Furnima's specialty is a variety of bits derived from old molding-plane profiles—ideal for renovation work.
2) Reliable Grinding offers special bits for interlocking joints. This lock-miter bit produces strong miters that won't skid out of alignment when clamped.
3) Reliable also offers a variety of male-female cutter sets for cutting interlocking frame parts for doors and panels. Need a special bit? Reliable can custom-make it to your specifications from a drawing or wood sample.
4) Furnima makes a slick finger-joint cutter that can join stock end-to-end, edge-to-edge, and in miters of any angle.
5) Amana's reversible ogee bit with slotter can make both male (stick) cuts and female (cope) cuts for frame parts. Restacking the bit's cutters makes the two different cuts possible.

Surprisingly, in most cases half-inch router bits cost just a few cents more than similar quarter-inch bits. Most router makers also offer bits, but those bits tend to be standard hardware-store items. For out-of-the-ordinary bits, I recommend the sources listed at the end of this article.

Keep the little guy
"OK," you say, "but I already have a quarter-inch router and an extensive collection of bits. If I buy a monster router, what happens to them?"

No problem. With a slip-in adapter (standard equipment with most routers) your half-inch router will take quarter-inch bits just fine.

A half-incher should *not* be your only router. You'll still want to use your quarter-inch router for light work and freehand operations (your big router will probably spend most of its time bolted to a router table). And for light-duty work such as laminate trimming, a bottom-of-the-line quarter-incher from Sears or Black & Decker (about $40) is perfect—light, compact, and easy to handle. It probably wouldn't hold up for long if it were your only router, subjected to long hours of hard use. But if you leave the heavy work to your half-incher, your light-duty router will probably last a lifetime.

Buying the big one
With the power, smoothness, and expanded capability the half-inch routers offer, it's no wonder they are proliferating fast. The current Trendlines catalog, for example, offers a whole page of half-inch routers and hardly any quarter-inchers.

The table below shows what's available in half-inch routers. The main thing to look for is power. I'd make $1^{1}/_{2}$ horsepower my low-end cutoff point. Two horsepower is even better. Remember, you are buying the router to swing big bits, and that takes a lot of power.

What's the cost of a half-inch router? List prices, as shown in the table, may seem high, but if you shop around, you can probably find a good 2-horse half-inch router for about $150. That's not much more than you'd pay for a good quarter-inch router.

If money were no object, I'd pick the Porter-Cable 518. This is a 3-horsepower workhorse with five electronically controlled speeds ranging from 10,000 to 22,000 rpm. Ideally, the larger the router bit, the lower your rpm should be. Huge bits like some of the new panel raisers really work best down around 10,000 rpm, and the 518 is the only router I know of that can provide those low-end speeds.

Unfortunately for me, money is an object, and the 518 lists for around $520—though I've seen it reduced to $345. So I'm currently using a Ryobi R-500. Shop around, and you can probably find one for about $150. That's most likely as low as you can go for a 2-horsepower router. The depth adjustment tends to bind up on mine now and then, but except for that, I'm happy—*by A. J. Hand.*

SOURCES FOR UNUSUAL ROUTER BITS
Amana Tool Company, 1250 Brunswick Avenue, Far Rockaway NY 11691, **DML Inc.,** 1350 S. 15th Street, Louisville KY 40210, **Ekstrom, Carlson & Company,** 1400 Railroad Avenue, Rockford IL 61108, **Freud USA,** Box 7187, High Point NC 27264, **Furmima Industrial Carbide, Inc.,** Box 308, Barry's Bay Ont. K0J 1B0, **MLCS Ltd.,** Box 53, Rydal PA 19046, **Reliable Grinding,** 145 W. Hillcrest Avenue, San Bernardino CA 92408, **ZAC Products Inc.,** 34 Renwick Street, New York NY 10013

portable radials

A radial-arm saw is a fine tool—if you have a roomy shop and you're content to do all your sawing there. But if you need a saw you can store in a corner or take to a job site, the conventional radial saw is not the tool.

Now there are two *unconventional* radial saws: portable models from Black & Decker and Ryobi. Neither the B&D folding saw (at 65 pounds) nor the Ryobi RPM bench-topper (at 53 pounds) is a featherweight, but both are easily carried to the job. And they don't hog a lot of shop space when they're unemployed. Better still, I found both of these saws compare favorably with stationary radial saws.

Full-size comparisons

How can you compare a 50- or 60-pound portable with saws that weigh two or three times that? Start with the motors: Most full-size radials have 1¹/₂- to 2³/₄-hp motors; the Ryobi and B&D portables have 2-hp motors.

In cutting capacity, these portable saws also compare well with the big ones. They will cut the cabinet woods and construction lumber most of us use—³/₄-inch boards and plywood, 2×4s, 2×8s. They will not rip a full sheet of plywood in half, however, or cut through 3-inch lumber.

List prices of the portables are high, but they often are sold for much less. One catalog currently offers the B&D for $329 and the Ryobi for $249.

For my shop test, it took me an hour to put the B&D saw together and align it, and less than a half-hour to do the same with the Ryobi. More parts of the Ryobi are preassembled, and there is less adjusting to do.

Both saws are sturdy, considering that lightweight materials are deliberately employed. And both have impressive ball-bearing rollers that guide the motor yoke on the arm.

Although the Ryobi saw has only an 8¹/₄-inch blade, its cutting depth capacities are virtually the same as those of the B&D, which has a 10-inch blade. Both could cut hardwoods satisfactorily at their full rated depths.

I also tried the saws with a carbide dado head set up to make a ³/₄-inch-wide cut. Both handled such cuts in hardwood. Then I tried the machines with molding heads on the arbors. (Personally, I am afraid to use molding heads on a radial saw regardless

of how rugged the machine is. But since both saw makers tout this capability, I tried it.) Taking moderate cuts, the saws performed satisfactorily.

The Ryobi, which has a high-speed universal motor and gear drive, is noisier than the B&D saw, but that arrangement gives it an attractive capability: You can rout with it.

The 18,500-rpm motor is geared down on the saw-blade end, but the other end runs at full speed, and has a $1/4$-inch collet to take router bits. To rout, you just take off the saw blade and up-end the motor.

While 18,500 rpm is a bit slow for routing—most portable routers turn at 23,000 to 25,000 rpm—it works just fine. And it has some interesting capabilities. It functions in much the same way as a router mounted under a router table, but here the router is above the work, so you can see the cut. It is stable enough to make finished cuts in hardwood from $1/8$ to $1/2$ inch deep, depending on the cutter. Successive cuts are a snap because you can quickly adjust the depth or move the yoke on the arm. With too heavy a cut, however, you can get enough deflection to make the cutter wander.

Moving experience

The folding mechanism on the B&D saw is easy to use: You remove the fence and the two rear table strips, unlock the column, and swing it down to the right. The table is mounted about 4 inches to the left of center to clear the arm and motor when the saw is folded. It takes just a few seconds to unlock and fold the saw, and the same to re-erect it.

The Ryobi saw can be moved assembled by locking the yoke on the arm. To make it more compact you can remove the column from the base (you should also remove the blade for safety). That takes about a minute and lets you store the saw in a 27-by-$27\frac{1}{2}$-by-14-inch space.

While these saws are truly portable, they must be fastened down whenever they are used. And don't attempt to fold the B&D saw or disassemble the Ryobi without first disconnecting the power—*by Phil McCafferty.*

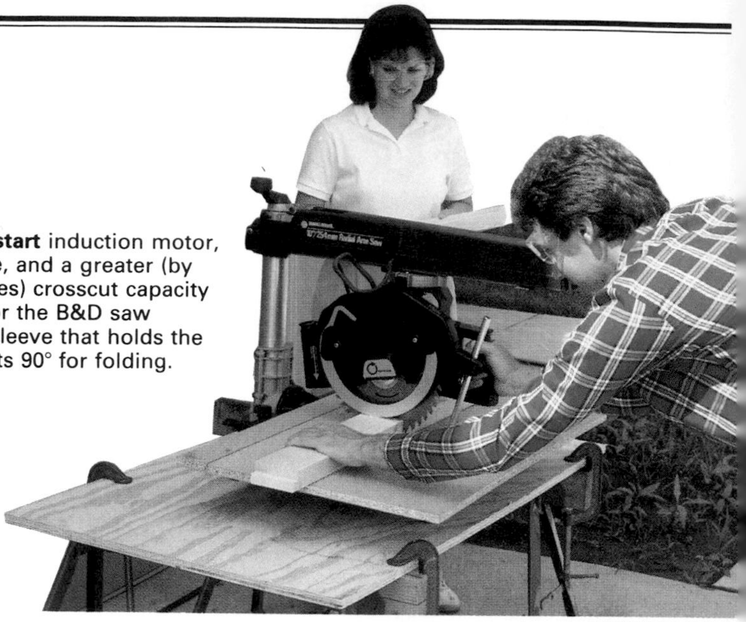

A capacitor-start induction motor, a wider table, and a greater (by about 3 inches) crosscut capacity are pluses for the B&D saw (right). The sleeve that holds the column pivots 90° for folding.

PHOTOS BY THE AUTHOR

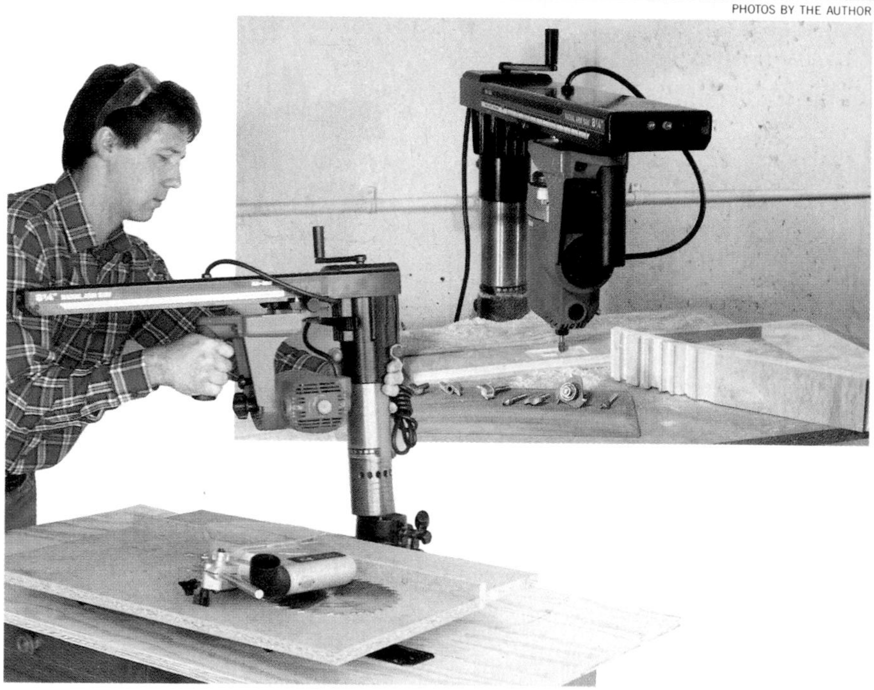

Flip the Ryobi saw's motor (above), and you have an 18,500-rpm router spindle. Easy adjustability and a good view of the work make this a fine routing machine. Elevation takes place at the top of the column on the Ryobi. Thus you can remove the column to store the saw.

How the totable radials compare

FEATURE	BLACK & DECKER FOLD-DOWN MODEL 1712	RYOBI RPM MODEL RA-200	TYPICAL "FULL-SIZE" 10" RADIAL
Suggested list price ($)	393	489	n.a.*
Motor specs (both double-insulated)	2-hp capacitor-start induction, 3,450 rpm	2-hp gear drive universal, 5,000 rpm main, 18,500 aux.	$2\frac{3}{8}$-hp induction
Motor brake	Manual	None	Automatic
Blade specs (in.)	10, $\frac{5}{8}$ arbor	$8\frac{1}{4}$, $\frac{5}{8}$ arbor	10, $\frac{5}{8}$ arbor
Table size (in.)	$21 \times 34 \times \frac{5}{8}$	$21\frac{3}{8} \times 27\frac{9}{16} \times \frac{11}{16}$	$26\frac{1}{2} \times 39 \times 1$
Carrying weight (lbs.)	65	53	n.a.
Smallest assembled cubic size (in.)	$10\frac{3}{4}$ H. × 41 W. × $29\frac{1}{2}$ D. (7.54 cu. ft.)[1]	$20\frac{1}{2}$ H. × $27\frac{1}{2}$ W. × 27 D. (8.75 cu. ft.)	n.a.
Maximum crosscut on $\frac{3}{4}$" material (in.)	$13\frac{5}{8}$	$10\frac{15}{16}$	$14\frac{1}{2}$
Maximum ripcut (in.)	$19\frac{7}{8}$	$19\frac{7}{8}$	$25\frac{5}{8}$
Maximum depth cut 45° (in.)[2]	$1\frac{7}{8}$	$1\frac{15}{16}$	2
Maximum depth cut 90° (in.)[2]	$2\frac{13}{16}$	$2\frac{1}{8}$	3
Miter index stops (deg.)	0, 45 left, 45 right	0, $22\frac{1}{2}$ left, $22\frac{1}{2}$ and 45 right	0, 45 left, 45 right
Bevel index stops (deg.)	0, 45, 90	0, 45, 90	0, 45, 90
Elevation range (in.)	5	$4\frac{1}{2}$	6
Column diameter (in.)	2.34	3.00	3.00
Arm materials	Die-cast aluminum frame with steel track, ball-bearing roller head	Formed steel frame with integral steel track, ball-bearing roller head	Steel or cast iron with ball-bearing roller head

*n.a.: not applicable; [1]folded; [2]with guards in place

Index